Velasquez *London*

PHILIP IV

SPAIN

A SHORT HISTORY
OF ITS POLITICS, LITERATURE, AND ART
FROM EARLIEST TIMES
TO THE PRESENT

BY

HENRY DWIGHT SEDGWICK

WITH A PREFACE BY
J. D. M. FORD, PH.D.

WITH ILLUSTRATIONS

BOSTON
LITTLE, BROWN, AND COMPANY
1926

THE ATLANTIC MONTHLY PRESS PUBLICATIONS
ARE PUBLISHED BY
LITTLE, BROWN, AND COMPANY
IN ASSOCIATION WITH
THE ATLANTIC MONTHLY COMPANY

DP
48
.S4
1926

II
THE ROMAN DOMINATION

It was not likely that the Romans would look on with indifference while Hamilcar's plan of annexing Spain to the Carthaginian dominions was put into execution. The imperial leaven was working by the Tiber as vigorously as in Carthage, and the Roman Senate had already assumed some sort of protectorate over the Greek towns on the Catalonian coast; so, when Hannibal attacked Saguntum, a town not very far from Valencia, the Second Punic War became inevitable. The city made an heroic resistance, but in vain (219 B.C.); and Hannibal, with his rear secure, marched northward, over the Pyrenees, through France, across the Alps, and down into Italy. The Roman Senate, never doubting ultimate victory, sent two generals of the great house of Scipio to cut off his base of supplies; they landed in Spain, but after some successes were defeated and killed. A third Scipio followed, with better luck; he routed the Carthaginian forces, captured their strong places, and, as Plutarch says, "greatly advanced the honor and estimation of the State of Rome." A few years later this Scipio crossed over into Africa and won the battle of Zama, which decided that Spain should become politically a part of Europe and not of Africa, and secured for the conquering general the title of *Africanus*.

At first the Romans only held the regions from which they had ousted the Carthaginians, but, dragged forward by imperial destiny, which always fattens on the inevitable difficulties that arise daily between a civilized people and barbarian neighbors, they pushed on in an irregular, opportunist fashion to a complete conquest of the peninsula. The process was long and bloody; nearly two hundred years of intermittent fighting were required before Spain was wholly incorporated in the Roman Empire.

Of all this military history I shall mention only the siege of Numantia (134–133 B.C.), because it is famous in Spanish tradition and literature, and ranks with the defense of Saguntum against Hannibal and of Saragossa against the French in Napoleon's time, as one of the three great glories of Spanish valor contending against overwhelming odds. Numantia is a town in Old Castile to the southeast of Burgos; and the lines of circumvallation that Scipio Africanus the Younger drew about the town may still be traced. I will also enumerate the names of some illustrious Romans who held high commands in Spain at one time or another, since such an enumeration reveals how early Spain became intimately drawn into the main current of Roman history: Cato Major, Tiberius Gracchus, Sertorius, Pompey, Julius Cæsar, Octavius, and Agrippa.

The conquest, as I have said, was slow but thorough and, at the death of Cæsar Augustus, Spain was as completely Latin as Italy itself. The less civilized race accepted in great measure the ways and usages of the conquerors, partly under compulsion, but chiefly from the instinct of imitation and the obvious advantage of abandoning the worse for the better. The discipline of the Romans, the military science of their officers, their roads, their coins and measures, their masonry, their carpentry, their smiths, their shipwrights, their system of government, their enforcement of order, their mode of conducting business, their oratory, their books, and whatever else belonged to Roman civilization, swept away the simpler and more faulty practices of the natives.

The proofs of this transformation are abundant and of several kinds. The first is to be found in the names of those cities which at one time were Roman camps, such as Lugo (Lucus Augusti) in Galicia; Astorga (Asturica Augusta) and Leon (Legio VII) in the province of Leon; Saragossa (Cæsar Augusta) in Aragon; Mérida (Emerita Augusta) in Estremadura; Braga (Bracara Augusta) in Portugal; and so on. The second consists in the Roman remains scattered about Spain in various places; the viaduct of mighty arches at Alcántara that carries a road over the river Tagus, broad enough for four carriages to drive abreast; the circus at what was once Itálica, near Seville; the theatre on the site of Saguntum; the bridge across the Guadiana; the aqueduct, circus, and theatre, at Mérida; and sundry ruins and vestiges of monuments at Torredembarra, at Huelva, and elsewhere.

It is impossible to stand beside the great double arches of the aqueduct at Segovia, which strides like Olympian Zeus across the valley, and not see in this perennial masonry a symbol of the Romans, matched with whom, other peoples that came for a time into Spain seem scarce more permanent than the swallows that skim and flutter past the mighty stones in pursuit of ephemeral insects. At Tarragona, too, where the Scipios established their headquarters, the aqueduct, gilded by the setting sun, is a most beautiful and majestic monument.

The third item of proof, as convincing as Roman aqueducts or Roman cities, is the list of Spaniards who became emperors or held in their time the highest places in Latin literature. Trajan, wise and just, a great warrior, the friend of Pliny, came from Itálica, a town that grew out of a Roman camp; Hadrian, celebrated for his love of beauty, his restless intellectual interests, and his administrative abilities, was also descended from one of Scipio's legionaries stationed at Itálica; Marcus Aurelius, the noblest of sovereigns and perhaps the best of men, although born in Rome, was a member of a Spanish family, the Annii; and Theodosius, the last great emperor, was Spanish-born.

As to Latin literature in the first century after Christ, — known in textbooks as the Silver Age, — several of the foremost names are Spanish. Lucius Annæus Seneca (4 B.C.–65 A.D.), *el Séneca español*, as Calderon proudly calls him, came from Cordova; philosopher, man of letters, playwright, tutor to Nero, minister of State, he was the most famous man of his time in all the Roman world, and his family, next to that of the reigning house, was the first in Rome. His father is known for a book on orators and oratory; his brother Gallio secured an immortality of renown when governor of Achaia, by his indifference to the religious disputes between certain Jews in Corinth; another brother was father to Lucan, the poet of genius and rhetoric, of passion and bombast. And, oddly enough, this note of extravagant emotion, so pronounced in Seneca and Lucan, has remained a dominant trait in Spanish utterance ever since. The clever modern critic, Azorín, asks: "*¿Por qué los españoles, oradores, políticos, periodistas, críticos, poetas, etc., pensamos en hipérbole?* (Why do we Spaniards . . . express our thoughts in such an exaggerated way?")

A third writer of the highest rank is Martial (42–102 A.D.) "*ex Hiberis et Celtis genitus,*" born at Bilbilis, now Calayatud, in Aragon. Toward the end of his life he left Rome, went back to his native land, and lived on a farm; here, he says, he enjoyed a rivulet, springs of fresh water, a grove, trellised vines, a rose garden, a vegetable patch, a dovecote, and so on; he writes gaily of these pleasures to Juvenal who, poor fellow, for his part, must be perspiring in his citified toga, as he climbs the steep hills of Rome. Bilbilis, Martial says, "has turned me into a regular countryman; I sleep like a top, get up at nine o'clock, don a tunic without regret for valet and well-pressed toga, saunter into the kitchen, where a noble fire and well-scoured pots greet me, and the farmer's wife, busily cooking, promises me a capital breakfast:

"*Sic me vivere, sic juvat perire.*"

Quintilian (35–95 A.D.), "*gloria Romanæ togæ,*" as Martial calls him, and saluted fourteen hundred years later by Fernán Pérez de Guzmán as *insigne Quintiliano*, makes the fourth illustrious Spanish figure in this period of Latin literature. He was born at Calahorra, a town on the river Ebro near the border between Navarre and Aragon, but lived all his life in Rome, where he kept a fashionable school and taught the youth of the aristocracy what an orator should know in order to become *vir bonus dicendi peritus*.

These men, of the highest rank in state and literature, were *cives Romani* quite as much as if they had been born on the banks of the Tiber, and show what an intimate and essential part of the Empire Spain had become. But stronger evidence still, stronger than all I have cited, is the Spanish language; for language is a creation of the whole people, fashioned, moulded, and shaped not merely by poets, orators, and scholars, but by men of all classes and occupations; and Spanish, *la lengua castellana*, as the Spaniards call it, is a Romance language. This little phrase means that Spanish has grown out of the language of the Romans, and offers eloquent testimony to the completeness of Roman dominion. The original Iberian speech — unless represented by Basque — seems to have disappeared; the Basque gave an uncertain amount; Greek contributed various words through the Romans; the Arabs added such nouns as were necessary to name the new customs, the new things, the new knowledge that they brought in; but these modifications and additions are so subordinate that to the ordinary reader Spanish seems to flow as direct from the Latin as Italian does.

Under the Roman rule, some time in the second or third century, the Spaniards were converted to Christianity. There is a tradition, generally believed in Spain, that Saint Paul and Saint James the Greater were both in Spain. Saint Paul in his Epistle to the

Romans says, "Whensoever I take my journey into Spain, I will come to you"; but except for this venerable tradition there is but vague, conjectural evidence to prove that he ever went to Spain, and none to show that Saint James went.

III

THE VISIGOTHS

THE dismemberment of the Roman Empire began in the early years of the fifth century. Spain shared the common lot. Tribes of barbarians burst their way over the frontiers, swarmed across the Rhine, invaded Gaul, and swept southward over the Pyrenees. Alans, Vandals, Suevi were the first comers. There is no need to follow the tangled threads of their inroads, their shifting fortunes, their struggles with the Empire and each other. The upshot was that the Vandals were pushed on across the Straits of Gibraltar into Africa; the Alans were absorbed and disappeared; the Suevi were crowded into the rough and rugged northwest corner.

The next invaders, the Visigoths, occupy our stage for nearly three hundred years; nevertheless, they contributed little to form the Spanish nation. They had scant statesmanship; they added nothing to the arts of agriculture, of mining, of breeding sheep or cattle; their ornaments were barbaric; they had no literature, and supplied but few if any words to the language, for such Germanic words as there are in Spanish had already been adopted by the Romans. The scant remains of churches built in Visigothic times testify that builders and carvers were bred upon Eastern traditions. The horseshoe arch came from Syria or Asia Minor. The best that can be said of the Visigoths is that they set an example of physical courage, personal independence, and self-respect, before the eyes of a poor-spirited population, and introduced some laws and customs that fostered and developed a higher standard of manliness. They were, however, by no means wild barbarians when they came. For two generations they had lived along the Danube both without and within the boundaries of the Empire; they had served in the Roman armies, had had dealing with Roman traders, and probably their young nobles had been bred in Roman camps or at the Roman court. At first, in the time of their weakness, they had been on friendly terms with the Empire; but after they understood their own strength they took to bullying, did as they pleased, and under their famous chieftain Alaric sacked Rome. From Italy they emigrated into southern Gaul, and there came into contact with Spain. At first they crossed the Pyrenees as friends and allies of the Spanish and Romans, to give aid against the barbarians that had preceded them; and in return for military service they received, according to custom, a share of the land. Later the more powerful Franks, pressing down on them from the north, forced the whole tribe over the border; but even then they did not profess to be masters or assume the rights of sovereignty until some time afterward, during the reign of King Euric (466–485 A.D.).

Once firmly settled in Spain, the Visigoths became a military aristocracy, scornful of the unwarlike natives and yet conscious of the superiority of Latin civilization; they preferred to live in the country, leaving the cities, for the most part, to manage their own affairs very much as they had done before. Probably the great bulk of the subject population — poor freemen oppressed by cruel taxation, serfs, and slaves — did not care very much whether Gothic chiefs or Roman bureaucrats levied the taxes and took the lion's share of the produce; but, naturally enough, the dispossessed upper classes both hated and despised their masters. The Roman gentry, with all their faults, were educated after the classical fashion; they had social conventions and definite notions of good breeding, and concerned themselves with literature, whereas the barbarians were illiterate; even the nobles with few exceptions, throughout the entire period of Gothic domination, could not write their own names; their manners were rude, and they wore coarse clothes that to the Romans were disgusting.

The task that confronted the Visigoths was to unite the various peoples of the peninsula, more particularly the Romanized natives and themselves, into one nation; in this they failed, and they failed signally. The task, it must be granted, was difficult, for the inhabitants were divided by differences of race, religion, and law. There were Goths, Romanized Iberians, — whom I shall call Spaniards, — Suevi, and Basques, and for three quarters of a century a large settlement of Byzantine invaders was established on the southern coast. Part of their task, it is true, they did accomplish, for the Basques were isolated, the Suevi overcome (585 A.D.), and the Byzantines expelled (625 A.D.), but the main problem, the fusion of Goths and Spaniards, remained unsolved. This fusion was hindered by the differences of law and of religion; and to these matters the more intelligent Gothic kings addressed themselves. About the middle of the seventh century two kings with outlandish names, old Chindasvint the father and Redesvint his son, combined after a fashion the Gothic and the Roman codes into one legal system, known in Spanish as the *Fuero Juzgo*, and did away with an old prohibition of marriage between the two peoples.

The barrier of religion, however, was much more serious. The Visigoths were Arians; they denied the dogma that the Father and the Son are of the same substance, while the Spaniards were orthodox Catholics. With such a religious cleft a united nation was impossible. In order to form a genuine political union one party or the other must give way; and the question was — which?

The Arian Goths had the advantage of being the dominant military caste, but the Catholic Spaniards were at least ten times as numerous, and their ecclesiastical hierarchy, which comprised virtually all the men of education, had succeeded to the moral, social, and political influence over the subject population that had been formerly held by the Roman administrative organization. As religion is of the essence of Spanish history, I shall narrate the circumstances of the triumph of the Catholic faith with some fullness.

The straining-point between the two creeds was reached under King Liovigild (*r.* 573–586 A.D.) the vigorous monarch that overcame the Suevi. His eldest son, Hermengild, married a Catholic princess. This girl and her Arian mother-in-law could not get on together peaceably, and therefore, in order to avoid unseemly bickering, Hermengild was sent to Seville as governor of the southern province. The

bishop of Seville at that time, Leander, was a man of
intellect, character, and force, and of blameless life;
he is reported to have been *vir suavis eloquio ingenio
præstantissimus vita quoque etiam atque doctrina clar-
issimus*, or, as we should say, a gentleman, an accomplished speaker, and a scholar of unimpeachable
orthodoxy. Between bishop and wife, Hermengild
was converted; and the Catholic party, over-hastily
surmising that their opportunity had come, broke out
into open rebellion and hailed him as their king. The
insurrection was put down and the unlucky prince
cast into prison, where he was put to death. The
Church rewarded this triumph of piety over filial duty
by canonization, and Saint Hermengild, both in the
calendar of saints and in many a painting, as saint
and martyr, enjoys an ecclesiastical immortality.
Leander fled to Constantinople. The masterful King
was wroth.

For the succeeding events I quote the narrative of
Saint Isidore, brother to Leander, of whom more in
the sequel:

Liovigild, mad with bestial Arianism, started in upon a
persecution of Catholics. He banished many bishops; he
confiscated Church revenues; he abolished ecclesiastical
privileges; he drove a multitude from sheer terror into the
Arian pestilence, and seduced still more by gold and
worldly advantages. He pushed his audacious heresy so
far as to baptize Catholics a second time, not merely
common folk but even priests, for instance Vincent, bishop
of Saragossa, who turned renegade and was hurled from
heaven to hell. Others he served still worse, chopping off
the heads of the nobles of chiefest sort, or driving them
into exile and laying hands on their property.

Happily for the orthodox, Liovigild died the next year and was succeeded by his younger son Reccared. Fernán Pérez de Guzmán, the poet and prose-writer of the great house of Guzmán (fifteenth century), whom I have already quoted, says of him:

> *Aquel rey*
> *christianisimo e clemente,*
> *gran zelador de la ley*
> *e amador de su gente.*
> *Perseguidor muy ardiente*
> *fue del error arriano.*

> That very gracious Christian King,
> Great zealot for God's commanding
> And loving to his people,
> An ardent persecutor he
> Of the Arian heresy.

This king read the signs of the times; a house divided against itself cannot stand. The minority must yield to the majority. He turned Catholic himself and persuaded various bishops and noblemen to do the same; then he convoked a council at Toledo (589 A.D.), which sixty bishops attended, together with the clergy of their dioceses. The King, opening the session with a speech, announced his acceptance of the Nicene creed and subscribed it with his own hand; the Queen followed, and all the clergy broke into a jubilant: *Gloria Deo Patri et Filio et Spiritui Sancto.* Orthodox resolutions defining the consubstantiality of the Father and the Son were passed, and all Arians were anathematized. Leander made the closing speech, which a very distinguished modern Spanish scholar calls "a sublime effusion." Among other things he said:

The peace of Christ has pulled down the wall of disagreement which the Devil had built up, and the house
that division was bringing to ruin stands united upon
Christ as its cornerstone. Let us all say, Glory to God
in the highest and on earth peace, good will toward men.

This action, however, did not at the time succeed
in bringing all the Goths or even a majority of them
into the orthodox Church, but in its later effect it was
of great moment; it dealt such a blow to Arianism
that, after the Mohammedan conquest, when the
remnant of the Spanish people began to lift their
heads, there were no Arians left; all Christians were
united in one Catholic faith, and Spain in due course
entered the commonwealth of Christian nations
subject to the Papacy.

Leander's younger brother, Isidore, succeeded him
as bishop of Seville; both have been canonized by a
grateful Church. Saint Leander is entitled, I imagine,
to the main credit for the work done at the Council
of Toledo, but the fame of Saint Isidore is far more
sonorous and widely extended. Isidore is the only
man of international reputation that Spain produced
during the whole period of Gothic dominion, and also
one of the most eminent men of letters — for the
author of *El poema del Cid* is unknown — between the
Silver Age of Seneca and Quintilian and the *Siglo de
Oro* of Cervantes and Lope de Vega. His renown
spread all over Europe and remained resplendent
until after Dante's time:

> *Vedi oltre fiammeggiar l'ardente spiro
> d'Isidoro.*

This chief book is an encyclopædia entitled *Etymol-
ogies*. This great collection of miscellaneous informa-

tion begins with an account of the studies proper for schoolboys, and proceeds to medicine, law, ecclesiastical rites and ceremonies, God, angels, prophets, priests, and heresies; then on to language, physiology, cosmography, architecture, surveying, mineralogy, agriculture, military science, games, ships, clothes, pots and pans; and, at that, the book is said to have been left unfinished. The immense admiration lavished upon this encyclopædia during the centuries of ignorance has been paid for by excessive depreciation to-day; it is denounced as stale and unprofitable, mere slender gleamings from the rich harvest of classical learning, with no original thought, no traces of personal experience, no records of observation. This disparagement is unjust. The flood of ignorance was rising fast; books were growing scarcer and scarcer. It was impossible for students in Seville or anywhere else to have access to a good library, so Saint Isidore gathered together, as if he were laying up provisions for an ark, whatever he judged would best suit their need. The book fulfilled its author's intention. "For centuries," it is said, "Saint Isidore was the battle cry of Spanish learning. . . . *Beatus et Lumen, noster Isidorus. . . . Isidorus, noster Varro, Isidorus, noster Plinius.*"

Such, in a general way, is the story of the triumph of orthodoxy in Spain. One evil consequence flowed from it. The Jews, who until then had been well treated, were now persecuted, sometimes most cruelly. They were excluded from public office, not allowed to hold slaves, made subject to ecclesiastical jurisdiction, forbidden to read books not approved by the Church, denied rights of trading, sometimes deprived of their children, often baptized by force, and so on. No wonder that the Jews wished to overthrow this régime and, when the Moorish deliverers came, aided them with a right good will.

One other famous saint of this period should be mentioned for the sake of those interested in popular subjects of painting, Saint Ildefonso, bishop of Toledo (658 A.D.); he wrote a book on the perpetual virginity of Our Lady, and in reward was divinely blessed by a gift, from her own hands, of a chasuble woven by the angels.

IV

THE MOHAMMEDAN CONQUEST

THE Gothic monarchy had other difficulties to face beside those caused by religious differences. The kings, following the dictates of nature, strove to make the crown hereditary, while the nobles clung tenaciously to their ancient Teutonic right of election, and also practised "the detestable habit of killing their king whenever he displeased them and putting another whom they preferred in his place." And while on the one hand they resisted the king's attempts to subject them to a rule of law and order, on the other they insisted on their own arbitrary ways of dealing with the inhabitants of their baronies. There was no idea of loyalty to a common good. The clergy cared only for the welfare of the Church; great landowners added farms to farms, acres to acres, swallowing up the small proprietors, as in Roman times; while the yeoman, hard put to feed their children, the serfs bound to the soil, and the slaves, looked on with the dull eye of animal indifference to political changes. These humble classes agreed, if on nothing else, in an endeavor to evade military service. Why should they fight? Nothing they had was worth fighting for. Why should they attend the muster? What profit was there in fighting to further the ambition of this or that arrogant baron, who hoped to rend some castle from his neighbor? Altogether the genius of disorganization was ready to wrench apart, cog from cog, wheel from wheel, the whole mechanism of the body politic.

When ruin came, nothing remained of Gothic kingdom or Gothic greatness except tradition and legend. Since the Visigoths had been military conquerors and their chiefs had been petty tyrants, Gothic blood was held in high estimation as proof of aristocracy, very much as Norman blood in England, and every great family, with what justice I do not know, traced its pedigree back to some Gothic nobleman.

Another tradition, which historians treat with more respect than I should suppose it deserved, is the magnificence of the Gothic capital, the imperial *nobilísima ínclita y esclarecida ciudad de Toledo*. This legendary magnificence of Toledo is largely due to the glowing imagination of Arabian historians, who were proud of the conquest and therefore wrote with dash and audacity: the Amalekites had built it, and Solomon had brought there many treasures, among them a table cut out of a solid emerald; but "as to this [Al Makkari, the historian, cautiously adds], God only knows." At any rate, at the time of the capture the conquerors found "twenty-five royal crowns of gold, twenty-one copies of the Pentateuch, treatises on plants and animals, recipes of simples and elixirs, vases full of precious stones, silken stuffs, robes of gold, rich armor," and suchlike. It would be idle to enumerate more, for "Toledo outdid the most extravagant description." To-day the city, stark and forsaken, sits on her hilltop high above the encircling river, like a queen, "nerveless, dead, unsceptred," but still royal, looking over the plain, now bare and barren, that in those ancient days was gay with gardens, orchards, and fertile fields, so prosperous that the grim castles scattered about merely served to emphasize the loveliness of nature.

The fall of the Gothic kingdom is wrapped about by legends that tarnish the name of the last Gothic king,

> Rodrigo, en quien fenescio
> nuestra gloria.

One of these is familiar to readers of Southey, Sir Walter Scott, and Lockhart. Near the city stood an enchanted tower, built by Hercules. Its gate was stoutly locked; and rumors of evil that would befall whosoever should dare to enter had fenced the place about with religious fear. In order to add physical security as well, a long line of Gothic kings, one after the other, had each affixed a lock to the gate. The warders asked Roderick to affix another; the King, in his boundless insolence, not only refused but said he should go into the tower. He broke the locks, forced the gate, and, disregarding portentous warnings, stalked into an inner chamber, opened a coffer, and, unrolling a painted cloth, beheld a picture of dark-visaged men on horseback, with turbans, lances, and bucklers, with swords dangling at their necks and bows and arrows at their saddlebows, and underneath the legend: SUCH MEN SHALL CONQUER SPAIN. The next day horrid sounds prophesied evil, and the tower collapsed in ruin.

This act of Roderick's, though of overweening insolence, did no more harm, it would seem, than to unveil the future; whereas another legend depicts

him as the cause or occasion of his country's sub-
jugation. A beautiful girl, Florinda, — also called
La Cava, daughter to a great nobleman, Count Julian,
warder of the southern ports, — was bred at the
royal court; the King saw her bathing and fell in love.
She rejected his suit; he used violence; she told her
father; he, in revenge, called on the Moors to cross the
Straits, and when they came he joined them with his
followers.

These legends, concocted by Moorish chroniclers,
are so familiar in books about Spain that I have narrated them; but the true circumstances of the invasion seem to have taken place in quite another
fashion. On the death of King Witiza (710 A.D.) his
eldest son assumed the crown; but the nobles, refusing
to recognize any hereditary right, elected one of their
own number, Roderick, Duke of Bætica, and crowned
him. The old royal faction looked across the Straits
for help. It so happened that only a few years before,
the Arabs, shouting, "Allah and Mohammed!" had
swept along the north of Africa, had conquered the
native Berbers, and had inspired them with roaring
zeal for the new religion; and now, at the very time
when these Mohammedans, puffed up by success, by
lust of conquest, and by pride of race, were impatient
for an opportunity to carry the crescent into western
Europe, Fortune held out both her hands.

The invaders were aided by Count Julian of the
legend, the governor of Ceuta, a town on the African
coast nearly opposite Gibraltar. Count Julian was
not a Goth but possibly a Byzantine or a Berber.
Besides this the Spanish Jews, eager to shake their
Christian oppressors from their shoulders, stood

ready to aid and abet the invaders of their own
Semitic race in a hundred ways, open or underhand.
For a year or two nothing more serious was done than
reconnoitring and plundering. In 711 A.D. a Berber
chief, Tarik, — who has left his name to the great
rock, Gebel-al-Tarik, our Gibraltar, — crossed over
with an army of Berbers. Count Julian was with him
and other partisans of the Witiza faction. They won
a victory over King Roderick near the Lago de la
Janda, which lies some dozen miles northeast of Cape
Trafalgar. Encouraged by this, the Arab governor
of North Africa, Muza, came over with an Arab
army and took chief command. A second battle was
fought; the Goths were again defeated. In one or
the other of the two fights Roderick was probably
killed. Cordova, Toledo, Seville, and Mérida fell into
the hands of the invaders; and Muza, deeming it no
longer necessary to affect the pretense of upholding
the Witiza faction, proclaimed the sovereignty of the
Caliph, and annexed Spain to the province of North
Africa.

The conquerors took several years (711–718 A.D.)
to overrun the peninsula. Their campaigns were
unsystematic, and they met different resistance in
different places. In the impetus of victory an army
crossed the Pyrenees. An Arab partisan says: "God
filled the hearts of the idolaters with terror and
alarm." For a time it looked as if Islam would drive
Christianity helter-skelter before it and overrun
Europe from Gibraltar to the Hellespont. But a
serious defeat at the hands of Charles Martel and his
fair-haired Franks at Tours (732 A.D.), the death of
their leader, and grievous dissensions among them-

selves, stopped their victorious career and obliged
them to retire and rest content with their conquests
south of the Pyrenees. As a consequence, according
to Mohammedan belief, "Europe remained in intellectual darkness for the next eight centuries," and
Spain alone was blessed by the enlightenment of
Islam.

The Spaniards — that is to say, the upper classes,
for during the Middle Ages only the upper classes
were able to make themselves audible — took a
different view from that of the Mohammedan author
whom I have quoted, and for hundreds of years be-
wailed Roderick's defeat. I quote the *Primera Crónica General* (thirteenth century):

Spain was broken into fragments; her children were dead
or in exile. Forgotten was the sound of her singing, and
her language was converted into alien words and into the
speech of a strange people. The Moors clothed themselves
in the gay attire of their spoils; the reins of their horses
were as fire, their faces were black as pitch, their eyes
shone like burning candles; their horses were swift as
leopards, and the riders fiercer than a wolf in the sheep-
fold at night. The vile people of Africa were now exalted
on high, for the noble Goths were broken in an hour,
quicker than tongue can tell. Oh luckless Spain! So great
was the slaughter that none were left to mourn. She lies
more dead than alive; her voice sounds as if from another
world, and her words as if they cried from underground:
"Is it nothing to you, all ye that pass by? Behold, and see
if there be any sorrow like unto my sorrow."

But, whether the conquest was in the interest of
higher civilization or not, the domination of the
Moors is a matter of the most far-reaching conse-

quences in the history of Spain, second only to the influence of the Romans. The reconquest took nearly eight hundred years, and during all that time a part of the country was always under the moulding pressure of Mohammedan laws, customs, and ideas. At first the whole peninsula, except the mountainous parts of the north and northwest, belonged to the Moors; then the dividing line between the two peoples moved slowly southward by irregular advances and recessions, halting long about the river Douro and again at the Sierra Morena, until at last nothing was left to them but the little kingdom of Granada. To-day, of the northern provinces Aragon bears most marks of the Moors, though careful observation would probably find traces of them all over; but these marks and traces are negligible compared with the Moorish stamp set upon Andalusia. There architectural monuments, dwellings, the ways and customs of the people, and still more conspicuously their eyes, features, and look, proclaim a Berber or Arab inheritance; and as the emigration to America was mainly from the south of Spain, a tincture of Moorish blood is probably to be found in almost all the Spanish-speaking peoples from California to the Argentine.

By the word "Moors" I mean all the Mohammedan invaders from Africa; but this is inaccurate, for in the beginning the two races, Arabs and Berbers, were quite distinct. The Arabs were the master race, both in intelligence and in civilization. As a guide to the differences between the two peoples at that time, I will quote what good observers say of them to-day:

The Arab, one of the finest types of all the races of mankind, tall, thin, fine eyes, aquiline nose, spare frame; walking with dignity; a horseman, poet; treacherous and hospitable; a gentleman, and yet inquisitive; destroying the civilization of every land he conquers, and yet capable of great things — witness Granada and Damascus; a metaphysician and historian; sensual and yet abstemious.

And again:

At the foot of a solitary palm tree you will see a man lying at full length, with long, narrow, dark-skinned face, scanty beard, head shaven and covered with a turban. . . . The whole life in that lazy, loose-lying figure burns in his big, brilliant, wide-open eyes, that reveal in their flashing depths a fiery soul far more instinct with life than the dried-up body that houses it. There is the dreamy, meditative spirit that divined the unity of God, imagined the sensual harem, the poetry of David, and the wisdom of Solomon. . . . The blazing sun impregnated his soul with the fierce delirium of Islam and the lazy fanaticism which rejects the organized bustle of European civilization.

On the other hand, the Berbers are —

short, squat men with high cheek-bones, small eyes, and square frames; great walkers, becoming horsemen only by necessity . . . strong, terrible, robust men, who do not fear snows and cold. . . . They are the greatest thieves and assassins in the world. . . . These people are the primitive inhabitants of Mauretania, the Libyans. Both in appearance and ways of living they are like the type of Iberians in Spain prior to the Roman dominion.

Many observers also say that the Arab is by nature skeptical, and believes in Allah for the sake of some material good, while the Berber is passionately religious.

These Mohammedan invaders gradually merged into one people, advanced in civilization, and reached their zenith in the tenth and eleventh centuries; but at the time of the conquest differences such as I have described separated the Arabs from the Berbers, and explain why dissensions arose between them, and how such dissensions enabled the Christians to regain their lost territories.

In the first exhilaration of triumph they worked together well enough, but when they settled down into a life of routine the differences made themselves felt; and the division of land, by which the Arabs assigned to the Berbers the barren plateau of Castile and took for themselves the delightful region of Andalusia, did not help matters. Moreover, at the very beginning, in addition to this cleft between races minor causes of disunion were at work. The Arabs were endowed with no more cohesion than the sands of their deserts; some came from Arabia, where one tribe was at swords' points with another, others from Syria; some were strict in religious observances and anathematized the lax, others were lax and laughed at the strict; and so on. As time went on, fresh immigrations of Berbers gave that race such a numerical superiority over their Arab tyrants that they not only ousted the Arabs from their higher place but virtually caused them to disappear as a separate race. And to make the muddle worse, beside these rifts among the conquerors, the subject people — who were far more numerous than the Moors — were divided not only by the old divisions between Goths and Spaniards, between Arians, Catholics, and Jews, but also by a new, deep-reaching cleavage. It might have been supposed that the domination of an alien, dark-skinned race would compress the subject people together, but on the contrary it split them afresh by a religious disagreement, for many were converted to Mohammedanism and became *renegados* or *muladíes*, — as they were called according to the Christian or the Mohammedan point of view, — while the rest, known as Mozárabes, remained true to the Christian religion. And among these last some were calm, vegetable Christians, while others were violent in the assertion of their creed. To unite and blend these discordant elements into one people would have taxed capacities for organization far greater than any possessed by Arab sheiks or Berber chiefs, each man jealous and suspicious of his neighbor. These sheiks and chieftains acted together only when attacked by the Spaniards, and often not even then, or when forced into subjection by a gifted and powerful ruler.

The history of the Moors in Spain is a tale of disintegration and defeat, followed by the rise to power of such a man as I have indicated; then his successors prove degenerate, and a new period of disintegration and defeat is ushered in. Of these shifting periods I shall speak briefly in the next chapter.

V

MOHAMMEDAN SPAIN

THE causes of dissension among the Moslems, enumerated in the last chapter, prevented not merely any national unity but also any permanently stable government. Nevertheless three dynasties arose in succession, and each for a time managed to bring the refractory elements into union and obedience. These three dynasties, the Omayyads, the Almoravides, and the Almohades, cover a period of five hundred years.

At first Moslem Spain was ruled by an emir who was subordinate to the Arabian governor of North Africa, and he in his turn was subject to the caliph at Damascus. Not long after the conquest, however, the ruling dynasty, the Omayyads, was overthrown by a rival family, the Abassides, and the seat of government was removed from Damascus to Bagdad. As a consequence of this shock to the caliphate, Moslem Spain seceded or dropped away from the central government, and straightway fell apart into quarreling fragments. As luck would have it, one of the Omayyads, by name Abd-er-Rahman, eluded his murderous enemies, escaped to Spain, and proved himself a man of great abilities. He forced the quarreling Arab and Berber chiefs to acknowledge his authority, declared Spain independent of the Abasside caliph at Bagdad, and established himself firmly as monarch of the Spanish Moors, with the title of Emir.

A long line of his descendants succeeded to the emirate with varying fortunes; some were strong or crafty enough to maintain their authority, but for the most part the permanent causes of discord — race, religion, tribal jealousy, personal ambition — reduced the emir's authority to a shadow. Conspicuous among these passing princes stands one brilliant figure, Abd-er-Rahman III (891–961), by whose ten talents Moslem Spain rose to the foremost place in civilization in all Europe. Abd-er-Rahman III was a good soldier, a wise ruler, a man of intellectual interests and varied tastes. He snapped his fingers at the successors of the Prophet in Bagdad, and assumed the title of Caliph for himself. He put down the disaffected, organized a regular army, adopted the principle of the *carrière ouverte aux talents*, encouraged agriculture, commerce, education, literature, and architecture. At a time when Rome was in eclipse and all the other cities of Europe — London, Paris, Venice, Antwerp — were untidy mediæval towns, Cordova shone like a golden bowl among vessels of clay, in all the strength and beauty of high prosperity. The accounts of Arabian chroniclers are, no doubt, colored by the imagined glories of a sun that has set; yet at the worst they do but magnify the truth. According to them, Andalusia, compared to Africa, was as a pearl is to glass beads; and Cordova was "the cupola of Islam." "Do not talk of the court of Bagdad and its glittering magnificence; do not praise Persia and China and their manifold advantages; for there is no spot on earth like Cordova." Students from all the world flocked thither "to learn the sciences of which she was the repository, to drink in knowledge from the lips of the doctors who swarmed there." Cordova was "the minaret of piety," the home of elegance and magnificence. She reckoned her mosques by thousands and her palaces by tens of thousands; chief among these, each more beautiful than the others, were the Palace of the Garden, the Palace of the Lovers, the Palace of Content, the Palace of Flowers, while meaner buildings were numbered by hundreds of thousands. The city with its suburbs stretched out ten miles long and at night the road was lighted all the way.

Praise be to God most high [one writer says] for allowing his humble creatures to design and build such enchanting palaces as these, who permits us to inhabit them as a sort of recompense in this world, and to the end that the faithful may be encouraged to follow the path of virtue by the reflection that, delightful as are these pleasures, they are still far inferior to those reserved for true believers in the Celestial Paradise.

The greatest of these palaces, the Azarha, almost a city in itself, built by Abd-er-Rahman for a favorite wife, has perished; but the ancient glory of Cordova may still be judged by its mosque, the Mezquita. To those who associate religion with the high-aspiring vaults of the Gothic cathedrals, the Mezquita is a strange, fantastic building, poetical rather than religious. Its builders, an out-of-door people, habituated to the uncircumscribed vault of heaven, thought to bring Allah nearer by shutting out with a low roof the fearful vastness of unlimited space; but within they honored him and Mohammed his Prophet with all the cymbals and psaltery of color. The ceiling was gaudily painted; "the gold that covered it glittered like lightning darting through clouds"; and mosaics of many colors gleamed and glistened in the radiance of ten thousand lamps, made out of Christian bells captured at Compostela. And yet, in spite of all this gayety, the long sequences of double arches that march through the files of a thousand columns produce a subtly mournful effect, suggestive of a litany, or a flight of sea birds migrating from home, that ply their wings in unison and sing together the same homesick, plaintive note. But whatever richness of material could do, that was done. The sacred recess for prayer, the mihrab, lined with ivory, ebony, sandalwood, and cinnamon, gold, silver, and lapis lazuli, shone like an inner chamber in Mohammed's Paradise.

This noble mosque was not constructed all at once, but at three several periods. Abd-er-Rahman I began it about the year 785 A.D.; Al Hakim II (r. 961–976) erected the first great addition; and the famous vizier Almanzor, the real ruler of the state in his day (939–1002), built the second enlargement, out of materials — it is said — of demolished churches, carried to Cordova on the heads of Christian captives.

The prosperity of Cordova endured for two hundred years. An Arabian geographer in the service of King Roger of Sicily, who wrote in the year 1154, breaks into eulogies of much the same nature as those that I have quoted.

At this point, while talking of the Moslems, I will speak of the second great Moorish city, Seville. The third, Granada, belongs to a much later period. Seville is like a reigning beauty: everybody in every age, whether out of admiration or convention, praises her. George Borrow, sailing up the river on his way to peddle Bibles, says:

The principal object in this prospect is the Golden Tower, where the beams of the setting sun seem to be concentrated as in a focus, so that it appears built of pure gold. . . . Cold, cold must the heart be which can remain insensible to the beauties of this magic scene.

Five hundred years earlier, Fernán Pérez de Guzmán said:

> *Esta cibdad tan notable*
> *e tanto cavallerosa,*
> *tan fertil e abundosa,*
> *tan dulce e tan delectable.*

> This city so notable,
> So full of courtesy,
> Of foison and fertility,
> So sweet and delectable.

There is no discordant voice in this chorus of praise throughout her history. But our present concern is with the time of Moorish dominion. The city lies on the Guadalquivir halfway between Cordova and the sea. "Seville is a young bride, her necklace the river." A proverb says: "If thou seekest bird's milk, by Allah, thou shalt find it in Seville."

The air is pure, the temperature mild [it is an Arab speaking]; the city is beautiful, its streets lined with fine buildings, its tower [the Giralda] unparalleled throughout the world, its dwellings beautiful with goodly courts, which are filled with orange trees, lemons, limes, and citrons. And the environs are still more beautiful. The banks of the Guadalquivir for thirty miles are covered with gardens, orchards, vineyards, yew trees, with castles and towers. The farmhouses are so white that they look like stars in a sky of olive trees; and fruit trees, melodious with singing birds, are so thick that they shade the pleasure boats which sail or paddle up and down, while the pleasure-seekers listen lazily to the singing. The region can be compared only to Paradise:

> Down on the river sweeps the breeze in play,
> Catches its watery robe and lifts the edge,
> The maiden river clutches bank and sedge,
> And hastes for refuge to the sheltering bay.

Naturally enough, the inhabitants are the merriest people in the world, witty, frivolous, jocose, a multitude of them poets (as everybody knows), and all play all sorts of musical instruments, timbrels, lutes, rebecs, viols, dulcimers, harps, sackbuts, guitars, flutes, and clarionets, and singing and drinking wine, for they only regard excess as forbidden; they have but one fault, which comes from perverted wit: they backbite outrageously, and anyone that does not slander his neighbors is cordially disliked.

Whether these eulogies on Cordova and Seville are deserved or not, cannot be told for sure. As the Arab historian Al Makkari prudently says: "God only is all-knowing." Nevertheless, modern scholars are hardly less complimentary:

Science, art, and literature flourished in Andalusia as nowhere else in Europe. Splendid buildings were erected, and luxury in domestic life was carried to a pitch of refinement undreamt of in the north. Women were given a place in society such as they possessed in no Christian country at that time or for many centuries later. The application of the Egyptian system of irrigation brought agriculture to a pitch never reached by Spain under Christian rule. Pottery with a gold lustre and beautiful glass were made. Fruit of many kinds was grown and preserved for winter use. Tubular stoves were used for heating houses, and soap was regarded as one of the first necessaries of life.

To these various praises I may add that during the reigns of the Omayyads (755–1031) their Spanish subjects were treated far better than the Moors were treated by the Spaniards after the reconquest. Christians were allowed to practise their religious rites and to govern themselves according to their own laws and customs, except that the Moslem emirs succeeded to the royal prerogative of summoning ecclesiastical councils and even of appointing bishops. The only distinction made between the renegados who changed their religion and those Christians — the Mozárabes — who did not, was to subject the latter to a heavy poll tax. Most of the subject inhabitants changed their religion — some from conviction, some to avoid the poll tax, and such as were slaves in order to receive freedom. Probably many in the lower classes were quite as much pagan as Christian, and ready to accept any gods that new masters should bring with them. The conquerors confiscated only the lands actually won in fight and those belonging to the Gothic Crown, to the Church, or to fugitive nobles; and as the Arabs were too proud to stoop to agriculture, these lands were leased to peasants, on terms of paying a certain share of the produce: those on lands belonging to the State, one-third; those on private estates, four-fifths. By this change the country people were gainers, for the great estates were broken up, and each family of peasants acquired its individual patch of land to cultivate. The Jews also were liberally treated, and as the Moslems were in many ways far more civilized than the Spaniards, their arts, such as irrigation, medicine, various processes of manufacture, and so forth, conferred great benefits on the country. All this applies to the earlier period of the conquest; for as time went on, and the Moslems felt their power firmly established, they began to violate their treaties and promises, imposed various irregular taxes, and did other tyrannical acts.

The decline and fall of the Moorish dominion was due far less to the attacks of the Spaniards than to their own inability to compromise. Every petty chief was bound to rule or ruin. Their own historians are explicit on this point: "They are the worst people to render obedience in the world; the most difficult to govern; their disobedience to their kings and rulers has become almost proverbial." One governor said: "They are like the camel, which complains whatever you do, whether you add to its load or unburden it. It seems as if God Almighty had created them to be continually engaged in war or in civil dissension."

Almanzor, the grand vizier who enlarged the Mezquita at Cordova and was so brilliant in government and terrible in war, died in 1002. The Omayyad dynasty, deprived of his abilities, collapsed within a generation and the emirate fell apart into little principalities, to the great relief of Christian Spain. The remnant of the Spanish people, at first cooped up in the mountainous regions of Asturias and Galicia, took advantage of the Moorish débâcle to recover towns, villages, and castles, and pushed so far south as to capture Toledo (1085) and, by the valor of Ruy Diaz (*el Cid Campeador*), even Valencia. It seemed as if they were on the brink of driving the invaders back across the Straits into Africa.

There was great alarm among the Moslems, but the local princelings and chieftains got together and asked a Berber clan, the Almoravides, who had recently made themselves masters of northern Africa, to come to their rescue. The leader of the Almoravides, Yusuf, a shrewd, able, energetic ruler, accepted the invitation and came. He defeated the Spaniards in a bloody battle (1086), recovered Valencia (1102), and — except for Toledo, which was lost forever — pushed the international boundary line back to where it had been under the Omayyads. But Yusuf did not fight for the benefit of the quarreling princelings; he treated Moslem Spain as a conquered province, and annexed it to his African kingdom.

The Almoravides, however, were not destined to stay in power long. They were originally a rude, fanatical people, used to a simple, hardy, abstemious life, but when once established in Spain, although they remained indifferent to the refinements of civilization, they very soon took eagerly to the vices that flourished luxuriantly in this pleasant garden of the world. They became gross, tyrannical, and hateful to their subjects. The African provinces rebelled and the shock of their rebellion reverberated in Spain. The Spaniards, seizing opportunity by the forelock, took Saragossa (1118), while the Moorish princelings in Andalusia, seeing their hated masters hard beset, and wholly indifferent to the fate of Saragossa, rose in arms and drove the Almoravides out. Then again, just as had happened on the fall of the Omayyads, the Moorish state broke up into bits. "Every petty governor, chief, or man of influence who could command a few followers, and had a castle where he could seek refuge in case of need, called himself 'Sultan' and assumed all the insignia of royalty."

The revolution in Africa was due to a religious sect of Berbers, the Almohades (Unitarians). They, in their turn, were invited by some Moslem chiefs into Spain to defend Islam from the Spaniards and, like their predecessors, though they went to rescue they stayed as masters, and Moslem Spain under the new dynasty continued to be a part of an African empire. The Almohades were pure Berbers, and tyrannized over such Arabs as had been left to such an extent that, as I have already intimated, they virtually wiped them out; as a consequence, from this time on the term "Moors," meaning Berbers of Arabian civilization, fairly applies to all the Mohammedan population.

I have no space to give to the Almohades, though it is said that "the new dynasty was far more enlightened and favorable to culture than the Almoravides had been." The wars with the Christians continued with shifting success, until Alfonzo VIII of Castile won the great battle of Las Navas de Tolosa (1212) and broke the power of the Moors forever. The fragments of the Moslem state fell bit by bit into the hands of the conquerors: Mérida, 1229; Cordova, 1236; Valencia, 1238; Seville, 1248, leaving only the kingdom of Granada, which, owing to discord among its enemies, continued to exist for two hundred and fifty years more.

This Moorish occupation of Andalusia for five hundred years produced ineffaceable effects; first, by the intermixture of blood, to which I have already referred; secondly, by the temper that centuries of warfare conferred upon the national character; thirdly, by the widespread adoption of Moorish manners and customs. Lesser results appear in art: witness the Mezquita at Cordova, the Giralda and the Alcazar at Seville, the Alhambra at Granada, and the influence that these buildings — and the taste they called forth — exerted upon Spanish as well as Mozarabic architects and decorators. Their physicians, such as the family of Avenzoar, are famous in the history of medicine. Their philosophers, Avencebrol, Avempace (*d.* 1138) of Neoplatonic renown, and greatest of all Averroes (1126–1198), who nearly rivals Saint Isidore in the extent of his European reputation, were certainly among the most distinguished thinkers in Europe, prior to Roger Bacon and Raimund Lull. Other eminent philosophers, Solomon ben-Gabirol (1021–1070), Moises-ben-Ezra (1070–1139), and Maimonides (1135–1204), were of the Hebrew race, and united their culture to the general intellectual sunshine that radiated from Cordova and Toledo. Both Arabs and Jews cultivated literature. And to learn the general effect upon manners and customs, we have but to look at the words that the Spanish have taken over from them, such as, *alcalde* (judge), *alguacil* (policeman), *alcabala* (tax), *tarifa* (tariff), *azote* (whip), *azucar* (sugar), *alquimia* (alchemy), *algebra*, and dozens of others. And one must remember that the Moors introduced into Spain cotton, silk, oranges, figs, almonds, sugar cane, and other fruits and vegetables.

VI

THE HEROES

I NOW return to the Spaniards. After Roderick perished, those Gothic nobles and persons of the upper classes who preferred to abandon their homes rather than submit to the conquerors gathered together in the mountainous regions of the northwest, and elected one of their number, Pelayo, to be their king. Pelayo is said to have been a Goth. A strong force of Moors went up against him. Learning of their approach, Pelayo dismissed most of his men to various places roundabout, and with a picked body took refuge in the far-famed cave of Covadonga. This cave is hollowed out of the rock "as if God had made it for a place of refuge." The Moorish slingers and archers closed in around the mouth, "but [as the *Primera Crónica General* records] Almighty God in His mercy fought on the side of His people, and the arrows, darts, and stones aimed at the cave were turned by His doing against the Moors themselves and wrought great slaughter. And by God's will through this unheard-of miracle more than 20,000 Moors were slain." The rest fled in confusion. Pelayo and his bands fell upon them and massacred many; those that escaped took refuge "on top of a mountain, but the mountain fell headlong with them into the river, and all perished by drowning or under the avalanche of rocks that fell upon them." The chron-

THE ALCAZAR AT SEVILLE

icler likens this deliverance to that of the Children of Israel from the hands of Pharaoh. But, miracle or not, some successful battle was fought; and as Fernán Pérez de Guzmán says:

*Desta pequeña centella
gotica se encendio
tanta lumbre, que alumbro
a toda España;*

*Bendito el emperador
Jesus, que asi respondio
a su fe, e favorecio
su devoto servidor.*

From this little Gothic spark was enkindled so great a light that it illuminated all Spain; blessed be our Emperor Jesus, who hearkened in such guise to the Faith, and showed favor to His loyal servant.

The poet was right. This battle of Covadonga (718 A.D.), though probably a small affair, had great moral results.

But I do not mean to tarry over the early story of the reconquest; it is a tale of battles, raids, burnings, and of the gradual recovery of town, village, grange, of barren fields and stark mountain slopes, until the Spanish lands reached to the river Douro; and then in the course of generations, as I have said, the boundary line between the two peoples traveled southward irregularly, until at last, after five centuries, the Christians reached the southern coasts. I shall take all such matters for granted, and proceed to speak of the heroes that hold a great place in Spanish legend and Spanish literature.

The first great national hero, if I am not giving too ample a significance to the term, is Saint James the

Greater, Santiago, the patron saint of Spain. A stanza in the epic poem on Fernán González says:

Fuertement quiso Dios a la Espanna honrrar,
quando al santo apostol quiso ay enbyar,
de Ingla-terra e Frrançia quiso la meiorar,
e sabet que non yaçió apostol en todo aquel logar.

Mightily the Lord God willed to honor Spain,
When the holy Apostle He willed there to send;
Over France and England He willed to set her first,
For know that no apostle's bones lie in either land.

The legend runs in this wise. Saint James, brother to Saint John and son to Zebedee, journeyed to Spain and preached in Galicia, but returned to Judæa, where he was put to death by King Herod; his disciples carried his body back to Spain for burial. In time the place of his tomb was forgotten, and the people of Galicia fell away into paganism. At last the tomb was found, but as to the manner of finding accounts differ. One version tells how a bishop was guided by a star to the spot, which in consequence became known as Compostela — *campus stellæ*, the field of the star. But I shall give another version. Charlemagne, lying in bed unable to sleep, beheld a vision. A path of stars led through Gascony, Navarre, across the Pyrenees into Spain, and proceeded westward to Galicia; this same vision was repeated several nights. On the last night Saint James appeared and said that his body was buried in Galicia, then held by the Saracens, and bade Charlemagne lead a great army along the road marked out by the stars and deliver the tomb, so that all Christians should be free to make a pilgrimage there forever. Charlemagne did as he was commanded; Archbishop

Turpin baptized the people of Galicia, and dedicated a basilica to the Saint. For this Charlemagne received his reward. When his soul appeared before the judgment seat and Satan had weighed down one balance with his sins, Saint James cast the basilica into the other balance, and turned the scales.

The cult that raised Saint James to be the patron saint of Spain seems to date from the early part of the ninth century, at which time the first church is said to have been built — not by Charlemagne but by Alfonso II, surnamed the Chaste. This church was destroyed by the Saracens under the great vizier Almanzor (997 A.D.), and its bells were carried off to make lamps for the Mezquita at Cordova. But after danger from the Saracens had passed the church was rebuilt, and in course of time Santiago de Compostela became a bishopric, then a metropolitan see, and for a time virtually an independent principality.

Saint James is of the first consequence in the history of Spain; his name became a national symbol, a sort of spiritual flag, and his tomb attracted pilgrims from all over Europe, especially from France. Pilgrims were on the road by the beginning of the tenth century, and continued to come in great numbers well into the sixteenth. The pilgrims' road, *el camino francés*, went by way of St.-Jean-Pied-de-Port and the Port de Cize, through the pass of Roncevaux into Spanish Navarre, and thence westward. A guidebook, carefully prepared, directed pilgrims and informed them what to expect. On the whole it was encouraging. The country between Pamplona and Logroño on the river Ebro abounded in meat, fish, good bread, the best of wines; in short, it was a happy

land, *cunctis felicitatibus plena.* The road ran on past
Carrión, a place of ill renown in the story of the Cid,
but described in the guidebook as a *villa habilis et
optima, omni felicitate felix,* on to Leon, *urbs regalis
et curialis,* to Triacastella in the province of Lugo.
Near here, at a quarry, every pilgrim picked up a
stone, and carried it to the lime pit at Compostela
for the benefit of the church-builders. The last stretch
of the road traverses valleys of chestnut, walnut, oak,
and stone pines, and is very beautiful in the spring
when the heather is in bloom and the patches of
golden gorse are new-gilded by the sun.

The cities along the route were apparently all that
is delightful, and abundant in much more than a
pious pilgrim should care for; but out in the country
the road was often beset with difficulties. The Gascons were robbers, the Basques exacted outrageous
tolls, the natives of Castile were vicious, and those of
Galicia more uncivilized still, bad-tempered and
quarrelsome. The peaks of the Pyrenees touched the
sky; and in Navarre there was a poisonous river to be
forded, where natives hung about with knives ready
for skinning, and urged travelers to let their horses
drink. In another river the fish were unwholesome.
Finally, these perils passed, when the pilgrims neared
their journey's end, before entering Compostela they
halted in a shady grove, bathed, and proceeded, clean
in body and refreshed in mind, up a steep slope and
through the Porta Francigena into the "most excellent apostolic city, overflowing with all sorts of
pleasantness as well as in possession of Saint James's
body, and recognized to be blessed and preëminent
over all the other cities of Spain."

Even in the sixteenth century pilgrims continued to come in great numbers, and with the increase of law and order the hazards of the way diminished; yet, such is the perversity of human nature, sophisticated Spaniards, although they conceded that *el camino francés* was enjoyable because travelers met all kinds of people, saw all sorts of costumes, and heard all varieties of speech, nevertheless complained that they were bored by having to say at every step, "God bless you" — especially the nearsighted, who, for fear of omitting the proper salutation, God-blessed all the trees by the wayside. At least Cristóbal de Villalón (sixteenth century) so reports.

Tradition and legend grew up about the Saint's memory. He would ride in the front ranks of the Christians as they advanced to battle against the Moslems; and he also did a great many wonderful things near his tomb. He built a church; he dug a well with his own hands; he hollowed out a seat in the rock on which he, Saint Peter, and Saint John used to sit; he produced a fountain by a stroke of his crook; he rowed in a stone boat. Even in 1587 pious pilgrims saw all these objects. Many were the votive offerings hung up in the church in gratitude for favors received.

The cathedral, as it stands to-day, was begun in 1078 or 1082, was building all through the twelfth century, and consecrated in 1211 in the reign of Alfonso IX, a year before the great victory of Las Navas de Tolosa. The nave, aisles, and transepts, the choir with its ambulatory and chapels, the vaulting, the triforium, are in the early Romanesque style and "of an extreme magnificence." The historical interest of these architectural forms lies in the fact that the church is, in great measure, similar to the church of St. Sernin at Toulouse, and indicates the hand of a French architect, and so adds its testimony to a great mass from other sources to prove how far-reaching were the French influences that came over the Pyrenees into Spain by *el camino francés*. But the most beautiful part of the building is the Pórtico de la Gloria, designed and carved with tender and elaborate devotion by Magister Matthæus, who spent twenty years at the task (1168–1188). Mr. George Edmund Street, a distinguished English architect who wrote the first authoritative book on Spanish cathedrals written in English, says: "I cannot avoid pronouncing this effort of Master Matthew at Santiago to be one of the greatest glories of Christian art," and Professor A. K. Porter calls it "the most overwhelming monument of mediæval sculpture."

Mr. Street and Professor Porter speak with authority; but the sculpture is primitive and, to my thinking, lacks the beauty of French Gothic. The uneducated pilgrim to-day, though he may be ashamed to confess it, is likely to derive more genuine enjoyment from the exterior of the church. The south side, with the great flight of steps that leads to the door of the transept, is flanked to the east ("damaged," Street says) by a noble clock-tower, solid as a donjon keep, and to the west by the picturesque wall of the cloister. The irregular and charming apse displays a round-arched arcade, gay chapels, and gallant statues evidently fetched from somewhere else. The long northern front has its own

Casas y Noboa

CATHEDRAL AT COMPOSTELA

(*Western façade*)

qualities too, and, more than the others, the western façade, where genius shows its power to handle even the late baroque style with triumphant success. Nothing could be more delightfully fantastic or more irrelevant to the solemn interior — flights of steps, upper storeys of pilasters, balustrades, niches, lofty towers ("pepper boxes," Street calls them), and what not. Nature, collaborating with the architect, whose design shows that he had anticipated her collaboration, has spread golden lichens over the great stones, planted tufts of grass and nodding plumes in chinks and corners, and given her benediction to the handiwork of man. This cathedral was the first great edifice built in Spain since the Mezquita at Cordova, and seems to sound a defiant challenge to the Moslem faith and prophesy the coming decisive victory.

Saint James, whatever we may think of his presence in Spain, was a real person; so was Pelayo. Our next hero, Bernardo del Carpio, is generally believed not to have touched earth at all, but to have lived solely in the imagination of patriotic bards and chroniclers; and yet his legend brings its quota of historical truth, for it indicates that the little kingdom of Asturias was fearful lest it be swallowed up in the great empire of Charlemagne. That Emperor did in fact invade Spain, and his coming — or rather his return — has been rendered memorable in French literature by the *Chanson de Roland*. The Spanish version of that retreat, narrated much later in Spanish ballads and chronicles, is very different. What actually happened is obscure. It seems that some Saracen chiefs, chafing under the rule of Abd-er-

Rahman I, the founder of the Omayyad dynasty, invited Charlemagne to come to their rescue. Charlemagne accepted, crossed the Pyrenees by the route I have described that led from St.-Jean-Pied-de-Port and the Port de Cize through the valley of Roncevaux, and descended upon Saragossa; but he was not able to take the city. A sortie of the garrison, or a concentration of the enemy's forces, or perhaps bad news from the Rhineland, obliged him to raise the siege and hurry. He took the road by which he had come, and with the main body of his army crossed the crest of the mountain range.

But I had best quote Eginhard, his biographer, who I understand is our principal authority:

Charles led his troops back without loss; but at the top of the Pyrenees he made acquaintance with the treachery of the Basques. The army was obliged by the straitness of the path to march in a long-drawn-out file. Meanwhile the Basques had stationed themselves on the very summit of the mountains, a perfect place for an ambush, as the woods were very thick; and they burst out from their place of vantage down upon the rear guard (which had the baggage train in its keeping), drove them in disorder into the valley below, hung on the flanks of the fugitives, and slew them all to the last man. Then, under cover of darkness, they plundered the baggage, and in a great hurry scattered every which way. The Basques had in their favor the advantages of place and of light arms, while the Franks were in a wretched position and encumbered by heavy armor. In the battle Eggihard, purveyor to the King's table, Anselm, Count of the Palace, and Roland, Count of the March of Brittany, were killed; and many more. It was impossible to punish the attack, for the enemy immediately scattered no one knew where.

The historical importance of this episode lies in the evidence it affords that religion was not the cause of any of the fighting mentioned. Christian Franks united with Moslems to fight other Moslems, and Christian Basques ambushed fellow Christians. The literary importance is incomparably greater, for Roncevaux, as a mountain pass, ranks next in fame to Thermopylæ; and the *Chanson de Roland* is a sort of mediæval *Iliad*. Of this pass, the pilgrims' guide-book that I have quoted says:

Near this mountain, to the north, lies the valley called Charles's Valley, where Charles and his army were bivouacking when his knights were killed at Roncevaux. . . . Afterward as you go down the mountain you come to the hospice, and to the church in which is the great rock that the mighty hero Roland split with his sword at the third stroke, from top to bottom. Then you come to Roncevaux, where the great battle was fought where King Marsile and Roland and Oliver and one hundred and forty warriors, Christians and Saracens, were slain.

In the church, also, so it was said, Roland's oliphant was hung, and might be seen there in Don Quixote's time. At present the only surviving mementoes are Bishop Turpin's slippers.

The Spaniards, however, did not accept either Eginhard's account that Charlemagne's rear guard was ambushed by Basques, or that of the French poet, that it was attacked by Saracens, guided by the traitor Ganelon; they produced a third version, according to which the men of Leon and Asturias defeated the French, and Bernardo del Carpio strangled Roland with his own hands. Various ballads express this first burst of national feeling against the French:

Con los mejores de Asturias
sale de Leon Bernardo,
puestos á punto de guerra,
á impedir á Francia el paso.

With the best men of Asturias
From Leon Bernardo goes,
With sword and spear to guard the pass
Against their Frankish foes.

As the story went, King Alfonso II, the Chaste, having no son, proposed to make Charlemagne his heir, but the patriotic nobles were horrified at this national dishonor, and with Bernardo at their head opposed the invaders at Roncevaux. There are other legends concerning Bernardo, his birth, his father's imprisonment and murder by the treacherous king, familiar to us in Lockhart's translations, but they lie outside our path. So, skipping a hundred years and more, I proceed at once to the next national hero, Count Fernán González (895?–970).

By this time the little kingdom of Navarre had appeared to the east, and the little kingdom of Asturias had spread over Leon and also over a good part of the region to the south, which the Spaniards had made secure by building many castles. This castellated region (Castile) was, until the time of Fernán González, a mere dependent province, whose counts were subject to the king of Asturias and Leon; but Count Fernán González, by shifting his sails to every wind, succeeded in securing local independence, so that within a generation or two Castile took its place as an acknowledged equal by the side

of the kingdoms of Leon and Navarre. Finally, after
a period of partnership with Leon, Castile absorbed
its partner and became the chief power in Spain.
What seems to have been disloyalty to his sovereign
in Fernán González lies interred with his bones, while
his romantic deeds flaunt themselves triumphantly in
chronicle and ballad: how he was imprisoned by the
king of Navarre and eloped with the king's daughter;
how he was imprisoned by the king of Leon and
escaped because his wife came in and exchanged
clothes with him; how he did this and did that, and
so forth. According to the *Primera Crónica General*,
his career begins with his election by the nobles of
Castile to be their Count, "because he was true to
his word [the power of patriotic pride is more powerful than the most obdurate fact], wise in judgment, a
very valiant and puissant knight." The *Crónica*
continues with a record of many flashing feats of
arms, performed against the Moors, the King of
Navarre, or the Count of Toulouse, whom in personal combat he ran through the body. But his great
renown is due to bearding his own sovereigns, in
particular King Ordoño III (r. 950–955), with whom
he quarreled over the boundaries between Leon and
Castile. As the ballad says:

> Sobre el partir de las tierras
> ahí pasan malas razones;
> llámanse hi-de-rameras,
> hijos de padres traidores.

Out of all these legendary stories one fact stands
clearly: that neither Christian lord nor Moslem chief
troubled his head much about patriotism or religion,
but acted under the spur of ambition or revenge.

Fernán González, however, has a secure place in history as the founder of the fortunes of Castile, a sort of *Pater Patriæ*, who gave the first great push to the movement that made the counts of Castile kings of Spain and *la lengua castellana* the language of Spanish literature.

VII

THE CID (1040–1099)

I PASS over another hundred and fifty years of forgotten feuds, to a time when the kingdom of Leon and Castile has spread well to the south of the river Douro and includes the ancient cities of Salamanca and Segovia, and when the little Christian kingdoms of Navarre and of Aragon, also the county of Barcelona, are well established along the southern slopes of the Pyrenees. In the Moslem territories the dynasty of the Omayyads has come to an end, and their subject states have fallen apart, as if a cord that bound a bundle of faggots had been cut. Here was an opportunity for Christian gentlemen adventurers; and we find Ruy (or Rodrigo) Diaz de Bivar, *el mio Cid Campeador*, rising to the height of the occasion. Cid is an Arabic title meaning "lord," given to Ruy Diaz by the Moors, and Campeador signifies "champion." This hero has a double personality. One was a man of flesh and blood, a condottiere of fortune, who led a troop of sharked-up adventurers to fight on either side, for or against Moslems or Christians, whether for hire or booty, wherever money was to be got; who broke treaties, cheated Jews, sacked churches, mocked all notions of loyalty, and did whatever primitive covetousness might suggest. Happily this groveling kind of history did not exist in those days; it was left to be dug up by the curiosity of modern scholars. The real Cid lives glorious in high romance, in chronicle and ballad, the hero of a militant nation. With the *Poema del Cid* Spanish literature begins; in fact, I believe that, except for a charter or two, it is the oldest monument in the Castilian tongue, as well as one of the noblest. In the *Poema del Cid* the personages are real, the localities mentioned are correctly placed, historical usages are truthfully depicted and the battles accurately enough. But perhaps, before speaking of the poem, I had better give the historical setting of the story.

Fernando I of Castile and Leon (*r.* 1037–1065) was the first monarch to assume the title, King of Castile. By his last will, setting a bad precedent that other kings were foolish enough to follow, he divided his monarchy up among his three sons and two daughters. The eldest son, Sancho II (*r.* 1065–1072), by despoiling his brothers and sisters managed to reunite the severed dominions; and on Sancho's death, his brother, Alfonso VI (1072–1109), succeeded to the reunited kingdom. Alfonso VI continued his father's energetic warfare against the Moors, and is famous for the recapture of Toledo (1085). Ruy Diaz, who is first heard of in the reign of Fernando I, was born at Bivar, a little place some three miles north of Burgos, probably about 1040. This makes him a contemporary of William the Conqueror, of Hildebrand (Pope Gregory VII), and of the Emperor Henry IV who knelt in the snow outside the castle of Canossa. Of his early life virtually nothing is known. The Cid's love for Doña Ximena, — the Chimène of *le grand Corneille*, — the quarrel between her father and his, the fatal duel, famous in ballad and drama, are not mentioned in the *Poema del Cid*, which begins its narrative just after a quarrel between the Cid and King Alfonso. The cause of the quarrel can only be conjectured. Perhaps it was because the Cid fought in the service of King Sancho when he dispossessed Alfonso. Another explanation is given in the *Crónica General*, compiled some five or six generations later. The nobles suspected that Alfonso had poisoned his elder brother, and Ruy Diaz obliged the King to go to church and purge himself by oath. A third account, which bears an odious look of probability, suggests that Ruy Diaz, while in the service of Alfonso, kept back some booty that belonged to the King. Whatever the cause, there had been a quarrel; and the poem begins with the Cid's banishment.

The first verses extant — for the opening lines are lost — secure the reader's sympathy. The banished Cid is leaving his house in Bivar; he weeps and casts longing looks backward:

> *Delos sos oios tan fuerte mientre lorando*
> *tornava la cabeça y estava los catando.*

But very soon the poet introduces a humorous touch. The Cid says to his faithful squire, Martin Antolinez: "I have spent my gold and all my silver; you see clearly that I have no money left, and I must have some for my troopers; I must get it, and I shall get nothing for the wishing. By your advice I propose to make two coffers. We will fill them with sand to make them very heavy, cover them with leather, and stud them well with nails; the leather shall be scarlet and the nails all gilded well. You shall go for me privily to Rachel and Vidas." Antolinez goes to the two

Hebrew money-lenders; he tells them that the coffers are full of gold taken from the Moors, and too heavy to carry; that the Cid wishes to borrow six hundred marks on their security, but that they must not open the coffers for a whole year. The two Jews think it over, decide that they need to make a little money, and ride out in high glee to the Cid's tent. The Cid greets them with a smile. They pay the money down and take the coffers with excessive obsequiousness:

> *Ya Canpeador, en buen ora çinxiestes espada!*
>
> Ah, Champion, in happy hour you girded sword!

The Jews are so obviously delighted with their bargain that the wily squire is able to wheedle them out of a recompense for his services as broker. It seems to me, though others think differently, that the poet saw nothing derogatory in playing a scurvy trick on Jews, and that the Spanish public has agreed with him; for one of these coffers is still shown in the cloister of Burgos cathedral.

The Cid then rode to the monastery of San Pedro de Cardeña, about six or seven miles southeast of Burgos (where his tomb and that of his wife, Doña Ximena, still are, and where their ashes reposed until they were removed to the cathedral). Here he found his wife on her knees praying to God for him:

> *Tu que atodos guias, vala myo Çid el Canpeador,*
>
> Thou that guardest all men, prosper my Cid, the Champion.

Their parting is full of tenderness; it was like "tearing nails from the flesh" —

> O Lady Ximena, my perfect wife,
> As dearly as my soul, I love thee!

But go he must. He rode south, across the Douro, as far as Alcalá de Hinares, a place destined to become famous as the seat of a university and the birthplace of Cervantes. Then follow ambuscades, forays, and martial enterprises against the Moors or the Count of Barcelona, in which the Cid won his earlier glory as well as his swords, "Colada" and "Tison." The most famous episode is that in which his standard-bearer, Bermuez, violating the Cid's command not to break ranks, dashes ahead into the very centre of the Mohammedan army and the Cid is obliged to follow. Of course a great victory is won, "a grand day for Christianity." The final exploit is the capture of Valencia (1087) and the defeat of a relieving army, when the Cid got his charger, Babieca, in his share of the spoils.

A hundred years ago Southey said that this epic is by far the finest in Spanish, and all the world agrees with him. Menéndez y Pelayo, one of the most erudite and accomplished of modern Spanish scholars and literary critics, says that the poem is the product of a mysterious art that works like Nature herself, and is of necessity lost in days of scholarship and printing. It is, he says, profoundly national, passionately patriotic, and manifests the qualities of the Castilian spirit: high temper, a grave discourse, a noble simplicity, dignified courtesy, loftiness without affectation, imagination solid rather than brilliant, and an ardent piety. To those that cannot read the Spanish, Ormsby's version, or bits of translation made by J. Hookham Frere, will give some idea of the versification. Frere is the man that translated Aristophanes so brilliantly and was sent as British envoy to Madrid by Canning in Napoleon's time.

The poem has often been compared with the *Chanson de Roland*. Comparisons are odious. To my mind it lacks the note of high tragedy, the intensity of emotion, the mastery of language, that mark the *Chanson de Roland*. If I had to make a comparison, I think I should fetch out *Marmion*.

There is a second episode in the poem, which recounts how the two princes of Carrión, insufferable snobs and blackguards, marry the Cid's two daughters, maltreat them beyond belief and, being forced to a judicial combat, are defeated; and how the rejected daughters marry the heirs to the thrones of Castile and Aragon. As a poem it is of much less interest than the part devoted to border warfare.

In this connection I will mention the tragic story of *Los Siete Infantes de Lara*. The epic is lost, but fragments sufficient to tell the plot were embedded, after the fashion of those days, in the *Crónica General*, and various passages have passed into ballads. The story is laid in the time of the great Vizier Almanzor. The Nobles of Lara attended the wedding of their mother's brother. A quarrel arose, insults passed, and the youngest infante killed a cousin of the bride; later there were further outrages and another death. The aunt planned vengeance and, by the treacherous contrivance of her husband, the seven brothers were basely killed. A young half-brother, Mudarra, born of Almanzor's sister, when he grew to be eighteen learned of this treason and put his uncle and aunt to death. The ballads that sprang from this lost epic, according to Gaston Paris, are among the very best in Spanish ballad poetry.

All Spanish ballads — *romances*, as they are

called — are a little disappointing to beginners because of their form. We are used to a swing and
rhyme, as in *Chevy Chase;* but these are in long verses
of sixteen syllables — usually divided in two by print-
ers — that end not with a rhyme but with an asso-
nant, that is, where the vowel in the terminal syllable
(I mean the last vowel that is stressed, disregarding a
final *e,* for instance, that is not) is the same, but the
consonants are or may be different.

VIII

ARCHITECTURE IN THE TWELFTH
AND THIRTEENTH CENTURIES

The Cid's career marks the triumph of Spanish arms over the broken fragments of the Omayyad caliphate, and ends with the advent of the Almoravides and the ensuing revival of the Moslem power. He died in 1099, the year in which that other romantic scourge of Islam, Godfrey of Bouillon, recovered Jerusalem. At that time Portugal was not yet independent, Leon not finally united with Castile, nor the county of Barcelona with Aragon; but for convenience' sake we may prematurely assume these changes to have been accomplished, and on our map for the twelfth century draw a rough-and-ready boundary line between Christians and Moslems that starts at Lisbon on the Atlantic coast, runs eastward along the river Tagus, and onward across the peninsula to the Mediterranean, at a point somewhere near the mouth of the Ebro.

Of political history during the one hundred and fifty years from 1100 to 1250 I shall say but little, and that incidentally, for anybody can readily get an idea of mediæval warfare by reading a chapter or two in Froissart or an act of Shakespeare's *Henry VI*. The space thus saved I shall devote to other matters.

In this stretch of time Spain produced but one great man, Saint Dominic (1170–1221), and his career belongs to Provence and Italy rather than to Spain. The only great achievement in literature is the *Poema del Cid*, of which I have just spoken, composed about 1140. So I proceed to the architectural monuments of the period, which lie scattered about in various cities and towns of northern Spain.

In these cathedrals and churches the inspiration, and the art that embodied the inspiration, whether Romanesque or early Gothic, came from France, although in most cases touched and tinged by various other influences. The earliest breath of French genius was felt at Compostela, where the cathedral of Santiago is — as I have said — very similar in the plan of its original construction to St. Sernin at Toulouse; for even if the cathedral was built first, and if ideas and formulæ passed to and fro across the border, and even if its first architects, Bernard, *magister mirabilis*, and Robert, were not Frenchmen, yet the plan is obviously due to the same trained conception of what such a church should be; and this conception, as well as the training necessary to carry it out, could only have come directly or indirectly from France.

In the eleventh century, when Rome lay enervated and feeble, a prey to unworthy political ambitions, the great Benedictine abbey of Cluny in Burgundy had risen to be the spiritual head of Latin Christendom. There many a famous prelate was bred, and the abbey had become a fiery furnace of reform. At that time national spirit had not yet made the Pyrenees the racial barrier that they finally became, and Spanish kings in moments of solicitude for their souls, or moved by the purpose of furnishing parishes recovered from the Moors with clergy of a piety more ardent than that which they found at home, — whether with or without some ulterior political motives, — turned for help to Cluny. In answer to their requests monks came, bringing with them definite notions both of religious practices and of church architecture. Auvergne and Burgundy are for the first period of Spanish architecture what the Île-de-France became for the second period.

The French influence radiated from Santiago of Compostela roundabout. You will perceive it in the cathedrals of Tuy, Lugo, and Orense in Galicia, all three built in the twelfth century; and farther away, in the cathedral of Ciudad Rodrigo, the *catedral vieja* at Salamanca, and the church of San Isidoro in the town of Leon, all built about this time; and also in the cathedral at Zamora on the river Douro, a city famed for its pride in that Scipio Africanus the Younger had said, "It is no easy matter to fight with the citizens of Zamora." And in Old Castile, at Ávila, the churches of San Vicente and of San Pedro, as well as the cathedral, bear the marks of a builder's art derived from Burgundian and Angevin sources.

That first great wave of French influence was due to the spiritual force that proceeded from the abbey of Cluny and dominated ecclesiastical matters, both moral and architectural, for generations. But success opened the door to comfort, luxury, pomp; the Order of Cluny became puffed up, seeking its own and more than its own; and under the leadership of Saint Bernard, the sterner-minded among the monks, idealists, believers in simplicity, shook the dust from their feet and founded a new order at Cîteaux. Thereupon a

second great wave of moral and architectural influence radiated forth from the Cistercian monasteries
and, having set its mark of simplicity upon the regions
of central France, passed on into Spain.

The earliest important monument of the Cistercian
order in Castile is the abbey of Las Huelgas, just out
of Burgos, where the first influences of the Gothic
style blend with the Romanesque in what Señor
Lamperez calls the *estilo románico de transición*. The
vaulting shows both Angevin formulæ and those used
in the Île-de-France. It is said that the earlier portions were constructed from 1180 to 1230, and the
rest from 1230 to 1279. Another famous Cistercian
edifice, which served as the burial place for the kings
of Aragon, the monastery of Poblet, is now sadly
damaged but noble still; the solid round arches and
the vault of its nave testify that they were built before the Gothic style came in. But at Poblet and at
Las Huelgas, as in the case of most great churches, the
edifice was not completed for scores of years, and each
new generation had its own architectural notions.

The hasty traveler who trips lightly down the centuries must perforce pass the minor churches by, and
even in front of the most famous cathedrals can tarry
for no more than a moment. Of all the ecclesiastical
buildings of the thirteenth century the cathedrals
at Burgos, Toledo, and Leon stand in the foremost rank, singing together, as the Bible says of the
morning stars, in a chorus of praise to God, Our Lady,
and the divinely given genius of France. Sometimes
a browsing reader comes across a patriotic Spaniard
who belittles the influence of France upon these and
other Spanish churches. In answer to this the testi-

mony of the buildings themselves is sufficient; but instead of attempting to enumerate their French borrowings or imitations I shall narrate briefly the channels by which French influence came into Spain; and to do so I must start some way back.

Sancho the Great (970–1035), King of Navarre, who extended his sway over Leon, Castile, and Aragon, believing that he had received divine help in his wars with the Moors and not wishing his gratitude to pass off in barren emotion, set himself to revive monastic life in the dominions reconquered from the infidels. This he proposed to do — regretting that he himself was not a monk — by introducing "the most perfect" of all ecclesiastical orders. He sent a company of religious men to Cluny to learn these perfect monastic ways, and on their return settled them near the northern border of Aragon in the monastery of San Juan de la Peña (1020). He also induced the hierarchy of Aragon to agree to choose its bishops from among these monks. Nor did he neglect Castile; at Oña he reformed the nunnery of San Salvador, *pulsis ex eo monialibus quarum vita parum vitæ monasticæ regulæ respondebat.* Altogether King Sancho flung the gates wide open to receive the ideas of Cluny.

On Sancho's death, his son Fernando I (*r.* 1037–1065), of whom I spoke when recounting the Cid's early career, carried on the same ecclesiastical policy. So did his son, the Cid's enemy, Alfonso VI (*r.* 1065–1109), whether from a considered approval of that policy or because he was influenced by one or more of his four French wives. Alfonso made the abbot of Cluny director of religious matters in Castile, and appointed Cluniac monks to the principal ecclesiastical positions in his realm. Don Bernardo, a Frenchman from Guienne, was made abbot of the monastery at Sahagún, the most important in Castile, and then, by the King's doing, metropolitan of Toledo, soon after that city had been retaken from the Moors (1085). Not content with these distinctions, Don Bernardo persuaded the Pope to raise the see of Toledo to be the first among the five metropolitan sees in Spain, thereby himself becoming primate. Other monks of Cluny were appointed to the bishoprics of Osma, Braga, Siguenza, Segovia, Valencia, and Coimbra; and, if further proof of the influence of Cluny is needed, at the instigation of the abbot the King substituted the Roman ritual throughout the redeemed Spanish territory in place of the old Mozarabic ritual, which the Christians had used for centuries while under Moslem rule.

Incidentally, King Alfonso VI also gave fresh impetus to this ecclesiastical policy by the marriage of his daughter Urraca to a Burgundian nobleman, Raimundo, and of his two illegitimate daughters to other French lords, all three of whom were cousins to his French wife, Constance. Don Raimundo, it is said, was one of the judges who sat in trial upon the Infantes of Carrión for the outrage that they had committed upon the Cid's daughters, but he plays a more historic part in this matter of introducing French architecture into Spain; for, in order to revive the depopulated cities of Salamanca, Avila, and Segovia, he brought in gentlemen from France, also master builders and masons. No doubt Don Raimundo had in mind the building of fortifications, citadels, with barbicans, sally-ports, and so forth; nevertheless it is probable that these French artisans, or their sons, built or helped build the churches in these three cities. The son of Don Raimundo and Urraca became King Alfonso VII (*r.* 1126–1157). He was all French by his father and half French by his mother, and naturally leaned still further toward French ideas. Within fifteen years he founded several Cistercian monasteries in Castile, Aragon, and Galicia, and more somewhat later.

Alfonso's son, Sancho III (*r.* 1157–1158), applied to the abbot of Cîteaux for help to defend his frontier. The abbot approved and, by the monastic conversion of a valiant body of men-at-arms into lay brethren, the famous military Orders of Calatrava and Alcántara were established under the Cistercian rule. Sancho's son, Alfonso VIII (*r.* 1158–1214), hero of Las Navas de Tolosa (1212), married a daughter of the Angevin Henry II of England, and this royal couple founded (1180) the Cistercian nunnery of Las Huelgas outside Burgos, to which I have alluded, famous in Castilian annals because Ferdinand III was knighted there (1219), Alfonso el Sabio crowned (1254), Edward Longshanks, Prince of Wales, knighted, and I believe married also, and several later kings crowned under its sacred roof.

The grandson of Alfonso VIII and his English Queen was Fernando III (*r.* 1217–1252), the conqueror and saint who holds a position in Spanish history like that of his cousin Saint Louis in French history.

And with him we pass out of the period of Romanesque architecture and enter that of the Gothic. As

the story goes, when young Fernando was eighteen
or nineteen and it was time for him to take a wife,
the Bishop of Burgos was one Mauricio, who is
commonly thought to have been an Englishman —
by which I assume that an English Angevin is meant.
Bishop Maurice was sent to Swabia to ask the hand
of Princess Beatrice, a daughter of the imperial house
of Hohenstaufen. He journeyed by way of Paris and
saw Notre-Dame, then in the course of construction,
and very likely other French cathedrals. The consequence was that the new cathedral of Burgos was
built in the Gothic style. The corner stone was
laid in 1221. In the *coro* — that portion of the
nave fenced off for the clergy, according to Spanish
fashion — stands his tomb, one of the noblest in
Spain.

The style of the main body of the building is
French Gothic. Street says that "in almost all the
details throughout the original work of the cathedral
there is little, if anything, to show that we are not in
France and looking at some of the best and purest
thirteenth-century Gothic . . . the whole being pure,
simple, and good." The steeples, the lantern, and the
"constable's chapel" are all much later, and so are
the rich accessories within. But I shall not attempt
any description; a cathedral is to be looked at — not
written about. To the citizens of Burgos it appears
labrada como por mano de ángeles, and a sensitive
French spirit, Frédéric Ozanam, says: "*Burgos
s'annonce d'abord comme un édifice jeune, élancé,
qui n'est point sans majesté, mais qui a surtout l'élé-
gance et la grâce.*" But a better tribute still is that
from the lady who asked what God would do with the

cathedral on the Day of Judgment: "*Pourquoi ces monuments n'auraient ils pas aussi leur immortalité ou leur résurrection?*"

The cathedral of Toledo, begun in 1227, is — so Borrow and many others have thought — "the most magnificent in Spain." The rocky hill on which the city stands is a fit base for this noble building. The western façade with its deeply recessed doors, its niches, buttresses, carved railings, and its magnificent tower, belongs to the fifteenth century; so does the Puerta de los Leones to the south; and, in fact, I believe nothing of the exterior belongs to the early Gothic of the first architects. But for those whose artistic education has been neglected, changes of taste, of fashion, of style, in succeeding generations, are like different growths in a forest. They add a richness beyond the compass of a single mind; each sets the other off, and by their very dissonance they create a magnificence that the simplicity of a single style cannot attain. The interior is glorious; the noble nave with its attendant aisles, the choir girdled by its double ambulatory, the arches, vaults, columns, together with grilles, retablos, tombs, sculpture, and glass, make this cathedral one of the royalest treasure-houses of art in all the world. The architect was Petrus Petri — Peter the son of Peter; and though some Spanish scholars have claimed him as a fellow countryman and call him Pedro Pérez, it seems more likely, from his intimate knowledge of French Gothic, that he was a Frenchman. At any rate, visitors to Toledo, whatever their notion of Petrus Petri's nationality, will unite in an amen to the prayer in his epitaph: O THOU THAT ART ALONE, THOU THAT RULEST

ALL THINGS, SHOW MERCY TO HIM THAT WROUGHT THIS THY TEMPLE SO WONDERFULLY.

The third of these glorious sisters, the cathedral at Leon, was begun somewhere about 1250. This cathedral, *Pulchra Leonina* (the Beauty of Leon), as it is called, rises — I quote Señor Lampérez — "in the pure lines of Rheims, Amiens, and Beauvais, and represents the complete triumph of the Gothic style of the Île-de-France and Champagne, liberated from the lingering traits of the Romanesque." As the cathedral stands to-day, the west front, except for the stately sculptured porch, is a little disappointing; the towers edge away from the nave, the spires lack grace, and the gable and pinnacles above the rose window are quite inadequate. But the building is all glorious within. "Let there be light," the architect said, and he designed the piers that divide window from window as slender and delicate as the weight of the roof would endure. His triumph — for which, to be sure, he paid by the necessity of rebuildings from time to time — was brilliant; the light pours in from aisle, triforium, and clerestory through the exquisite glass, which glaziers of the thirteenth and succeeding centuries, grateful for so rare an opportunity, wrought in a fashion worthy of the highest heavens of effulgent glory in Dante's Paradise. There the pilgrim loses himself in the purification of heavenly color and, filled with an emotion he cannot express in words, wanders forth into the cloister, where in the shadows cast by crocket, finial, and balustrade from the cathedral roof, he muses upon the meaning of life and the vanity of all that is not religious. *Omnia vanitas præter amare Deum et illi soli servire.*

IX

ALFONSO EL SABIO (1221-1284)

As the last chapter concerned itself solely with architecture, I slurred over the great series of Christian victories in the first half of the thirteenth century, which dislodged the Moors from all the regions of the South except the little kingdom of Granada, where, thanks to the quarrels among the Christian States, the last Moorish dynasty maintained itself for two hundred and fifty years longer. Alfonso VIII, who built Las Huelgas, the aristocratic nunnery outside Burgos, won the great battle of Las Navas de Tolosa in 1212. His grandson Fernando III, who founded the three great Gothic cathedrals at Toledo, Burgos, and Leon, continued the triumphant war. So did his valiant contemporary the King of Aragon, Don Jaime *el Conquistador*, of whose career a Frenchman says: "*Rien de plus intéressant que l'histoire de ce beau colosse barbare, brave, généreux, brutal, vantard, malin, et naïf.*" They are the two heroes of the glorious campaigns that followed. They raged in Andalusia like Diomed and Ajax over the Trojan plain. Mérida was taken, 1228; Badajos and the island of Majorca, 1229; Minorca, 1232; Ibiza, 1235; Cordova, 1236; Valencia, 1238; Murcia, 1241; Jaen, 1246; Seville, 1248; and Cadiz, 1262. These victories represent the brutal aspect of the religious fervor that found, as I have narrated, its nobler expression in pointed arches, clustered columns, and flying buttresses. "The tumult and the shouting dies." Hardly a tourist seeks the sloping plain beneath the Sierra Morena, where the battle of Las Navas de Tolosa was fought; but the religious awe and majesty embodied in the Gothic cathedrals draw aliens and foreigners to visit them from all over the world.

This energetic thirteenth century was full of achievements, and I shall now take a hasty glance at what it accomplished in literature.

There is, or was, a few miles from Nájera, near the river Ebro, the little village of Berceo. Here Saint Millan, a saint of much repute in Spain, was born, and also, several generations later, a poet named Gonzalo. This Gonzalo de Berceo (1198–1264) was successively pupil, deacon, and priest in a Benedictine monastery hard by, and seems to have spent his life in simple monastic duties, which, however, left him sufficient leisure to write several long poems: *The Life of Saint Dominic of Silos; The Life of Saint Millan; On the Sacrifice of the Mass; The Martyrdom of Saint Lawrence*, as well as lauds to Our Lady, and hymns, and such things. These poems, I should suppose, would no longer be read in the United States by anybody not ambitious for a Ph.D., but they have their little niche in the columbarium of literary fame, and for two reasons: first, they are the earliest Spanish poems whose author is known; and second, they introduce a new kind of poetry, which Spaniards call the *mester de clerecía*, quite different from the epic or the popular ballads.

One practitioner describes the style in these terms:

Mester es sin peccado, ca es de clerecia,
fablar curso rimado per la quaderna via
a sillavas contadas, ca es grant maestria,

which, freely interpreted, means that the poem is written in stanzas of four lines of fourteen syllables each (or sometimes twelve or thirteen), all ending in one rhyme, with the stress on the sixth syllable in each half-line, and composed in an academic style, such as would be acceptable to educated men. Hookham Frere translated a few stanzas from one of Berceo's poems, if the reader should be curious to see a sample.

An unsympathetic Beginner is tempted to think that Berceo exercised unnecessary ingenuity in putting into rhyme stories that could have been told much better in prose; but his more appreciative countrymen suggest that he has something in common with Dante, and praise the mystic fervor of his verses to the Virgin. However, as scholars are apt to champion the object of their study, I shall not quote their opinions, but rather that of a clever modern critic, Azorín, who describes Berceo in this somewhat over-imaginative fashion:

From before the window of a monastic cell a gracious landscape stretches away: green meadows, soft as velvet, a clear smooth-sliding brook, with a clump of poplars mirrored in its limpid surface. Within the white walls of the cell a monk is writing verses. He is describing a landscape. This landscape is green and neatly beautified; it is studded thick with fragrant flowers; clear waters jet forth from pebbled fountains, in summer fresh and cool, in winter, warm. Groves of trees stand in the fields and lift their rounded tops in sharp outline against the blue sky, while here and there young pomegranates and fig trees, delicate and sensitive, withdraw timidly from the rough thickets of old trees — young pomegranates, with twisted trunks and flaming blossoms, that stand a-tiptoe on hillocks and peer curiously at the horizon; fig trees, moist epicures that shun the cold, fold themselves in their dense foliage, and crouch in the damp bottom of the hollows. Many other fruit-trees may be seen in the close and in the garden. From the fields roundabout — especially at the twilight hour of vespers — a sweet, grateful fragrance creeps into the monk's little cell. How good to be there! And how pleasant it is, after writing for a long stretch, to look out upon this landscape and sip leisurely a goblet of good wine, light, pellucid, fragrant wine, from those very fields.

The intellectual story of Spain in the thirteenth century, however, is dominated by another man, King Alfonso X, el Sabio, the Wise or Learned (1221–1284), the son of San Fernando, said to be "one of *los grandes civilizadores* in the annals of mankind." Like Prospero, "in the liberal arts without a parallel," he dedicated himself "to closeness and the bettering of his mind," far too much for a king called upon to perform hard political tasks. Mariana, the Spanish historian, says: "*Dum cœlum considerat observatque sidera terram amisit.*" However, his reputation was such that, after the death of the Emperor Frederick II (1250), some of the electors of the Holy Roman Empire, looking upon him as heir — through his mother — to the Hohenstaufen claim, chose him as their candidate in opposition to the Englishman, Richard Duke of Cornwall. Alfonso was not able to do very much to enforce his claim. Once he sent a body of twelve hundred horse to Genoa, but beyond that he did little more than make a stout assertion of his claims and show a

gracious hospitality to Italian envoys, whether a
Ghibelline from Pisa or the Guelph Brunetto Latini
from Florence. The King had excuses enough for
not undertaking a struggle for the imperial crown.
The election was not popular in Spain; the Popes
played fast and loose; and Castile was poor. His
real faults were neglect of political duties at home,
heavy taxes for the sake of his imperial ambitions,
a prodigal mode of living, and the foolish taking up
and laying down of doubtful claims on Navarre and
Gascony. In consequence of what he did and what
he did not do, first his brother and then his son
rose in rebellion, supported by the larger part of
the barons, who were always ready to grasp at any
chance of enlarging their own independence. After
a few years of civil war Alfonso died (1284) and
his son, Sancho IV, reigned in his stead. As Fernán
Pérez Guzmán says, Alfonso's career was full of
vicissitudes:

> *Siempre vivio trabajado*
> *por muy varias e diversas*
> *fortunas tristes adversas,*
> *e al fin desheredado.*

> His life in troubles sore he passed
> Through mishaps multifarious,
> Ill-fated and contrarious,
> And lost his kingdom at the last.

But Alfonso's place in history has to do with quite
other matters. What that place was, as it appeared
to his contemporaries, is told by his nephew, Don
Juan Manuel, of whom I shall soon speak:

Among the many good qualities that God gave to King
Don Alfonso, son to that holy and fortunate king, Don

Fernando, He gave him the desire to foster learning as much as ever he could; and Alfonso did so much for learning that, from the time of King Ptolemy until now, no king nor any other man can be named who did as much for it as he did. So great was his wish that his subjects should have more knowledge, that he caused to be translated into Castilian all the learning that concerns theology, logic, the seven liberal arts, and all the mechanical arts. He had the sacred books of the Moors translated, in order that the errors which Mohammed, their false prophet, put into them should be patent. Besides, he caused to be translated all the Hebraic law, even the Talmud, and that very secret learning that the Jews have and call Cabala. And he did this in order to make it plain that the Jewish law was nothing but a prefiguration of what we Christians have, and that they, as well as the Moors, were in such great error that they would lose their souls. Besides, he turned into Spanish all the canons and statutes that I shall speak of. Nobody can tell how much this noble king did, especially for the increase of knowledge and enlightenment. . . . He had many good books written, which treated fully of hunting, hawking, and fishing, in great detail both as to theory and practice. And he did it all so excellently that it is obvious that nobody could better it or add to it, or do it as well as he did.

This favorable opinion has maintained itself unshaken for six hundred years. A Spanish scholar says:

Alfonso el Sabio dominated the century both in literature and in general culture, not only before his accession to the throne but also after his death, so completely that its law, prose, poetry, and whatever influences came in from the East are all due to him. . . . He was our first and greatest legislator, the earliest of Spanish prose-writers and one of the best, the founder of Castilian prose, the best historian, and the best lyrical poet of his time; and besides all this, he brought in the science and civilization of the Arabs and the Jews, whether of Spain or the East, and in short gave the push that started all Spanish culture. His accomplishments did not merely consist in what he himself wrote, or in what he caused others to write, but in the immense influence of his royal example, and most of all in his championship of the Castilian tongue, which he substituted where he could for the traditional official Latin.

Three of Alfonso's works are preëminent, the *Crónica General, Las Siete Partidas,* and *Las Cantigas de Santa Maria.* The *General Chronicle* (a history of Spain) is as long, perhaps, as two volumes of Macaulay's *History of England;* it begins with the book of Genesis, lightly passes on to the story of Rome, which it tells at great length, and then proceeds to the doings of the Visigoths, and the history of Spain proper until the death of Alfonso's father, San Fernando. It is in the main a transcription of whatever Alfonso's scholars and scribes could find that bore upon the history of Spain in Ovid, Lucan, Suetonius, Orosius, Arabian and Spanish historians, Castilian minstrels, or in the works of Saint Isidore, and so on. The most interesting episodes are those that concern Bernardo del Carpio, Fernán González, and the Cid, all taken, I understand, from epics upon these heroes.

Las Siete Partidas, so called because of its division into seven parts, is a book of laws, almost as long as Blackstone's *Commentaries;* it has been thought to be an attempt — and if so it was certainly not a very successful attempt — to create a uniform code out of the multitudinous local laws and charters. Whatever its purposes may have been, its provisions are in part direct commands and in part paraphrases, or explanation and exhortation, such as a father might use in order to unfold gently to his children the reasons for family rules. Its eulogists say that it is of the greatest historical importance in that it influenced legislation for hundreds of years, not only in Spain but also in the Spanish colonies in America, including Louisiana. But, though it may be superior to the code of the Emperor Frederick II, enacted at Melfi (1231) for the Kingdom of Sicily, I should doubt very much if it can boast of any superiority over the contemporary treatise, *De legibus Angliæ*, by Bracton. It seems to preserve without condemnation very primitive customs, due I presume to the Visigoths, such as that a father, if poverty-stricken, may sell his son; or if starving during a siege and possessed of no other food, may eat him.

Of course Alfonso did not write the history or the code himself. He employed a staff of scholars, over whom he stood like a schoolmaster, directing, instructing, polishing; and for this he is fairly entitled to the praise of having conferred upon Castilian prose all those qualities of breeding, and elegance, of freedom from alien and vulgar words, or turns of phrase, that are implied in the familiar adjective *castizo*, so dear to Spanish critics.

The King's poems, *Las Cantigas de Santa Maria*, are not written in the Castilian dialect for which he did so much, but in that of Galicia, where at the time, it seems, the influence of the Provençal troubadours had advanced the arts of lyric poetry far

beyond what they were in Castile. These hymns to
the Virgin, according to Fitzmaurice-Kelly, are "of
incomparable beauty, pregnant with mystery and
terror." They were also much admired at the time,
as royal poetry often is; at any rate, the seeker after
culture, if he has the leisure, after studying the
poems in a printed book, will do well to look up the
beautifully illuminated codex in the Escorial, with
its charming miniatures, which, like the ecclesiastical architecture, betray the delicate touch of
French genius.

X
MEMORABILIA OF THE FOURTEENTH CENTURY

AFTER the death of Alfonso el Sabio several kings follow from father to son. Their reigns are full of rowdy noise. The rubric at the head of their biographies may well read: Alarums, excursions, retreats, and flourishes. Nothing could be more tedious than to investigate the civil wars in Castile, or the quarrels between Castile, Aragon, Navarre, and France. The Moors of Granada, although they sometimes chose to take the initiative and try their luck in a foray, were on the whole let alone and, consequently, they had leisure to irrigate their valleys, grow the musk rose and the myrtle, and in due course to build the Alhambra. They withdraw to the back of our stage and leave the space by the footlights to the victorious Castilians, who step forward and enact some famous romantic episodes.

Sancho IV (r. 1284–1295), the rebellious son of Alfonso el Sabio, succeeded to his father and most deservedly was confronted by rebellion in his turn. During his reign the first of the romantic episodes to which I have alluded took place. Nobody, I think, mentions the town of Tarifa — not only Spaniards, but all travelers, George Borrow, Richard Ford, their predecessors or followers — without stopping to praise Guzmán el Bueno. His place in drama and story is among the foremost. He was governor of

Tarifa on behalf of King Sancho when the town was
besieged (1294) by rebels who captured the governor's
young son, dragged him out into full view of the de-
fenders, and threatened to kill him unless the town
were surrendered. Guzmán refused, and to emphasize
his refusal flung a knife down from the walls. The
rebel leader picked it up and stabbed the boy to death
before his father's eyes.

Sancho IV was succeeded by his son Fernando IV
(r. 1295–1312), of whom I have nothing to say; and
Fernando by his son Alfonso XI (r. 1312–1350) who,
by those that have a knowledge of the political history of the time, is, in the language of red-backed
guidebooks, "favorably spoken of." During his
reign there was a fresh outcrop of wars with the
Moors, in one of which another romantic episode
occurred that redounds to the honor of a favorite
hero with those whose good fortune it is to have
been bred upon *Tales of a Grandfather*, and links
the story of Spain to that of Scotland. There have
been many ties between England and Castile: Alfonso
VII married Eleanor Plantagenet; Edward Longshanks married Isabella of Castile; two daughters of
Pedro the Cruel married the dukes of York and
Lancaster, sons to Edward III; Enrique III married
Catherine of Lancaster; and there have been military
alliances, though not often, from the days of the
Black Prince to those of the Duke of Wellington. For
long generations there was a religious and sentimen-
tal relation between Ireland and Castile, and Irish
names, Richard Wall, O'Reilly and O'Donnell, are
familiar in Spanish history. But I do not recall any
other direct contact with Scotland than this.

Robert the Bruce, hero of Bannockburn, died in 1329, and the good lord Sir James Douglas, better known as the Black Douglas, set forth to fulfill his promise to carry the Bruce's heart to the Holy Land. He got as far as Flanders, where he

kept alwaies his port and behaviour with great tryumphe, with trumpettis, and clarions, as though he had been kyng of Scottis hymselfe. . . . And whan he had thus taryed there the space of XII dayes, he hard reported that Alphons, kyng of Spaigne, made warre ageynst a sarazyn kyng, of Granade; then he thought to draw to that partie, thynking suerely he could nat bestowe his tyme more nobly, than to warre ageynst goddis ennemies; and that enterprise done, then he thought to go forth to Jerusalem, and to acheve that he was charged with. And so he departed, and toke the se toward Spaigne, and arryved at ye port of Valence, the great; then he went streight to the kyng of Spaigne, who helde his host ageynst the kyng of Granade sarazyn, and they were nere together, on the fronters of his lande; and within a while after that, this knyght, syr [James] Duglas was come to ye kyng of Spaigne, on a day, the kyng issued out into the felde, to aproche nere to his ennemies. And ye kyng of Granade issued out in like wyse on his parte, so that eche kyng myght se other with al their baners displayed. Than they arenged their batels eche ageynst other. Than syr [James] Duglas drewe out on the one syde, with all his company, to the entent to shewe his prowes the better. And whan he saw these batels thus ranged on both parties, and sawe that ye bataile of ye kyng of Spaigne began somewhat to advaunce towarde their ennemies, he thought than verelye that they shulde soone assemble to gether to fyght at hande strokes; and than he thought rather to be with the formest than with the hyndemoost, and strake his horse with the spurres, and al his company also, and dashte into the batelle of the

kyng of Granade, criyng "Duglas, Duglas!": wenyng to
hym [that is, he thought] the kyng of Spaigne and his host
had folowed, but they dyd not; wherfore he was deceyved,
for the Spaignysshe host stode styll. And so this gentle
knight was enclosed, and all his company with the sara-
zyns, where, as he dyd mervelles in armes, but fynally he
coulde not endure [he lifted high his arm and flung the
heart of the Bruce into the thickest of the enemy crying
"Go thou first, as always," and fought his way toward it]
so that he and all his company were slayne.

This Alfonso XI was an excellent Christian on
paynim battlefields, and his failure to support the
Black Douglas must have been an accident; but he
sowed tares at home that sprang up like the dragon's
teeth. With that evil harvest I shall concern myself
later, for in this chapter an observance of chronology
brings me back to literature, and with no violent
transition, since Don Juan Manuel (1282–1348), to
whose story I address myself, was not only a distinguished man of letters but a very valiant and quarrelsome soldier, and occupies the front of the stage
throughout this reign in whatever battles, skirmishes,
and double-dealings political history records. Don
Juan was a nephew of Alfonso el Sabio, and though
several other members of the royal family were distinguished by their intellectual attainments and their
contributions to literature, he ranks next to his
uncle, of whom he was justly proud, as the eulogy I
quoted testifies. Literature, however, was the pas-
time of his later years; during his youth and earlier
manhood, notwithstanding the testimony to the contrary adduced by the gravity, dignity, and self-re-
straint of his literary style, he was a sort of Castilian

Hotspur, quite capable of killing "some six or seven dozen," Moors or Christians, before breakfast and crying, "Fie upon this quiet life!" His daughter was betrothed to Alfonso XI, and as the King put her away, Don Juan rose in wrath, leagued with the Moors, and wrought what vengeance he could. In his later life, as I say, he took to literature and wrote a good many books; the only one generally remembered is *El Conde Lucanor*, which, according to Fitz-maurice-Kelly, is "one of the books of the world." It is a volume of short stories set in a framework after the fashion of the *Arabian Nights*. In place of Scheherazade, who told tales to the Caliph, Patronio, a sort of chamberlain, tells them to his master, Count Lucanor. Each story begins in the same way. The Count, puzzled over what he should do in a certain case, consults Patronio, who gives his counsel under the guise of an anecdote in which the same question is involved. The Count acts upon the advice, and the issue is invariably prosperous. These tales were picked up anywhere, partly from Oriental sources. Several of them are very familiar to us through La Fontaine's *Fables*, such as "The Fox and the Crow" and "The Man, the Boy, and the Donkey." Others we know indirectly, as, for instance, the story in which a dutiful wife maintains that mares are cows because her husband says so: a theme that Shakespeare adopted in the *Taming of the Shrew*. If I were to venture an opinion, Don Juan's talents have been sometimes overrated; he cannot lay claim to originality, for two books of Oriental stories had already been translated and had brought this literary form into popularity; and, although a Spanish scholar says that Don Juan is "*un estilista muy superior*," yet his style, however admirable for its direct, simple, child-like qualities, cannot compare in grace or vigor with Boccaccio's style, which though scarce twenty years later already exhibits the rich luxuriance and mastery of the Renaissance.

At the very time that Don Juan Manuel was busy with ambition, vengeance, or literary pursuits, there lived in the little town of Hita, near Alcalá de Henares, an archpriest in humble circumstances named Juan Ruiz, whose fame in recent years has far outstripped that of his princely contemporary. He wrote a book entitled *El libro de Buen Amor* (The Book of Rightly Directed Love). In dealing with an accepted classic it is much more suitable that I should put forward, at least at first, the opinion of a Spanish scholar. So I quote — chiefly, I confess, in order to put the reader on his guard against Spanish patriotism — Don Julio Cejador, only regretting that the rich colors of the original are sadly dimmed in my pale translation:

In our literature [he says] three peaks rise toward the stars and stand high among the topmost creations of human genius, *Don Quixote* among novels, *La Celestina* in drama, and *El Libro de Buen Amor* in satire, in lyrical poetry, and also in the drama, in fact, in every kind of literature, for all styles are mingled in the creative ebullitions of this unique poet. . . . In sinewy vigor, in flow of language, in strength of roaring life, in careless sincerity and openness of heart, the archpriest of Hita surpasses all the artists of the world. . . . He is like the Titan Polyphemus whom Homer describes, transplanted into literature. . . . Compared with this work of a real primitive in art, Greek literature is a sort of almond paste. For strength only Æschylus can be compared with him. He would feel at home pedestaled among the primitive artists of Egypt (for he would be among those that could understand him), or elbowing Ezekiel or Isaiah, spirits cast in the same mould — a truly colossal, masculine artist.

Nothing is known concerning this poet excepting what he himself says in the poem. He states that his name is Juan Ruiz, that he was born in Alcalá de Henares, that he was archpriest of Hita, that on one occasion he was entrusted with some important clerical duties by the Archbishop of Toledo (at that time a great historical personage, Cardinal Albornoz), and subsequently kept in prison for years by the same prelate. It is also apparent from the poem that the author has read a certain amount of canon law and various books then in vogue. Outside the poem the only item of evidence that touches upon this story is a record that in 1351 some other person was archpriest of Hita, and it is assumed, therefore, that Juan Ruiz was already dead by that time. All the scholars accept these biographical statements as facts, for no very good reason that I can see; nevertheless they differ among themselves as to the correct interpretation of the whole story, which purports to be an autobiographical confession of the poet's love affairs and at the same time professes to expose the evils of sensual love and to counsel a love of holy things. Some say, and I agree with them, that Juan Ruiz wrote coarse stories for the sake of entertaining readers who like such stories; while others maintain that he was a great moralist and merely wrote in the first person dramatically, as the most effective way of exposing the vices of the clergy, his contemporaries.

The book, though published as if it were a single poem, is really a collection of stories, fables, apothegms, and hymns, all loosely stitched together. The main story, which is taken almost verbatim from the Latin, is a disreputable love-affair in which there are three characters: Don Melon, who is assumed to be the author in person, Doña Endrina, and Trotaconventos (nunnery-messenger), a go-between. It is but fair to say that this version is much more decent than the original.

The fables, of which many are interwoven, are exceedingly well told; and the *serranillas*, which I should have supposed to be imitations of the French *pastourelles*, are, I am told, a native Spanish form and realistic pictures of mountain wenches. To my taste his proverbs are by far the best ingredient in the whole book:

> *Buen dinero yaze en vil correo*
> (Good money may lie in a cheap purse).
> *So mala capa yaze buen bevedor*
> (Under a bad cloak you may find a good drinker).
> *Más fierbe la olla con la su cobertera*
> (The pot boils best with its cover on).
> *El buen callar, cien sueldos vale en toda plaça*
> (A wise holding of the tongue is worth
> a hundred pence everywhere).

Of the miscellaneous episodes, I find the combat between Don Carnival and Lady Lent (which he takes from the French) much the most entertaining; it is roysterous, jolly, and full of youthful gayety. Lady Lent wins the fight on Ash Wednesday, but forty days later Don Carnival and Señor Amor make their triumphant return and everybody shouts for joy:

> *Dia era muy ssanto de la Pascua mayor:*
> *el sol salya muy claro é de noble color;*
> *los omes é las aves é toda noble flor,*
> *todos van rresçeber cantando al Amor.*

Bright on Easter morning, the holiest of days,
The sun rose up resplendent with noble golden rays,
And men and birds and flowers burst out in roundelays
And sallied forth to greet Lord Love and glorify his ways.

All the world turns out to do homage to Love — cavaliers, squires, clerks, priests, friars, monks, nuns, novices, dancing, singing, and playing every instrument you can think of, and shouting scraps of hymns: *Venite, exultemus! Te Amorem laudamus! Alleluia! Alleluia! Mane nobiscum, Domine!*

At the end of this book, probably in order to include all the poet's writings, come hymns to the Virgin, and a poem on the clergy of Talavera. This poem is a satire with the following simple plot: Don Gil Albornoz, the Archbishop, has sent orders to the clergy of Talavera to put away their concubines. It falls to the archpriest to read this pastoral injunction to the priests of the district; as he reads he bursts into tears, and all the clergy present protest angrily and put forward their several defenses. One says that it would be "an outrage upon charity to send away Orabuena, my niece"; another, that "my Theresa is a poor orphan girl," and so on. The credulous apologists of Juan Ruiz — believed to be himself the archpriest — say that the story proves first, that the Archbishop deemed him a person to be trusted;

second, that it was because he executed the injunction
that the clergy out of revenge bore false witness
against him and caused him to be put into prison. As
to all this fine flight of imagination, untrammeled by
any evidence whatever, I am quite incompetent to
judge. I confess, also, that the praises heaped Pelion-
on-Ossa so eruditely and patriotically by Don Julio
Cejador lie beyond the limits of my uninstructed
sympathy, for I could not for a moment put Juan
Ruiz in one category with Cervantes or Chaucer,
with whom it is the Spanish custom to compare him.
Nevertheless I bow to the general judgment upon the
skill of the poet's workmanship, upon his accomplished art in happy condensation of phrase. I feel
constrained to tell the Beginner that, to my thinking, of poetry in our English sense — simple, sensuous, impassioned, grave, gay, lively or severe, in all
the gamut from "Tam O'Shanter" to the "Lines
Composed near Tintern Abbey" — he will find no
trace whatsoever in *El Libro de Buen Amor*. But
others more competent to judge disagree with me.

XI
THE HOUSE OF TRASTAMARA

ONE must always remember that, while royal personages strut across the stage of history, far in the background the nameless multitude grunt and sweat at their daily routine — yokels feeding pigs, coaxing or belaboring obstinate little innocent-eyed donkeys, shepherds tending sheep, sunburnt husbandmen driving antique ploughs, or harvesting such crops as could brave the poor soil and marauding soldiers, girls carrying water jugs or washing clothes in the brook or in the town wash-basin, young men chaffing them, mothers chasing dirty little brats, old grandams gossiping, apprehensive of a Moorish raid or the character of the young lord of the castle, guilds jealous of each other, parents match-making, priests mumbling prayers, monks asking alms, cavaliers splashing mud, students, apprentices, and suchlike. I assume all these supernumeraries and the physical setting of the Spanish scene, the great dusty barren plateau of Castile, the long lines of jagged mountains that bound almost every horizon in Spain, the towered cities, the river beds now dry, now filled with torrents, the rich verdure of Andalusia, the lovely gardens of Murcia and Valencia — and asking my reader to "step lively," I return to the political dramatis personæ, who are now booked to play a bloody tragedy:

Don Pedro, King of Castile
Don Enrique of Trastamara, his bastard brother
The Black Prince, Lord of Aquitaine
Le Sieur Du Guesclin, French condottiere

If the play had been written by Sophocles, the chorus would have uttered solemn strophe and anti-strophe upon jealousy between brothers and the rival ambitions of England and France, each striving to win Castile to its interest.

Don Alfonso XI (r. 1312–1350), I have said, sowed dragon's teeth. He neglected his wife for Doña Leonor de Guzmán and left a large illegitimate family, of which Don Enrique, Count of Trastamara, was the oldest. This prince married a daughter of Don Juan Manuel, the author of *El Conde Lucanor*. I cannot record all the steps of Tragedy as she strides on to the last act. On the King's death, his legitimate son, Don Pedro, succeeded to the throne and not long afterward the Queen mother caused Doña Leonor, her preferred rival, to be poisoned. The bastards and their partisans looked to their own safety and revenge. Don Pedro may or may not have been an accomplice; but suspicion clung to him, and he also found many other ways of raising up enemies. He slighted the Castilian nobles by loading certain favorites with honors and riches; he was vengeful and frightfully cruel; and, following in his father's footsteps, he abandoned his wife, a French princess, for the beautiful Doña Maria de Padilla, and elevated her kinsmen to the chief offices of state. Froissart, a younger contemporary, describes him in this way:

Ther was a kyng in Castell, called Dampeter, who was full of marveylous opinyons, and he was rude and rebell

agaynst the commandementes of holy churche, and in
mynde to subdue all his cristen neyghbours, kinges, and
princes, and specially the king of Aragon, called Peter,
who was a gode true cristen prince, and had as than taken
fro him parte of his realme, thynking to have all the
remenant; also this kynge Dampeter of Castell had thre
basterd brethrene. . . . Theldest was called Henry. . . .
This king Dampeter hated them so that he wolde nat
suffre them to come in his syght, and often tymes if he
might have gotten them, he would have stryken of their
heedes.

Here, then, according to Froissart, were three sets
of enemies: the royal house of Aragon, the bastard
brothers, the slighted nobles, with their respective
followers and friends; and to them the rash King
added a fourth, France, by the ill treatment of his
wife, poor Queen Blanche, who did not live long;
rumor promptly asserted that he had poisoned her.

The inevitable consequence of Don Pedro's mis-
behavior was armed rebellion. England and France
were then in the grapple of the Hundred Years' War,
and of course deeply interested in the affairs of Castile. England, in order to strengthen her hold on
Aquitaine, supported Don Pedro, and sent the Black
Prince with an army of English and Gascons. France,
therefore, sided with Henry of Trastamara and sent
her high distinguished soldier Du Guesclin, with his
White Company of free lances, across the Pyrenees.
The fortunes of war shifted. First they declared in
favor of Don Enrique, for Bertrand Du Guesclin
turned the scale; and Enrique was crowned king
(1365). Then the Black Prince, glorious under the
laurels of Cressy and Poitiers, aided by his brother

John of Gaunt, won the great victory of Nájera
(1367). The story of this battle should be read in
Froissart. The Englishmen and their allies were out-
numbered five to one, but the Black Prince, "chefe
flour of chivalry of all the worlde," welcomed the
onset, and made a brief prayer:

> Very God, Jesu Christ, who hath formed and created
> me, consent by your benygne grace, that I may have this
> day victory of myne enemyes, as that I do is a ryghtfull
> quarell, to sustayne and to ayde this kynge, chased out of
> his owne herytage, the which gyveth me courage to
> avaunce myselfe to restablysshe hym agayne into his
> realme,

and he gave the command: "Avaunce baners, in the
name of God and saynt George!" The field was hard
fought; the Spanish slingers "clave and brake many
a bassenet and helme," while "the archers of Eng-
lande shotte fiersly and hurte spanyardes grevously,
and brought them to great mischefe." Enrique of
Trastamara bore himself right valiantly; three times
he rallied his men and led them to the charge again;
while "kyng Dampeter was greatly chafed, and
moche desyred to mete with the bastarde his brother,
and sayd 'Where is that horeson, that calleth hymselfe kynge of Castell?'" Finally the French troops
in Enrique's army were overcome, Du Guesclin and
many noblemen were captured; the Spanish levies
gave way and fled.

At first it looked as if Don Pedro would be firmly
seated upon the throne, but he alienated the Black
Prince by his failure to fulfill his promise to deliver
up to the English sundry castles, and disgusted him

by his cruelty. So the Prince marched back to France. Without his help the King was no match for Don Enrique and Du Guesclin; and before long he was captured — not without treachery — in the castle of Montiel (1369). The story of his death is one of brutal hatred and rage. The two brothers met in a tent; at first they did not recognize one another; then they grappled; Don Enrique fell underneath, somebody helped him to get uppermost (but stories differ), and he drove his dagger into his brother's body. In this fashion the bastard line of Trastamara ascended the throne.

In time the two lines reunited, for Don Enrique's grandson, afterwards Enrique III (*r.* 1390–1406), married a granddaughter of Don Pedro, and their son Juan II (*r.* 1406–1454) succeeded to the claims of both houses.

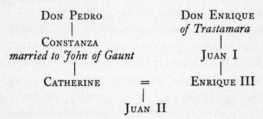

Catherine of Lancaster was sister to Henry IV of England, and therefore aunt to Prince Hal — Henry V, the hero of Agincourt. On her marriage, in compliment, I presume, to the English usage of styling the heir apparent Prince of Wales, the title of Prince of Asturias was conferred on young Enrique, her husband (1388). Catherine after her husband's death acted as Queen Regent during the infancy of her son, so I quote a contemporary description of her:

The Queen was tall and very stout, her complexion fair but very red, and her body and carriage were more like a man's than a woman's; she was very well-behaved and discreet of person and reputation, generous and magnificent, but very much under the influence of favorites. She had had a bad attack of the palsy, which left its mark on her limbs and her speech.

A more interesting person, one of the ancient Spanish noblemen, a typical Castilian of the mediæval school and, unless we except royalty, the most distinguished Spaniard of his time, is described by the same observer as follows:

Don Pedro Lopez de Ayala (1332–1407), high chancellor of Castile, was a gentleman of great lineage. . . . He was tall, slight, well made, a man of authority and rare good sense, very sagacious both in peace and war, and held high positions under the kings of his time. . . . He was affable in his manners, high-bred, conscientious, God-fearing, devoted to the liberal arts, and spent a great deal of time over literature and history; for although he was very much a man of the world and of great experience in affairs, his natural bent was towards learning; so he gave much time to reading and studying, not law, but philosophy and history. It is due to him that certain books are known in Spain, such as Livy, the *Fortunes of Princes*, the *Morals* of Saint Gregory, *De Summo Bono* of Saint Isidore, Boethius, and the story of Troy.

This eminent personage ran a career somewhat like that of Don Juan Manuel. He followed the banner of Don Enrique de Trastamara and was taken prisoner by the Black Prince at the battle of Nájera. Later the Portuguese captured him and shut him up in a cage for fifteen months. It is difficult to see when he did his literary work; but he wrote a long poem, or rather a sequence of poems, such as hold a place in the temple of national classics seldom visited except by scholars, and a chronicle of the reigns of Don Pedro, Don Enrique II, Don Juan I (*r.* 1379–1390), and Don Enrique III (*r.* 1390–1406), which is not only readable but also, I surmise, accurate and just. He belongs to the noble band of Spanish classics.

You will find it frequently stated in books about Spain that loyalty is a peculiarly Spanish trait, and the great dramatists of *el Siglo de Oro* never tire of using it as an important factor in their plots. But you will find that Don Pedro Lopez de Ayala, like Count Fernán González, the Cid, Don Juan Manuel, or any other early Spanish hero, took loyalty to the king but little into their reckoning; they were loyal to self-interest. Indeed, it seems to a random reader that political loyalty did not exist as a virtue until the great kings Charles V and Philip II attained absolute power, and that then it became a fashionable virtue.

XII

THE REIGN OF JUAN II (*r.* 1406–1454)

JUAN II, son to Catherine of Lancaster, was a poor weak creature, like his cousin Henry VI of England. He was but an infant when his father died, and his uncle Don Fernando de Antequera assumed the regency; but Fernando was elected to the throne of Aragon on the failure of the royal line there, and the Queen Mother took his place. When Juan came of age he did what his favorite Don Álvaro de Luna bade him do, and after Don Álvaro's death he obeyed his wife, Isabel of Portugal. Little need be said of general politics during his pitiful reign. Fernán Pérez de Guzmán, the Brantôme of his day, sums them up:

> From this time on what countless wrongdoings, injuries, uprisings, imprisonments, banishments, confiscations, usurpations, riots, villainies, robberies, wars with the Moors, followed hard on one another? Who could recount all this? *Ca la antigua é loable costunbre de los castellanos á tal punto es venida, que por haber el despojo de su pariente é amigo, le consentian prender ó matar.* (For the ancient and praiseworthy ways of the Castilians have reached the point that in order to share in the spoils of friend or kinsman, they will agree to lock him up or kill him.)

Out from among these rapacious Castilians one great figure stands conspicuous. For two and twenty years Don Álvaro de Luna (1407–1453), the royal favorite, governed the kingdom. Constable of Castile, Grand Master of Santiago, he added riches to riches, estate to estate, until his vassals numbered twenty thousand men. He was a little, thin-faced man, of a fine figure, a capital rider, excelling in martial sports, well-mannered when he wished to be, a good talker though he hesitated a little in his speech — altogether very much of a man. His great fault was avarice. And at last he fell. His fall was caused by an alliance of the King's second wife with the envious, angry noblemen whom he had roughly handled. The miserable King forswore himself and, forsaking his friend, privily went over to the Queen's faction. The conspirators surrounded Don Álvaro's palace in Burgos; he would have defended himself, but when the King plighted his royal word for his safety he gave himself up. His enemies hurried him through the farce of a trial and chopped off his head (1453), to the King's everlasting shame. His career may be compared to Wolsey's.

The curious pilgrim will find memorials of him in various places: at Segovia, a modest, charming palace, now in a sorry state but still proud of his heraldic device of a crescent moon; at Valladolid, the crossways where he was beheaded; and in the cathedral of Toledo, the magnificent chapel of Santiago built by him, in which his daughter set up a noble tomb, with his effigy lying at full length in all the dignity of death. And the poet Jorge Manrique has dedicated to his memory a stanza in his famous *Coplas* that will outlive the marble monument:

Pues aquel grand condestable,
maestre que conoscimos
tan privado,
no cunple que del se fable,
sino solo que lo vimos
degollado.
Sus ynfinitos tesoros,
sus villas y sus lugares,
su mandar,
que le fueron sino lloros?
fueronle sino pesares
al dexar?

Spain's haughty Constable, the true
And gallant Master, whom we knew
    Most loved of all;
Breathe not a whisper of his pride,
He on the gloomy scaffold died,
    Ignoble fall!
The countless treasures of his care,
His villages and villas fair,
    His mighty power,
What were they all but grief and shame,
Tears and a broken heart, when came
    The parting hour?   — LONGFELLOW

The King seems to me to have been a contemptible creature; nevertheless it would not be fair to pass over without a word the praise that Fernán Pérez de Guzmán bestows upon his judgment, his discretion, his power of conversation, his love of music and poetry. But one cannot forget his plighted word to Don Álvaro, once his dearest friend; so I leave him at that, and pass on to the group of men of letters who give to his reign whatever distinction it has.

Menéndez y Pelayo says that this literary group constitutes the portico of the Spanish Renaissance. I begin with a cousin of the King's:

Don Enrique de Villena was short and stout [I am quoting Fernán Pérez de Guzmán once again], his complexion dark but of a healthy color. He was by nature, as his life showed, inclined to the liberal arts and learning rather than to knightly exercises or to such conduct as befits courts and the great world. He was given no teacher, and nobody forced him to study; on the contrary, his grandfather, the old Marquis, who wished him to be a young gallant in the days of his youth, tried to stop him. Nevertheless, at an age when boys are driven by main strength to school, in spite of them all he set himself to learn, and he was so quick-witted and intelligent that he readily mastered any study to which he applied himself. It is obvious therefore that nature had made him what he was. Moreover, on the other hand, Don Enrique was indisposed and alien not only to knightly accomplishments but also to everything except study. It is astonishing how stupid and incompetent he was in the management of his household and his property. Besides other learning, he interested himself in astrology, so that people said in jest that he knew much about the sky but little about the earth; and in his love of books he did not confine himself to proper Christian studies, but went in for the ignoble arts of divination, interpretation of dreams and sneezes, and so on, which do not befit a prince of the blood nor any good Christian. For this reason the kings of his time made little account of him, and gentlemen did not respect him; nevertheless, he was very intelligent about poetry and a good poet himself, and very well and widely read in various matters of learning, and he could speak many languages.

Don Enrique's grandfather, the Marquis of Villena, the seigneur of the old school who had been taken prisoner, together with Ayala and Du Guesclin, in the battle of Nájera, when the Black Prince defeated Enrique of Trastamara, frowned upon boys becoming mollycoddles over their books, and naturally wished his grandson to become a riding, fighting, pleasure-loving Castilian grandee like himself. But now he is best remembered as a grandfather.

The grandson left many literary works. As to all these, the *Art of Poetry*, *The Labors of Hercules*, and so forth, I shall refer the reader to Ticknor, hereby stating by the way that Don Enrique translated the *Divine Comedy* at the request of his friend the Marquis of Santillana, and pass on to the only book that interests me. And I justify my omissions by the authority of Professeur Ernest Mérimée, who berates "*la naïve crédulité, l'indigeste érudition et le manque de talent de l'auteur.*"

This book that interests me is the *Art of Carving* (1423). The pilgrim will find a copy, as part of the appropriate furnishing, in that charming house at Toledo erroneously said to have been occupied by the great painter El Greco. But I must warn the reader that Mr. Fitzmaurice-Kelly denounces the book as "compact of curious counsels and recipes, expounded with horrid eloquence by a pedant who tended to gluttony." This is the disdainful judgment of a man steeped in the nobler pleasures of scholarship; but all men do not turn up their noses at a good dinner. There is a sect of Epicureans that worship the stomach, and Villena, holding *nil humani alienum*, was interested in their ritual.

He begins with a description of the carver's instruments, which he says are among the things that distinguish men from beasts. First he talks of the carving knife, and discusses its material, shape, temper, and various uses; then forks: (*a*) that with two prongs, which "takes up a slice of meat and sets it down without touching the fingers to it"; (*b*) the three-pronged fork, "a sort of trident that holds the meat while you carve it"; and (*c*) the long-handled fork that serves for toasting. The individual fork, I believe, if used at all in those days, was a great rarity and seems to have been unknown in Spain. Villena then discourses upon the corer, an implement for taking out the core of apples, and upon the oyster-knife, as well as on napkins, table knives, and spoons. The carver, he says, has all such things in his charge and he must see to it that everything is clean. During dinner the carver's function is to carve at the king's table, where he is provided with various cloths for wiping his implements, and with bowls — one to wash his knives in, another to put bones in, and so on. When he is not carving he must keep his eye on the king, and if he sees any crumb or spot on his face or clothes he must make a sign, privily, so that it may be immediately removed. Apparently the carver had general charge of the waiters, for it is prescribed in connection with his duties that while the king drinks his plate shall be lifted aside, lest some drops of wine fall into it; and that for each course a fresh plate must be forthcoming.

The nicety of the carver's art may be estimated by the different dishes to be carved: peacocks, pheasants, geese, ducks, partridges, pigeons, chickens, venison, beef, mutton, lamb, pork, and a great variety of beasts, birds, fish, fruits, and vegetables whose names are strange to me. In particular, cutting up a peacock is a task worthy of a Flemish artist, and the delicate cross-slicing of a young pig would have delighted Charles Lamb. The melon, of course, is to be cut lengthwise, the slices fairly thick, the seeds scooped out, and the rind cut off to where the green begins, and then cut athwart so that each morsel may be easily put in the mouth. Pippins are to be quartered, and bergamots cut across in slices about an inch thick.

Well! Mr. Fitzmaurice-Kelly is no doubt right to spurn these vulgar matters of eating and drinking, and Professeur Mérimée equally right to find Villena vapid and dull; but it must be remembered that his friend, the Marquis of Santillana, a very important person in literature, wrote a lament upon his death, in which he calls him a *rico tesoro* and *el mayor de los sabios del tempo presente* (a rich treasure and the wisest man of their generation). Alas! Time, fashion, and textbook-writers often deal scurvily with famous men. So does superstition. In his old age Villena was reputed to devote himself to the black art, and after his death his books were burned, and his name handed on to succeeding generations as that of a wizard.

XIII

THE PORTICO OF THE SPANISH RENAISSANCE

THE next figure in this group of literary men in the reign of Juan II is the redoubtable Marquis of Santillana, Íñigo Lopez de Mendoza (1398–1458). Santillana came of a family already distinguished for its literary abilities, and destined to become still more so. I do not remember to have read of any group of kinsmen, anywhere, of such eminence in literature. Pedro López de Ayala, Fernán Pérez de Guzmán (1378–1460), Jorge Manrique (1440–1478), Garcilaso de la Vega (1503–1536), and Diego Hurtado de Mendoza (1503–1575) were all, in their several generations, of his kith and kin. All are Spanish classics. In person Santillana was handsome and of a good figure, and in private life a quiet, agreeable, well-bred, cultivated gentleman. Hernando del Pulgar (1436–1492) says: *"Dentro de sí tenía una humildad que le facía amigo de Dios"*; but in public life he was an ambitious, covetous, revengeful man, one of those envious noblemen who hounded Don Álvaro de Luna to his death. And afterward, with a vulgar lack of magnanimity, he wrote moralizing verses called the *Doctrinal de Privados* (the Lesson of Favorites), in which his fallen enemy is made to confess manifold sins and wickednesses.

In literature, Santillana was governed by his

admiration for the great Italians, Dante, Petrarch, and Boccaccio. You will remember that he persuaded Villena to translate the *Divine Comedy* — and he is entitled to whatever praise may be due for preceding by a hundred years the more successful Italian imitators, Boscán and Garcilaso de la Vega. But the times were not ripe, and his premature efforts to write sonnets in Spanish attained little success. He seems to be peculiarly unfortunate in that Petrarch touched upon some of his themes before him and François Villon on others after him; but to his friend, the poet Juan de Mena, he appeared to be a "perfect lover of sweet poesy . . . a friend to whatever duty bids . . . and a fortress that stands foursquare against Fortune's worst." And in spite of Petrarch's sonnets and Villon's *Ballade des dames du temps jadis,* Fortune did not do her worst; on the contrary she dealt most kindly with him. For in among his verses, like the rosy fragrance of arbutus out from among the winter's withered leaves, you find a delightful serranilla, composed in a form borrowed, it may be, from Provence and Galicia, but in substance of his own fancy, *La Vaquera de la Finojosa:*

> *Moça tan fermosa*
> *non vi en la frontera,*
> *como una vaquera*
> *de la Finojosa.*

It has achieved immortality and stands at the top of those poems among which, far lower down, is Thackeray's ballad:

> Beauty is not rare
>   In the land of Paddy;
> Fair beyond compare
>   Is Peg of Limavaddy.

Besides these two poets, Santillana and Villena, if indeed Villena is to be reckoned a poet, there is a third, Juan de la Mena (1411–1456), who is usually rated by scholars much higher than the other two. But in my judgment — after a very cursory examination, I confess — all that he wrote is not worth a stanza of *La Vaquera de la Finojosa*. His most notable work, the *Labyrinth*, is said to be fashioned on the model of the *Divine Comedy* and consists of an allegory of human destiny. No Beginner should concern himself with this poem. The substance is dull and the style villainous. Fitzmaurice-Kelly politely speaks of "exalted rhetoric and resonant music"; I should prefer the words of another English scholar, "florid verbosity," a trait, as I have said, that often mars Spanish prose and Spanish poems from earliest times down to to-day. Some scholars deem this trait an inheritance from the original Iberian stock; others ascribe it to Oriental influences; others still, with special reference to Juan de Mena, to some strange property in the soil of Cordova where he was born — for Seneca and Lucan, who were prodigal of high-flown rhetoric, were also born there, as was likewise the later poet Góngora, renowned for his fantastic phraseology. I am glad to see that the French scholar, Ernest Mérimée, says that Juan de Mena "*est à peu près illisible.*" As far as I am concerned he might have stated the case more strongly still. When the reader who is rash enough to undertake Juan's eulogy upon Santillana comes upon nine ladies, looking like rose petals besprinkled with snow, with sceptres in their hands, sweeping down from the sky to honor Santillana, he thinks upon the baroque ceilings of Jesuit churches in foreign parts, wearily yawns, and closes the book. However, Santillana expresses admiration of him, and one should give great weight to the opinion of a contemporary. My rash and ignorant prejudices, of course, are not intended to be set down in answer to grave questions on an examination paper. In life Juan de Mena was a good fellow. Here, at last, is an instance of loyalty. Don Álvaro de Luna, in the days of prosperity, had been his patron, and after Don Álvaro's fall Juan de Mena, although he held at court the position of *secretario latino e historiador* and must have been dependent for his post on the favor of the rival faction, remained loyal to the memory of the fallen favorite.

To the ill-educated foreigner the prose of the period seems more readable than the poetry. I have quoted several times *Generaciones y Semblanzas* by Fernán Pérez de Guzmán (1378–1460). These are short biographical sketches of eminent contemporaries and, for anyone concerned with the history of Spain of that period, very interesting and agreeable. Pérez de Guzmán writes, as the phrase is, like a gentleman, with measure and restraint, but he is also vivid, and displays a master hand in choosing salient traits of character. And there is another book of very great interest, *Historia del gran Tamorlan, e itinerario y enarracion del viage y relacion de la embajada, etc.* It seems that Enrique III had sent ambassadors to Prester John, Lord of the Eastern Indies, to the Sultan of Babylon, to Bajazet at Constantinople, and to the great Tamerlane,

Whose looks make this inferior world to quake;

and it happened that certain of these Spanish ambassadors had been present at the bloody battle in which Tamerlane defeated Bajazet, and had seen Bajazet shut up in a cage. Doubtless they felicitated the conqueror on his victory. In consequence Tamerlane sent his ambassador, Mahomad Alcagi, with rich presents of jewels and captive ladies, to the King of Castile. The beauty of one of these ladies, a granddaughter of the king of Hungary, was celebrated by an Italian poet, Francisco Imperial, who had settled at Seville and wrote in Spanish. Here we have perhaps the first entrance into Spanish literature of the premature Italian influence that affected Santillana, Juan de la Mena, and their contemporaries, so much to their hurt. The captive lady was treated with all respect, and married a gentleman of distinction. In return for this expression of Tatar politeness, Enrique III sent Don Ruy Gonzalez de Clavijo as his ambassador to Tamerlane. Clavijo sailed from Cadiz on May 23, 1403, and finally arrived at Samarkand. This *Historia* is the ambassador's account of what he saw, together with what he learned of Tamerlane's life. He sailed along the Mediterranean coasts to the Ægean Sea and on to Constantinople, where he saw a great many churches that he describes, especially Santa Sofia, and so forth. He found the Greeks very devout, " *salvo que ha en ellos muchos errores en fecho de la fe.*" From Constantinople he traveled eastward, passing among others Calmarin, the first city erected after the Flood, and so on, till he reached Samarkand. The most interesting part of the narrative is after his arrival among the Tatars, where he saw Tamerlane himself in silk and jewels, with a high white hat on his head; he was so old that his weary eyelids closed. This book has been translated by the Hakluyt Society.

Another prose-writer, Alfonso Martínez (1398–1470 ?), archpriest of Toledo, is held in high esteem by scholars. I have dipped into his book on the failings of women, and there is a good deal of lively low-comedy, comparable perhaps in its primitive way to Lady Gregory's plays; but mediæval satire upon women is, on the whole, the dullest stuff imaginable, and the scale of this little book will not permit me to say more of him here.

XIV

LOS REYES CATÓLICOS

AFTER the turbulent reign of Juan II comes the turbulent reign of Enrique IV (1454–1474). The causes of trouble were the same, favoritism and weakness of character. The King's chief favorite was Don Beltran de la Cueva — and the Queen's, too. The barons were infuriated. They said that Don Beltran was the Queen's lover, and nicknamed the little princess Juana La Beltraneja; and they did not rest content with evil words. The King had a younger half-brother Alfonso, and a half-sister Isabella; the barons put this boy at their head and forced the King to acknowledge the truth of their charges against the Queen and to designate Alfonso as his successor. A little later the King changed about, and then the rebels proclaimed Alfonso King. This was going too far, and a reaction set in. Loyal noblemen rallied to the lawful King and won the victory of Olmedo (1467); but they do not appear to have followed it up with any vigor, for the rebel barons held together and on Alfonso's death put up Isabella. The King lost courage, and a pact was made by which he again stigmatized the Princess Juana as illegitimate, and appointed Isabella his heir. Even after this, however, the weathercock King once more changed about and acknowledged Juana as his daughter. When he died the issue could only be settled by the arbitrament of arms. Isabella triumphed, and became Isabella the Catholic, Queen of Castile. Princess Juana was sent to a nunnery.

Already, several years before (1474), Isabella had married Ferdinand, heir to the throne of Aragon. On his father's death Ferdinand became King, and the two countries were virtually united. This union of the two crowns is one of the most important events in Spanish history. Castile, being three times the size of Aragon, as a natural consequence became the dominant partner; and yet Aragon determined their joint destiny, for Aragon was already an imperial State, entangled in the skein of European politics. Here I must make a digression, in order to explain the situation.

In 1137 the Count of Barcelona became King of Aragon, and the two States, united under the common designation of "Kingdom of Aragon," became an essentially maritime nation and, as time went on, still more so. One hundred years later, Don Jaime *el Conquistador* (1213–1276) conquered the Balearic Islands. His son Don Pedro married (1262) Constanza, daughter to Manfred, the Hohenstaufen King of the Two Sicilies, "*biondo, bello, e di gentile aspetto*," and so acquired a claim to that kingdom, in opposition to the House of Anjou. By the revolt known as the Sicilian Vespers (1282) this title was made good as to Sicily, but it remained in abeyance as to the mainland until the reign of Alfonso V of Aragon (*r.* 1416–1458), who secured the crown of Naples as well. Sardinia was also appropriated, and robber bands of Catalans seized the duchy of Athens. These possessions, especially the Italian provinces, were the source of endless woes to Spain. The situation of the Spanish peninsula, thrust out toward both North and South America and the West Indies, seemed to mark Spain out from among all the countries of Europe — not forgetting England — as the explorer and colonizer of the Western Continent. But luck went against Nature's intentions. Portugal, which should have been Spain's Atlantic coast, split off and became an independent, often a hostile, kingdom. And Aragon, a Mediterranean Power, dragged her mate into the European broils of which Italy was always the centre. Aragon, therefore, brought a tragic dowry. But, in spite of this, the benefits that accrued to the united kingdom from the union were enormous. It is true that in the reign of Ferdinand and Isabella there was no union beyond that caused by the marriage of the two sovereigns; nevertheless, the two countries were virtually one, and I shall henceforth speak of the united kingdom as Spain, reminding the reader that Navarre (south of the Pyrenees) and Granada were still to be incorporated.

Los Reyes Católicos, the Catholic Sovereigns, as they are called (scholars, oddly enough, translate *reyes*, which may mean *king and queen*, by the word *kings*, which includes males only), were confronted by four serious problems: first, law and order; second, the conquest of Granada; third, the imperial policy of Aragon in Italy; and fourth, the western route to Cathay and the discoveries of Columbus.

The first problem was the most immediate. During the troubled reigns of Juan II and Enrique IV the great vassals of Castile had acted as if they were independent lords. Enrique IV, out of his foolish favoritism and a desire to secure loyal adherents, had given away right and left the property of the Crown, estates, castles, towns, with the consequence that all the grandees and barons were fighting over the spoils, while lesser robbers, imitating their betters, infested the roads, pillaged outlying granges, and waylaid travelers. As a contemporary says: "Every day there was some fray, every day murder or bloodshed." To correct this state of things Queen Isabella, for she was sovereign in her own kingdom, acted with vigor. Galicia was the worst place of all. She sent two judges there with a strong force; they destroyed forty-six castles, executed many criminals, imprisoned, fined, and terrified, and reëstablished the royal authority. And both there and throughout Castile two important measures were adopted.

In former times the municipalities of Castile had got together for the sake of mutual defense against robbers, high and low, and had organized a constabulary force, called a *Hermandad* (Brotherhood). This system was now revived and enlarged. A body of two thousand troopers was formed under the orders of a central council, appointed by the municipalities but really under the control of the sovereign. Each village furnished a trooper. When a crime was committed, a hue and cry was raised, the troopers mounted and scoured the country, spreading the alarm from town to town. When criminals were caught summary justice was done. This system ousted the barons of their old judicial prerogatives and at first they objected; but under pressure they gave way, and the Holy Brotherhood rendered immense service to the peaceable population. It did its work so well that in twenty years' time it became almost unnecessary, but the institution remained, and in Don Quixote's time the *Hermandad* was still a word of terror to evildoers.

The second measure was more radical. The Sovereigns (I speak of them as acting together) revoked all the grants made by Enrique IV. This was a knock-out blow at the insubordinate barons. But the Sovereigns had taken the precaution to secure the approval of the Cortes (Toledo, 1480) and, with the towns and commoners in solid ranks at their back, they put the measure into effect. By this means the Crown recovered a vast extent of crown-lands, and was able to reward its supporters by a reduction of taxation. Besides these two measures, the Sovereigns adopted a third, directed to the same end of diminishing the powers of the great nobles. The three military orders, Santiago, Alcántara, and Calatrava, had been founded in the earlier days of the reconquest for the purpose of defending the frontier against the Moors, and their Grand Masters possessed power inconsistent with royal authority. The reader will remember that Don Álvaro de Luna was Grand Master of Santiago, and acted as if he were king. They received very large revenues, and had the power of appointment to numerous honorable and lucrative offices. Queen Isabella procured the election of the King as Grand Master of each Order, and so, at one stroke, enfeebled the nobility and strengthened the Crown.

The solution of the second problem, the conquest of Granada, took ten years. I refer the reader to the

pages of Washington Irving for a romantic account
of this romantic war: of the fatal quarrels of the
Moors among themselves; of the Sultan Muley Abul
Hassan, his son Boabdil, his brother El Zagal; how
El Zagal supplanted Muley Abul Hassan; how Boabdil in his turn drove his uncle from Granada;
how the crafty Ferdinand set one against the other;
how Hernando Pérez de Pulgar, *el de las Hazañas*,
burst into Granada by night and nailed an Ave
Maria on the very door of the mosque; how the city
at last capitulated; how Boabdil breathed forth *el
ultimo suspiro del Moro;* how Ferdinand and Isabella
rode in, triumphant; and of all the picturesque
episodes that adorn the final act of the reconquest.
The terms of the capitulation were very favorable,
including full guaranties of civil and religious liberty.
These terms, however, were not kept; perhaps
Ferdinand never intended to keep them. But this
breach of faith is but one item in the harsh story
of Spain's dealings with disbelievers, and had better
await a later chapter.

In order to say something of the third problem,
I must make a digression. In 1266 the French House
of Anjou dispossessed the Hohenstaufens of the
kingdom of the Two Sicilies. In the course of time
the House of Aragon, as I have related, claiming
the Hohenstaufen title, recovered first Sicily and
afterward the mainland; but the mainland, the
kingdom of Naples, passed to an illegitimate branch,
and Ferdinand conceived the idea of recovering it
for himself, as representing the legitimate branch.
The House of Anjou, however, had not forgotten
its claims. So these two claimants, Louis XII of

France and Ferdinand of Aragon, agreed to conquer the kingdom of Naples together and go halves (1500). As usually happens in such cases, the robbers fell out over a division of the spoils, and Ferdinand, thanks to his own cleverness that won Machiavelli's admiration, and to the military genius of Gonsalvo de Córdova, *el Gran Capitán*, secured the whole (1504), and Naples became a dependency of the Spanish monarchy under the local government of a Viceroy.

As to the fourth problem, the Spanish policy toward the New World, I need not recount the familiar tale. Columbus hung about the Spanish court; Isabella would and would not; Fray Diego de Deza and other Dominican monks met in the monastery of San Esteban at Salamanca, and decided that Columbus was right; he sailed from Palos on August 3, 1492, in the Santa Maria. Fortune lifted him up and cast him down. His death, in a little house in Valladolid (1506), passed unnoticed by the world. All these things are in other elementary histories, and Christopher Columbus belongs to the whole world.

XV

CONTEMPORARY JUDGMENTS ON FERDINAND AND ISABELLA

THE King and Queen were a remarkable couple, in their respective ways the most gifted sovereigns in Spanish annals. It happens that, among others, the two cleverest observers in Europe recorded their opinions of them; so, instead of summarizing what modern historians say, I shall quote the contemporaries.

Machiavelli, in Chapter XXI of *The Prince*, says:

Nothing raises a prince so high in public estimation as enterprises of great moment, and the exhibition of rare qualities. In our time, for example, there is Ferdinand of Aragon, the King of Spain. He may be considered a self-made potentate, because from having been a weak king he is now renowned as the foremost sovereign of Christendom; and if his deeds be considered, they will be found great and at times very remarkable. In the beginning of his reign he conquered Granada. That conquest was the foundation of his proud position. He went to work at this in a leisurely fashion, and thereby avoided the danger of being interfered with. Moreover, the war occupied the thoughts of the Castilian nobles and kept them off rebellion; and, in consequence, before they were aware of what the King was doing, he had established the royal authority over them. Incidentally he acquired a great reputation. He maintained his armies with money raised from the Church and the people; and in that long war he got the military experience that has won him so much renown. Beside this he always used religion as a cloak for undertaking great enterprises, and under pious guise practised great cruelty. For instance, he despoiled the Moriscos and expelled them from his kingdom. There is no better instance of a policy of hypocrisy. Covered by this same cloak, he made war in Africa, undertook the expedition against Italy, and finally attacked France. In this manner he has always accomplished great exploits, and kept his subjects in suspense and admiration, busy with speculations as to how he would come out. And one enterprise has begotten another so quickly, that there has been no interval of time between for any objectors to concert measures against him.

And in the following passage, Machiavelli obviously refers to Ferdinand:

Everybody agrees that it is praiseworthy in a prince to keep his word, to practise honest dealing and eschew guile. Nevertheless, in our own times, we know by experience that those princes who have practised guile and made little account of their word have achieved great things; we know that in the end they got the better of men who acted upon principles of loyalty. We must remember that there are two ways of carrying on a contest: one is according to the rules of fair play, the other by brute force. The first way befits men, the second befits brutes. But as the first is often unsuccessful, it is necessary to have recourse to the second. . . . Since a prince, then, is obliged to play a brute's part, he should enact both the lion and the fox. . . . A prudent king cannot, and should not, keep his plighted word, if that would turn to his disadvantage, or if the motives that induced him to plight it have passed away.

Machiavelli **never** went to Spain, but he was familiar with Spanish policy in Italy, and he kept his eyes wide open on European affairs.

The other observer to whom I refer is Guicciardini, who for a time was ambassador from Florence to the Spanish court. In his report to his government, he says:

The feats that Ferdinand has accomplished, his words, his ways, and his general reputation prove that he is an extremely sagacious man. He is very secret, and unless obliged to does not communicate important matters; he could not be more patient. He leads a very regular life, assigning times for this and that. He likes to know about all the affairs of the kingdom, great and little, and has them go through his hands; and though he exhibits a willingness to hear everybody's opinion, he makes up his own mind, and directs everything himself. He is generally considered avaricious, but I can't tell whether this comes from his nature or from the constraint of great expenses, for his income is small in proportion to the magnitude of his affairs. But he means to proceed in orderly fashion and limit expenses as much as he can. He is good at knightly exercises, and keeps them up; he makes a show of great piety, speaks of holy things with great reverence, and ascribes everything to God. He also makes a great parade of worship and attendance at church, as indeed the whole nation does. He is no scholar, but very friendly to the humanists. He gives audience freely and answers petitions with great dignity, and there are few who are not satisfied with what he says. But rumor has it that he often departs from his promises — either because he did not mean to keep his word, or because events make him change his mind — and that then he pays no heed to what he had said. My opinion is that he can dissimulate better than any other man. . . . In short, he is a very notable king and has many talents; and the only criticisms upon him are that he is not generous and that he does not keep his promise.

Guicciardini enumerates the various difficulties that confronted the sovereigns, somewhat as I have done, and then proceeds to a consideration of Queen Isabella, who had died eight or nine years before:

And in all these achievements the Queen's prowess was equal to the King's, or rather by universal consent the greater share was attributed to her, for all the principal affairs of Castile passed through her hands. She had the dominating control; and even in matters common to them both it was not less advantageous to persuade her than her husband. Nor was this because the King lacked ability, for his subsequent career has proved how great that was; but because the Queen was so exceptional a person that even the King gave way to her. Or perhaps he acquiesced in her excellent plans because Castile was her kingdom. It is said that she was a great lover of justice, and a lady of the best breeding, and made herself greatly beloved and feared by her subjects. She was generous, of a high spirit, and very ambitious of renown, as much so as any woman of the time, no matter who. They say that, though the King was naturally inclined to gaming, nevertheless out of respect for her he rarely played, and only at the simple games; and this is confirmed by the fact that after her death he played often and for high stakes at games of little repute, and spent more time at them than became a king who carried so many kingdoms on his shoulders.

What Guicciardini says concerning the Queen's equality with the King is more than confirmed by a distinguished German visitor from Silesia:

I must note here a paradox in this kingdom of Castile, for the Queen is king, and the King is her servant. . . . This is so completely so that the nobility fear the Queen more than the King, who in whatever he does merely carries out the Queen's orders and wishes. If the King wishes to send off some letters, he cannot affix the seal of State without the Queen's permission; she reads them all, and if she comes upon anything that she does not like she strikes it out in the very presence of the King. Whatever is decided between her and Cardinal Mendoza, a very powerful Spanish nobleman, the King has to put into execution.

And another Italian, Lucio Marineo, after having first described Ferdinand, describes Isabella in this way:

As to her figure, stature, and beauty, whatever I have said of the King can be said of her. Whatever in the King expressed dignity, in the Queen was also clothed with grace and charm; the presence of both was touched with majesty, but in the opinion of most people the Queen was the handsomer, and had a quicker intelligence, a larger heart, and a more serious nature. She was an excellent Queen, a great lover of virtue, desirous of praise and spotless fame. She was very abstemious, being what is commonly called a teetotaller, for she not only did not drink wine, but had not even ever touched it. She was much in love with her husband, and was jealously alert to see if his affections wandered, and if she found that he cast glances of admiration at any lady in waiting, she very prudently found some tactful way of getting her out of the palace. . . . She spoke Spanish with elegance and great dignity. She did not know Latin, but she took pleasure in listening to Latin speeches and sermons, for she thought highly of the language when well spoken; and after the wars in Spain were over, although she was still very busy with important matters, she wished so much to know it that she began to take lessons, and made so much progress that she not only was able to understand the ambassadors and orators but could easily translate Latin into Spanish. As to Church matters, it is hard to say whether she was more diligent or more generous, for she possessed both virtues to perfection. She kept a great many chaplains and choristers. . . . Besides, when there was a bishopric or other high ecclesiastical office to be filled, she took more account of virtue, good character, and learning, than of riches or high birth, even if the candidates were her relations.

Such were these remarkable sovereigns.

XVI

THE RELIGIOUS POLICY OF THE CATHOLIC SOVEREIGNS

RELIGION is of the essence of Spanish history, both in times of prosperity and in times of decadence, so I shall devote this chapter to the religious policy of the Catholic Sovereigns. The polar star of their domestic policy is plain enough — homogeneity, one crown, one country, one faith. They desired to wear down the differences between Castile and Aragon, to bring all the peninsula under a single authority, to make all the population Christian. In their hearts, from the very beginning they knew what they wanted: to conquer Spanish Navarre; to drive the Moors from Granada; to obtain Portugal by marriage; to make their government strongly autocratic and to assimilate local institutions; and finally, to convert or get rid of non-Christians. Isabella was a devout Christian; she did not divide religion from life; she did not regard Church and State as separate bodies but as one, which (with the reservation of spiritual deference to the Pope) should be guided and governed by the sovereigns. Ferdinand concurred. He professed to believe that religion was to the State what the blood is to the human body and, as Machiavelli observed, gained great secular advantages from his pious professions. Both sovereigns were agreed that religious policy was an inseparable element in statecraft, and that religious unity was a virtual necessity, in order to secure political homogeneity. Here, then, we have the key to their treatment of the Jews and Moors.

One other detail. During the Middle Ages the Church had shared the general degradation of social life; its prelates usually had been noblemen, who were distinguished from the secular members of their class only by vestments, croziers, and abstention from the marriage ceremony. Both King and Queen desired to purify the national Church, to convert it into a prop of the throne.

This general religious policy, upheld by the piety of Isabella and the political sagacity of Ferdinand, is closely associated with two great prelates, Cardinal Mendoza (son to Íñigo López de Mendoza, the literary Marquis of Santillana, whom we know) and his successor, Cardinal Ximénez de Cisneros (1436–1517).

Ximénez went to school at Alcalá de Henares, to college at Salamanca, and practised canon law in Rome. On his return to Spain he attempted to assert some claim to a benefice and was put in prison for six years. Perhaps he learned during these years the need of ecclesiastical reform. He became a protégé of Cardinal Mendoza, and seemed destined to a distinguished career; but he threw up his position and retired to a Franciscan monastery in Castile. He was elected provincial of the order, and undertook his first works of reform. In 1492 he added another item of interest to that *annus mirabilis* by accepting the office of confessor to the Queen. He won golden opinions; he was said "to equal

Saint Augustine in wisdom, Saint Jerome in austerity of life, and Saint Ambrose in zeal."

On the death of Cardinal Mendoza (1495) and by that prelate's dying advice, Ximénez was made Archibishop of Toledo, Primate of Spain, and finally Chancellor of Castile. Besides these dignities Cardinal Ximénez has many titles to his high reputation. He was a man of spotless personal character and of great ability. He was also a scholar. He founded a university in Alcalá de Henares, the town of his schoolboy days, and he published there his famous polyglot Bible — one of the great works of sixteenth-century scholarship, in which Saint Jerome's Latin is printed in a central column between the Hebrew text to the right and the Greek of the Septuagint to the left (as Ximénez himself says), "like Christ crucified between the two thieves." He was an ascetic; and, if we are inclined to judge his policy harshly, we must remember that he was a thorough reformer at a time when Rodrigo Borgia, Pope Alexander VI, also a Spaniard, was leading a life of profligacy and practising a cynical statecraft that rivaled or outdid, in Machiavelli's admiration, even that of King Ferdinand.

I have glanced at Ximénez's life partly because he is considered one of Spain's great men, partly to show that deeply religious men supported Ferdinand's policy toward the Moors. Ximénez did much more than support; he played into the King's hand. After the surrender of Granada the Spanish authorities attempted to persuade the Moors to become Christians. Conversion made little headway; Ximénez denounced the authorities as weak-kneed, got himself put in charge, went to Granada, argued, bullied, bribed. He made a bonfire in the public square of all the pernicious infidel books he could lay hands on — illuminated copies of the Koran, priceless manuscripts of one kind or another. Finally the Moors could bear it no longer. Rebellion started up in the country roundabout. This was put down, not without difficulty; towns and villages were sacked and burned, men, women, and children murdered without mercy. The revolt also was taken as a justification for breaking the terms of the capitulation. The Moors of the district — and also all the Moors of Castile — were given their choice between baptism and exile (1499–1501). Those who chose to stay and be baptized are known as Moriscos, that is, Christian Moors. The Moors in Aragon were protected by powerful interests, and were allowed to stay for another hundred years.

It is difficult to judge this policy, for it is difficult to make out what sort of people the Moors were, so great is the bias with which historians have taken sides. The Arabian chroniclers, such as Al Makkari, whom I have cited several times, are brimful of patriotic eulogies upon their own people, although by no means without censure on various points, and many modern scholars dwell upon the industry of the Moors, their patience under hard labor, and their frugality. On the other hand, from this time on the Spaniards seem to have regarded the Moors somewhat as the people of California regard the lower classes of Japanese laborers. I find a modern Catalan scholar who says that the Moors in Spain caused only harm, and were a great hindrance to the development of any real civilization; and, to offer a comparatively recent bit of evidence, George Borrow was told by the British consul at Tangier that after living among them for ten years he had learned that "no people in the world were more false and cruel, that their government was one of the vilest description . . . and invariably acted with bad faith."

It is a matter of common observation that a white race and a dark-skinned race often find it very difficult to maintain pleasant relations with one another. Each dislikes the other's ways, habits, ideas, food, and everything that is characteristic of the other. Benevolent persons who live a thousand miles away, among a homogeneous people, are apt to blame these racial likes and dislikes. But I am getting rather beside the mark, for, though the Spanish people disliked the Moors, Ferdinand and Isabella expelled them primarily because non-Christians tended to prevent that homogeneity which they regarded as essential to national prosperity.

XVII

THE JEWS AND THE INQUISITION

Expulsion as a solution of the Moorish problem
may perhaps be regarded as the natural sequel to
centuries of warfare, but no such excuse can be offered
for a similar policy adopted toward the Jews. The
best that can be said is that the two problems, what
to do with the Jew and what to do with the Moor,
were similar, and that it was natural to pursue
a similar policy in both cases. I repeat, the pole
star that guided the Catholic Sovereigns was the
unification of Spain; only through religious homogeneity, so they believed, would it be possible to
establish order under a strong central government.
Up to this time the Spanish attitude toward the
Jews had been uncertain and shifting. Centuries
before, when the reconquest was well under way,
the Jews had been treated with more or less consideration, but about the middle of the thirteenth
century matters changed for the worse and perse-
cutions began in earnest. The Crusades seem to have
stirred up the populations of Europe to fits of angry
fanaticism, and the Church had adopted a stern
policy. Jews were obliged to live in a quarter of
the town by themselves, to wear a distinctive dress,
and they were debarred from almost all occupations
except money-lending. The necessary consequence
of this was resentment on one side and suspicion and

dislike on the other; every usurer was thought to be a Shylock, and horrible stories began to be told, how Jews stole Christian children and cut their hearts out. In Spain the prejudice against Jews seems to have been due, originally, not to their alien religion, but to their crafty ways of driving hard bargains; in Castile it was found necessary to limit by statute the rate of interest to thirty-three and a third per cent, and Jews were denounced for *insatiabilis avaritia* and *voracitas*. Juan Ruiz calls them *pueblo de perdicion,* and even the kindly Sancho Panza proclaims himself *el enemigo mortal de los judios.* Jews were commonly employed, on account of their training and natural aptitudes, as farmers of the revenue and collectors of taxes.

But whatever the causes of dislike may have been, the Church in Spain took alarm and preached against the Jews; ecclesiastical denunciation was followed first by hostile legislation and then by riots and massacre. In order to escape these evils a great many Jews asked to be baptized, and affected to become Christians.

And here it must be remembered that dislike of Jews was not peculiar to the Spanish people. Edward I had banished them from England; Philip Augustus and again Philip IV had banished them from France; German States, one after another, had done the same; Austria, I think, had cast every Jew into prison; and in Andalusia the Almohades had been so cruel to the Jews that great numbers of them fled into Castile and Portugal. In fact, up to this time the rest of Europe had been far less tolerant than Spain; travelers from other Christian countries were shocked to find how many Jews there were there. One visitor, as early as 1154, for instance, notes down that in Lucena and Tarragona, towns in Granada and Aragon, all the inhabitants were Jews. In 1484 a German traveler reports that all the customhouse officers were Jews; that in Barcelona and Saragossa there were more converted Jews (*conversos* or *marranos*, as they were termed) and unconverted Saracens than Christians; and, after traveling about, he concluded that the same was true all over Spain.

Priests, borrowers, and populace were united in one common dislike; but the Jews possessed great financial abilities, they were in control of the important branches of commerce, they commanded capital, and were ready to put their talents and their money at the service of royalty, and therefore royalty had usually been on their side. In the beginning of Queen Isabella's reign the Jews held so many high positions under the government that public rumor asserted that she was not merely the protectress of Jews but even the daughter of a Jewess. Add together, then, race prejudice, religious prejudice, envy, resentment, and the general belief — probably well justified — that ninety-nine out of a hundred *conversos* were hypocrites, who in public professed Christianity but in secret practised their Hebraic rites, and one can understand how popular pressure, supported by the accepted maxim of statecraft that religious unity was essential to national unity, induced the Catholic Sovereigns to adopt the policy they did. And remember that the prejudice against the Jews was not confined to the

uneducated classes. The clever, skeptical Guicciardini, in the report to his government that I have already quoted, says, after referring to the multitude
of criminals in Galicia when Ferdinand and Isabella
came to their thrones:

There was also another beastly, disgusting pest, for the
kingdom was full of Jews and heretics. The greater part of
the population was smirched with this wickedness. All
the chief offices, all the government places in the rural
districts throughout the kingdom were in their hands.
Their power and number were so great that it was plain
that, unless this pest was stopped, all Spain in the course
of a few years would abandon the Catholic faith.

All these motives had already been working together, but nothing decisive was done until the conquest of Granada gave the final push to the policy
of national unification; besides, the Sovereigns were
prudent and dealt with one problem at a time.

The fatal step was taken in the most famous year of
Spanish history, 1492. It is a harsh story; the petition, "His blood be on us and on our children,"
was granted to the full. The royal edict of expulsion
recited the spiritual evils suffered by Christians
from communication with Jews who, it said, were
"always endeavoring to seduce them from the Holy
Catholic faith and convert them to their own damnable beliefs," and ordered all Jews to leave Spain.
Permission was given to sell their belongings and
take away the proceeds; but Shylock could not have
put more ingenious stipulations into Antonio's bond.
Buyers, knowing that Jews must sell whatever they
could not carry, offered what prices they pleased; and
a prohibition against the export of gold, silver, or

coin would have taken away with the left hand
whatever the right hand had grudgingly relinquished,
had it not been that the Jews, not easily caught
napping, were able to save something by means of
bills of exchange. Of course many Jews suffered
themselves to be baptized; but this step cast the
poor people from the frying-pan into the fire, for
they were then subjected to the jurisdiction of the
great institution that played so portentous a rôle
in Spanish national life for the next two centuries.

The Inquisition had originated centuries before,
during the pontificate of the great Pope Innocent
III, at the time of the Albigensian heresies. It
sprang out of a bishop's duty to watch over his
flock; for it was his primary duty to detect the
deadly disease of heresy, in order to save the sick
if possible, and to prevent contamination from
spreading. The functions of this original Inquisition
were never, as I understand, very clearly distinguished from a bishop's regular duties; but we need
not concern ourselves about that, for the Spanish
Inquisition has its own definite history. It is said
that in the reign of Juan II many converted Jews
had ranged themselves with the enemies of Don
Álvaro years before his fall, and that he, in order
to have back at them, applied to Rome to set up
the Inquisition in Castile. But Don Álvaro lost
the game, and his head. Some twenty-odd years
later his plan was revived and approved both by
clergy and laity. The Catholic Sovereigns supported the project, and Pope Sixtus IV authorized
them to appoint inquisitors with all the powers of
judges of the ecclesiastical courts (1478). This was

one of the chief moves in the royal plan to subject
the national Church to the sovereign. This tribunal,
which supplanted the jurisdiction of the bishops,
became a part of the civil government of the realm,
and in a few years set to work. The first auto-de-fe
was held in Seville (1481). How many victims were
burned at the stake is uncertain. Henry C. Lea
says seventeen, others say two hundred and ninety-
eight. In the space of eight years seven hundred
were put to death, and five thousand were sentenced
to imprisonment for life or to other severe punish-
ments.

Mr. Lea says that the people did not approve.
It would be impertinent in me to dissent. But there
is no record of protest, no outcry, no shout of horror;
the ceremony was elaborate; the square where the
sentence was read and the place of execution —
usually, I believe, outside the walls — were thronged.
I have quoted the hard-headed Guicciardini on the
subject. Zurita, the sixteenth-century historian,
refers to the apostasy of many professed converts,
and says:

For this reason they [the Catholic Sovereigns] set up the
Holy Office of the Inquisition, which proved the best means
that could be devised for the increase of our Holy Faith.
It not only uprooted heresy and error at the time, but it
seems to have been created by divine inspiration in order
to guard Spain in the future against innumerable pesti-
lential errors and heresies, by which for our sins the greater
part of the Christian world is now infected and ruined.

The strongest argument in its defense is that it
saved Spain from the civil wars that raged in France
and Germany.

Of this tribunal a Dominican friar, Fray Thomas de Torquemada (1420–1498), stands in the world's estimation as the guiding genius. Torquemada was appointed Chief Inquisitor in the year 1483. It is hard to do him justice; the hangman that performs the duties put upon him by the community in which he lives bears a bad name with everybody. Dr. H. Graetz, the historian of the Jews, says:

His heart was shut tight against pity, his lips breathed forth death and destruction; he was a combination of the bloody hyena and the subtle, poisonous snake.

Mr. Lea says:

If we cannot wholly attribute to him the spirit of reckless fanaticism which animated the Inquisition, he at least deserved the credit of stimulating and rendering it efficient in its work by organizing it and by directing it with dauntless courage against the suspect, however high-placed, until the shadow of the Holy Office covered the land and no one was so hardy as not to tremble at his name.

In his private life, Torquemada was an ascetic. He was careful to observe the rule of Saint Dominic; his dress was poor and unadorned, he ate no meat, he had no linen on his back or on his bed. If he surrounded himself with a troop of horse it was to guard himself in the discharge of his duties; if fines passed into his hands they were paid out in building religious edifices. He always had the courage of his convictions, and spoke out his mind to royalty itself. He was a fanatic, as the phrase goes; that is, he believed literally and with all his might that God, man's Creator and Judge, had appeared on earth, and had declared: "It is profitable for thee that one of thy members should perish, and not that thy whole body should be cast into hell."

And, so far as I can judge, he embodied the Catholic ideas of religious duties current at that time. He is described as "*spiritualis pater dilectissimus . . . Inquisitionis Hispanæ autor dignissimus.*" His friends describe him as a man of admirable good-sense, remarkable prudence, full of virtue and sanctity. On the other hand, Protestants are severe upon him, and it is natural, and apparently pleasant, for people bred upon gentler notions of right and wrong to heap condemnations on his head. Cruelty, however, is no personal prerogative of Torquemada or of the Spanish Inquisition. It is common to all human beings who have been unnerved by fear. Read how, in the next generation, the German upper classes punished the uprising of the Anabaptists; how the English in 1857–59 blew Sepoy mutineers from the muzzles of their cannon; how the French troops from Versailles in 1871 shot down the Communists by thousands; read what man the brute does, whatever his nationality, when the cloak of civilization falls from his shoulders; and perhaps we shall be more just to Torquemada, the fearless Inquisitor.

XVIII
LITERATURE UNDER FERDINAND AND ISABELLA

TURNING our backs upon the political doings of the Catholic Sovereigns, upon war and the Inquisition, we return to those achievements of their reign that cost no sorrow at the time and have stirred hundreds of thousands of readers since then with deep, agreeable, and sometimes noble emotions. Perhaps I do the course of Spanish literature a little violence, but I look upon it as a series of periods:

XII	Century		*Poema del Cid*
XIII	"		Alfonso el Sabio
XIV	"		Juan Ruiz
XV	"	⎰ Juan II	The Portico
		⎱ Los Reyes Católicos	⎧ Jorge Manrique ⎨ *Amadis of Gaul* ⎩ *La Celestina*

In the reign of Juan II we passed through the portico to the literary Renaissance in Spain; and now in the reign of Ferdinand and Isabella we enter the first garden, court, or chapter, of the great period of Spanish literature, *El Siglo de Oro*, the Golden Age. This preliminary period is spoken of as the early Renaissance. It might be called the Age of Printing, since the first book printed in Spain was in the year of Queen Isabella's accession (1474).

Don Jorge Manrique (1440–1478) was a member of a very eminent family. His grandfather, Leon Pero Manrique, was one of those who banded together against Don Álvaro de Luna. His father, Don Rodrigo, was a turbulent fellow of the highest rank, who obtained the office of Grand Master of the Order of Santiago. One of his uncles was the Marquis of Santillana (author of *La Vaquera de la Finojosa*), and another, Goméz Manrique, was distinguished as soldier, orator, and poet. Don Jorge led a life of poetry and war. As an enthusiastic young Spanish author — who keeps citing the authority of *el Conde* Ticknor — says: "The ferocity of Mars and the gentle smile of the Muses were always disputing over that interesting existence which in the end succumbed to the former." This Spanish sentence means that the poet was killed in battle. Don Jorge's companions, out of revenge, decided to put six prisoners to death in sight of the enemy. These six were chosen by lot; one of them, who had a wife and children, was spared because his bachelor brother insisted on taking his place. I note this trait of chivalric self-sacrifice, the first that I have come upon since the time of Publius Scipio, because it seems to me that loyalty and other qualities that mark the knight and gentleman come in with the authority of the Crown and the establishment of law and order. Like literature and art, they are the gifts of civilization. From this time on the gallant Castilian gentleman, valiant, dignified, and courteous, steps forward to found those conceptions of honor and duty which we associate with the Castilian character in the days of Spanish glory.

Don Jorge's fame rests upon one poem, *"Las Coplas,"* — stanzas on the death of his father, — which Longfellow's translation has made familiar to the English-speaking world. This poem holds a rank among the best of its kind, in the same class with Villon's *"Ballade des dames du temps jadis"* or Gray's "Elegy in a Country Churchyard." Its subject is the transitoriness of life:

> *Nuestras vidas son los rios*
> *que van a dar en la mar,*
> *que es el morir:*
> *alli van los señorios*
> *derechos a se acabar*
> *y consumir;*
> *alli los rios caudales,*
> *alli los otros, medianos*
> *y mas chicos,*
> *allegados son yguales*
> *los que biven por sus manos*
> *y los ricos.*

> Our lives are rivers, gliding free
> To that unfathomed, boundless sea,
> The silent grave!
> Thither all earthly pomp and boast
> Roll, to be swallowed up and lost
> In one dark wave.
> Thither the mighty torrents stray,
> Thither the brook pursues its way,
> And tinkling rill;
> There all are equal; side by side,
> The poor man and the son of pride
> Lie calm and still.

Foreigners and Spaniards are agreed as to the merits of the masterpiece, so I shall content myself with a quotation from the modern critic, Azorín:

Jorge Manrique — what shall I say of him? Jorge Manrique is a creature of air, subtle, fragile, delicate like a slight shudder that passes over us and bids us think, or the breeze that wafts our spirit towards an ideal far away. . . . How can I put into words the distant notes of music, when someone plays a nocturne of Chopin's, or the memory of a rose that is withered, or the remembered rustling of exquisite garments worn by a woman, once the light of our life, who has vanished long since and forever . . .

¿ Que fueron sino rocios
de los prados?

What were they but dews upon the meadows?

The second great literary monument of this period is the mediæval romance, *Amadis of Gaul,* or, as Menéndez *y* Pelayo calls it, the first modern novel. The story — which seems to have come from French sources, probably by way of Portugal — had long been well known in Spain, for our old acquaintance the Chancellor Pero López de Ayala mentions it; but the first Spanish version was made by Garci Rodríguez de Montalvo, probably about 1492. Amadis is the perfect knight of romance, of prowess immeasurable, and his lady love, Oriana, quite worthy of his devotion; giants, dragons, monsters, enchanters, knights-errant and such like, are plentiful as blueberries on top of a New England mountain. The beginner may easily make acquaintance with all this in Southey's translation, but I warn him that if he expects to find any such interest or charm as there is in Sir Thomas Malory's *Morte d'Arthur* he will be sorrily disappointed. The only persons that I ever heard had read it, did so out of love of *Don*

Quixote; and their interest is due to Don Quixote's passionate purpose to imitate Amadis, especially in the rôle of *le beau ténébreux,* as Amadis is called when he withdraws to the wilderness and eats his heart out because of some misunderstanding concerning Oriana. In fact Amadis is almost a character in Cervantes' novel. When the priest and the barber were examining and burning the Don's books of chivalry —

the first that Master Nicholas put into the priest's hands were the four volumes of *Amadis of Gaul.* The priest said: "This is an odd coincidence, for I have heard say that this was the first book on chivalry printed in Spain, and that all the others started from this; and so I think that as the founder of a wicked sect we ought to accept no excuse, but condemn it to the flames."

"No, Sir," said the barber; "for I have heard, as well, that this is the best of all the books of that kind, and so it should be forgiven."

"You are quite right," the priest answered, "and for that reason its life shall be spared for the present."

Amadis was an enormous success. Everybody read it — nobles, courtiers, city people, country folks; and, of course, it provoked many imitations; for instance, to cite only from Don Quixote's library, *Las Sergas de Esplandian, Amadis de Grecia, Don Olivante de Laura, Florismarte de Hircania, El Caballero Platir, El Caballero de la Cruz, Espejo de Caballerías, Palmerin de Oliva, Palmerin de Ingalaterra, Don Belianís, Tirante el Blanco.* The number of these books grew so great and their contents became so fantastical that not only were they forbidden to be printed, sold, or read in the American colonies, but the puritanical members of the Cortes even petitioned for a similar prohibition in Spain, and asked that those already printed should be burned.

The third great achievement of this literary period is *La Celestina* or *La Comedia de Calisto y Melibea* (1499). This is a drama, or rather a novel cast in dramatic form; it was never intended for the stage, being much too long for any such purpose. The plot may have grown out of the episode in *El Libro de Buen Amor* where the old go-between, Trotacon-ventos, carries messages from Don Melon to Doña Endrina. You will find it told at length in Ticknor. Very briefly, it is this: Calisto catches sight of the lovely Melibea and falls desperately in love with her; by the advice of his rascally servants he employs an old bawd, Celestina, who finally succeeds in persuading Melibea to grant her lover an opportunity to speak to her. It all ends in tragedy; the lover is killed by falling from a ladder as he is leaving her house, and she flings herself from the housetop. Spanish critics are all agreed that this is a great book, and their judgment is final.

The story is brutal. There seems to be a certain stoical, almost callous element in the Spanish nature, that accepts the brutality of life without wincing. Their painting and their sculpture often display a fierce disregard of the womanish element in us. At any rate these Spanish critics are not troubled by the brutality which overwhelms the less enduring foreigner. Most of the scenes are low, gross, sensual, feverish, foul, with all that is basest in man. But Azorín, speaking of the author, merely says:

Nobody in his time, or since, has surpassed him in putting such a variety of emotions into one book; nobody has been more gentle (*apacible*), insinuating, sarcastic, jovial, boisterous, pathetic, and tragic, than he. Nobody more than he has made prose laugh and cry alternately, supplicate and threaten, dissolve like an iridescent dream, or etch deep lines of realism. Neither before nor since have the pages of any book contained such passionate cries, so ardent, so dolorous, so modern. The author of *La Celestina* and Cervantes have lifted human emotion to the heights, and inasmuch as they have done that they are the loftiest writers of prose.

I think it would have been impossible for an American to have written this; to me the book is a sort of bludgeon.

Other Spanish critics compare the story to *Romeo and Juliet*. That the two plays have certain elements in common is true: a youth, a maiden, and human nature. All plants have their roots underground; but the author of *Celestina* concerns himself with the root and Shakespeare with the flower. Ticknor seems to me right-minded. He says:

The play is full of life and movement throughout. Its characters, from Celestina down to her insolent and lying valets and her brutal female associates, are developed with a skill and truth rarely found in the best periods of the Spanish drama. Its style is easy and pure, sometimes brilliant, and always full of the idiomatic resources of the old and true Castilian. . . . The great offence of the *Celestina*, however, is that large portions of it are foul with a shameless libertinism of thought and language.

On the other hand, James Mabbe, the Tudor translator, says in his preface:

Doubt I not, but it will meete with some detractors who, like dogges that barke by custome, will exclaime against the whole worke, because some part of it seemeth somewhat more obscene than may sute with a civill stile: which as I do not deny; so sithence it is written reprehensively, and not instructively, I see no reason why they should more abstaine from reading a great deale of good, because they must picke it out of that which is bad; than they should . . . hate honey, because it is hived in straw. . . . They that are learned in [the book's] language, have esteemed it [in comparison with others] as Gold, amongst metalls; as the Carbuncle amongst stones; as the Rose amongst flowers.

This is the same sort of defense that Juan Ruiz makes, and most others who write licentious books. I give it for what it may be worth. There is no doubt that *La Celestina* is a most notable book, that the bawd herself may rank, in her way, with Iago, Falstaff, Sancho Panza, or Achilles; but I think that this book as well as *El Libro de Buen Amor* supports what to most people would appear the exaggerated opinion of an English author (I quote from a preface to a book on art), who insists upon the "brutal, witty, materialistic Iberian skepticism of the Spanish," and says that Spain is "utterly unromantic . . . the most materialistic of lands."

Celestina was written by Fernando de Rojas (1475–1536), who, according to Foulché-Delbosc, was a Jew by race. It has been translated into English, French, German, Dutch, Italian, and Latin, and its place is secure among the world's classics.

These, then, are the three great literary monuments in the reign of *los Reyes Católicos*. If I had more space, I should mention other pioneers; such as Antonio de Nebrija, the great scholar who wrote the first Castilian grammar, and worked at Cardinal Ximénez's polyglot Bible; such as Juan de Encina, who wrote plays for acting, though they are no more than eclogues with — I understand — some musical accompaniment; and various other persons.

XIX

CHARLES V IN SPAIN

Queen Isabella died in 1504, and the crown of Castile passed to her daughter, Mad Joan. This unfortunate woman had married Philip, son to the Emperor Maximilian and — through his mother — grandson to Charles the Bold, the great Duke of Burgundy. By this marriage Spain acquired the Netherlands, the cause of so much woe to both countries. Joan's father Ferdinand and her husband Philip agreed that Joan was incapable of ruling, and for a time there was a dangerous rivalry as to which of the two should act in her stead. Philip insisted on his rights and became King Philip I. He was a handsome man, a lady-killer, much concerned with his appearance: "*Monsigneur avoit une robbe de satin brochiet violet et une robbe de velour violet plaine de drap d'or. A lendemain, Monsigneur avoit une robbe de satin noir plaine de martres de sables.*" His poor wife adored him and, if she was crazy by nature, became far crazier from jealousy. Philip died two years later, and the tale of how she clung to his dead body touches the most pathetic notes that human history is capable of. His memory is usually spoken of with disrespect, but a Flemish friend says that he "*en bref a accomplit ce que pluseurs acomplissent en moult de tampz, car son âme plaisoit à Dieu.*"

On Philip's death Ferdinand became regent and

again directed the affairs of a united Spain. It was then that he conquered Spanish Navarre, and extended the realm from the Straits of Gibraltar to the Pyrenees. On his death (1518) Cardinal Ximénez assumed the regency for a few months, until the arrogant young heir came down from Flanders to take his crowns, and, in the summary fashion of a disdainful master, dismissed the aged statesman as if he had been a retainer of the royal bedchamber.

Before sketching the events of the young monarch's reign, I shall quote the description of the country that Guicciardini draws in the year 1513:

The kingdom is thinly populated; there are some fine cities, Barcelona, Saragossa, Valencia, Granada, and Seville, but they are few for so large a country, and the other towns for the most part are of little account. The southern regions are far the most fertile, but only the land in the neighborhood of the cities is cultivated. Wool, silk, wine, and oil are exported in large quantities. There is sufficient wheat for the home market, and, if the nation were only industrious and given to trade, their iron, steel, copper, hides, and other products would make them rich. But as it is, the country is very poor, not from lack of natural resources but from the laziness of the people. The men are proud, and think that no other nation compares with theirs. They speak with extreme deliberation and try to appear of more consequence than they are. They dislike foreigners, and are discourteous toward them. They are more warlike, perhaps, than any other Christian nation; agile, quick, and good at the manage of arms; they make a great point of honor, and prefer to die rather than submit to shame. Their light cavalry is excellent, their horses very good; and the Castilian infantry enjoys a great reputation, higher, whether for defense or siege, than the infantry of any other country. It is a matter of dispute whether they or the Switzers are better in the open field. . . .

Spaniards are thought to be shrewd and intelligent, but they are not good in liberal or mechanical arts; all the artisans at the King's court are French, or foreigners of some sort. All Spaniards look down on trade and put on airs as hidalgos and prefer to be soldiers or (before Ferdinand's time) highwaymen than to engage in trade or any other such occupation. It is true that in some parts of Spain they weave and make rich stuffs, as in Valencia, Toledo, and Seville; but the nation as a whole is opposed to industrial life. The country people follow their example, and till the ground much less than they might. Spaniards are fond of show; wear fine clothes abroad; ride a stylish horse; but at home, in the house, they live in a beggarly fashion hard to believe. They do not care for literature; and you hardly ever meet among the nobility, or in any class, anybody who knows Latin. In outward appearance they are very religious, but not so really. They are very ceremonious, full of fine words and hand-kissings, and everybody is their "lord" and they are "at his disposition"; but their fair words are not to be taken literally. They are avaricious and great dissemblers.

Guicciardini adds that, as he was curious to know why so warlike a people had been so often conquered, Ferdinand explained to him that Spaniards, although very well fitted for fighting, were so insubordinate that they never profited by their fighting qualities, except when they found leaders who could make them obey. In summing up, he concludes:

The present success — for Spain is no longer a subject people, but a dominating people — is due to the union of Castile and Aragon and the sagacity of Ferdinand and Isabella.

All this is probably true; but it does not explain why Spain played the master part in European history in the reigns of Charles V and Philip II. For a guess, I attribute it to these factors: the fighting qualities of the race, a romantic imagination set on fire by the discoveries and conquests in America, religious enthusiasm, and the stimulus to national pride caused by the sudden elevation of a people, but lately held in mean estimation, to the foremost place in Europe.

Some of the credit or blame for Spain's brilliant career is due to the ambition and determined character of Charles V. Even at the age of seven this little darling of Fortune showed his purpose to excel: *"il veult apprendre et entendre lettres en latin et à jouer de tous instrumens et bastons invasibles et diffensibles autant que grand prince ou povre gentilhomme en peult savoir. Et ne fait à douter que c'est le plus beau commencement de prince ou de roy et la plus belle apparence de prince magninime et vertueux que l'on vit en longtemps."* In 1517, already lord of the Netherlands and Franche Comté, he came down to assume the crowns of Castile and Aragon, speaking little or no Spanish, and surrounded by a swarm of greedy Flemings to whom he gave rich offices in State and Church, and so laid a broad base for ill will between the two countries. In later years the Spaniards reversed the account and took from Brabant, Hainault, and their neighbors what perquisites they could; but in the beginning the Flemings had their innings. Flemish favoritism excited the greatest indignation in Spain; people grumbled; they demanded that Spanish offices should be filled by Spaniards, and that Spanish gold should not be taken out of the country in the pockets of greedy foreigners. Charles did not listen.

Worse soon followed. His grandfather, the Emperor Maximilian, died, and he offered himself as candidate for the crown of the Holy Roman Empire in opposition to the French King, Francis I. Public opinion in Spain was strongly against Charles's candidacy; popular apprehension seemed to sniff from afar the ills that must come of Spain's entanglement in European politics. Charles paid no heed, but borrowed vast sums from the Fuggers, — the great international bankers, — in order to bribe the Imperial electors. On receiving news of his election, he announced that he was going to Germany. Again the country protested. Again Charles flouted public opinion; and to crown his impolicy, as he was leaving, appointed a Fleming, Cardinal Adrian, to be Governor-General of the kingdom during his absence. The cities of Castile objected to a tax levy; they did not think that they should be called on to pay the bills for these imperial doings. Charles was obstinate and autocratic. Their indignation overflowed, and he had scarcely set sail before they banded together into a confederacy, *las comunidades*, and raised the standard of open revolt. Juan de Padilla of Toledo led them, and for a time matters looked black for the royal authority; but class dissensions and personal rivalries weakened the confederates, and their army was completely crushed by the King's forces in the battle of Villalar (1521).

From this defeat the commons of Spain and the ancient parliamentary body, the Cortes, never recovered. The first Cortes in Castile had been held in or about 1250, although it is said that in Leon a Cortes had been assembled as early as 1188. The nobles and the clergy constituted separate bodies, though the three sometimes sat together. The Cortes, however, was merely a consulting body with no legislative powers whatever. Its one privilege was the right to present a petition for the redress of grievances, which the king was at full liberty to reject. The king might convoke it or not, at his pleasure. When he did so he would ask, if he chose, its advice in matters of public policy, demand a grant of taxes and the ratification of certain acts, in especial the appointment of his successor, and then close the session. Nevertheless, the Cortes had considerable moral power. If the king was in need of popular support against the nobility he was gracious and would listen to advice; when he was strong and prosperous, he was likely to be brusque and masterful. In the troubled times of the fourteenth and fifteenth centuries it seemed not unlikely that the Cortes might become as powerful as the Parliament in England, but Ferdinand and Isabella had no liking for democratic institutions, and now by this unsuccessful rebellion the commons virtually lost everything.

Under these circumstances the King naturally was very unpopular with his Spanish subjects; but in course of time, after he had lived for years in Spain, he became as good a Spaniard as anyone, and though he always acted as absolute master, the people felt proud of their valiant king, champion of the Catholic Faith, the arbiter of the destinies of Europe, and the old antipathy between them passed wholly away.

XX

THE FATAL FOREIGN POLICY

SPAIN'S dealings with foreign countries during Charles's reign are multifarious and complicated, and I can do no more than touch upon them. At the bottom of all the troubles was the quarrel with France. For this quarrel there were grounds in plenty. One was over Naples, which you will recollect King Ferdinand took from Louis XII. Another was Milan. The dukedom was a fief of the Empire, and on the failure of the Sforza line would, according to feudal law, revert to its overlord, and therefore Charles claimed it; but Francis, as heir to the earlier line of the Visconti, also laid claims. Besides these grounds of dissension, Francis had taken the defeat of his candidacy for the Imperial crown in bad part, and out of jealousy, and also from apprehension of the enveloping power of Spain, had adopted a policy of thwarting Charles wherever he could. This apprehension was not unreasonable, for if Charles, King of Spain, Emperor of the Holy Roman Empire, Lord of the Netherlands and Franche Comté, were to possess Lombardy too, France would be fenced in on all sides by an enemy of vastly superior power and resources.

The hostility of these two great kings affected all the politics of Europe. Secular affairs in themselves, therefore, were turbid enough, but at the very beginning of Charles's imperial reign religious quarrels muddled them far worse. In 1520 Martin Luther published his treatise *On the Babylonian Captivity of the Church of God*, and launched the Reformation. European politics became a horrid mess in which Charles, Francis, Henry VIII, the Lutheran princes of Germany, the Pope, and the Grand Turk, all did their best to gain an advantage over one another.

Of all Charles's European career I shall refer only to one or two salient incidents. In 1521, when he was on the way to his coronation at Aachen and the *comuneros* were in revolt, France, believing that she spied her chance to recover Spanish Navarre, which had been swallowed up by the crafty Ferdinand in 1512, sent an army across the Pyrenees by the old road via St.-Jean-Pied-de-Port and Roncevaux, and captured Pamplona. After the defeat of the *comuneros* the French were speedily driven out again, and the campaign is remembered only for the sake of a young soldier in the Spanish garrison. This soldier received a severe wound. During his convalescence he renounced a worldly life and dedicated himself to what he conceived to be the greater glory of God. From this self-consecration sprang the Order of Jesus. Ignatius Loyola is one of the greatest of Spaniards, but his career belongs to the story of Rome and of the world.

In 1525 the war between Charles and Francis over Milan was in full swing. The Emperor's generals won the great victory of Pavia, and captured Francis, *la soberbia de Francia*, as Lope de Vega calls him. The captive King was taken to Madrid. A treaty was made. Francis pledged himself to renounce all claims to Italy and to perform other conditions that, if performed, would have reduced France to the position of a second-class power, and finally, as a guaranty of faith and friendship, to marry the Emperor's sister. The marriage Francis made; but, once across the French border, he renounced the other clauses of the treaty, and war was renewed.

In 1527 an event took place without a parallel since the days of Attila. The Imperial army in Italy, under the command (if such a word may be applied to an army that does not obey) of the Constable Bourbon, getting no pay and scanty provisions, decided to provide for itself. It marched on Rome and sacked the city, amid horrors unspeakable. Nevertheless, but three years later the unfortunate Pope Clement VII, who had barely escaped with his life, was obliged to pretend that Charles was in no wise responsible, and to crown him with the Imperial crown. The consecration took place at Bologna, in the ancient church of San Petronio. Sword, globe, sceptre, and crown were bestowed with great ceremony. There was much bandying of compliments. At parting, the Pope suffered the Emperor to hold the stirrup for him to mount, "not to me, but to Him in whose place I am." That evening in the *piazza* before the church a fountain spouted red wine and white, and a roast ox, stuffed with poultry, as well as other good cheer, was served to the populace. As the Flemish secretary adds, "*le tout conclud avec grand silence et concorde, que semble venir par permission divine.*"

Other important episodes in Charles's career I must give more baldly still. He put himself at the head of Roman Catholicism and fought infidels and heretics. In 1535 the Emperor, by the capture of Tunis, won great and glorious fame as a Crusader. In 1537, again at war with Francis I, he invaded Provence but was driven bootless back, a repulse memorable because the great poet Garcilaso de la Vega lost his life in a casual fray. In 1541 the Emperor attempted to take Algiers but was beaten off with great loss, more by tempests than by the Turks. In 1543 he defeated the Lutherans at Mühlberg, and touched the zenith of his fortunes. In 1552 he was obliged to fly for his life to escape being taken prisoner by Maurice of Saxony. Nevertheless, the ups were many and the downs were few.

I have enumerated these episodes in the great Emperor's brilliant career in order to make clear how little Spain's true interests were concerned with these ambitions for which she shed her blood and wasted her treasure. What benefit did she get from holding the Netherlands, or subjugating Milan? What salvation did she win by leading the cause of the old ecclesiastical order in its bitter struggle with the Reformation? There are Spaniards, the great scholar, Menéndez y Pelayo, for one, who take an emotional view of Spain's heroic efforts to stem the current, onward or wayward, of human happenings; who feel a greater pride that Spain lost an empire for a spiritual cause than if she had led the course of material progress for centuries, as England has done; but those who are not sure what or where religious truth may be, who fix their eyes on the pages of economic history, see in these magnificent but vain efforts a mere prodigal and profligate waste of men

and money that inevitably brought about the national decline of later centuries. And the harm done
by the Emperor's policy did not end here.

Memorable as were the Spanish feats in Europe
under the Emperor Charles, there were others of far
more enduring results across the ocean. From the
opening of the century explorations proceeded rap-
idly. Many adventurers, Spanish and Portuguese,
followed in the wake of Columbus: Pinzon, Hojeda,
Solis, Pedrarias, Hernandez de Córdova, Magellan,
Balboa, Hernando de Soto, Ponce de Leon, Coronado,
and many more, sailors, soldiers, gentlemen pirates,
conquistadores,

Comme un vol des gerfauts,

as the poet says, swarmed about the western shores
of the Atlantic Ocean. Hernando Cortés hacked his
ships to bits on the Mexican coast, and gave Charles
the kingdom of the Montezumas (1519–1520).
Francisco Pizarro presented him with the kingdom
of Peru (1533–1534). But the Emperor, though he
was quite ready to accept territories upon which the
sun never set, and to confer heraldic honors and
high-sounding titles, paid little heed to America,
except to keep an observant eye on the independent
humors of his freebooting subjects.

At last, in 1556, the great Emperor, weary with the
burden of a turbulent world, laid down his crowns
and retired to the monastery of Yuste, which lies on a
mountain slope, clad with forests of oak and chestnut, between the Tagus and the stark Sierra de
Gredos. There he spent his last days, walking about
the garden, feeding birds and fishes, or watching

Torriano of Cremona contrive, with infinite patience and an ingenuity bordering upon wizardry, the nice mechanism of fantastic clocks, and yet always thinking upon what was going on in the great world and the doings of his son Philip.

XXI

BOSCÁN AND GARCILASO

ALL textbooks on Spanish literature will tell you of
many highroads, not to mention lanes and bypaths,
that lead hither and thither, in this opening period of
El Siglo de Oro, as the Spaniards call, with no very
definite limits, their epoch of literary glory. One
path will take you to the literature that sprung from
the discovery, exploration, and conquest of America;
another to the humanists, Luis Vives (1492–1540),
Juan de Valdés (1501–1541), and other admirers of
the great Erasmus; another to the first and best of
the rogue stories, *Lazarillo de Tormes* (1553), to
Guzmán de Alfarache by Mateo Alemán (1550–1609),
and the long line that leads finally to *Gil Blas*, and
on beyond *Gil Blas* to *Huckleberry Finn;* another
path to Guevara (*d.* 1545), whose *Dial for Princes*
won great renown throughout Europe; another to
Diana of Jorge de Montemayor (*d.* 1561) and pastoral poetry; other paths elsewhere.

The main avenue leads straight to Italy. Men
of letters, a hundred years before, had adopted
Italian fashions as best they might, but they could
not carry the Spanish public with them. The passage
of a century had removed many difficulties, and the
union of the kingdoms of Naples and Spain under one
crown took away the rest. If there were space, we
could track the rise and progress of the movement.

Intelligent Spaniards who visited Italy with Alfonso
V of Aragon at their head were dazzled by the brilliant performances of the Italian intellect, and wished
that Spain might profit by them. Italian scholars,
such as Lucio Marineo — whose description of
Ferdinand and Isabella I have quoted — and Peter
Martyr of Angleria, went to Spain, became pro-
fessors at Salamanca, or taught the young aristocracy at the royal court. Influences shot to and
fro between Spain and Italy like shuttles. The
Spaniard Rodrigo Borgia, Pope Alexander VI,
gathered a Spanish society of ladies about him, dis-
respectfully referred to by a puritanical Roman as
puttane Spagnuole, who encouraged the Spanish playwright Encina. Vittoria Colonna, who had married
a Spanish nobleman and was interested in Juan
de Valdés, patronized another Spanish playwright,
Torres Naharro. And so on. Famous Italians went
to Spain on diplomatic errands, Francesco Guicciardini for one; Baldassare Castiglione was another,
doubly renowned, as the author of the *Book of the
Courtier* and because Raphael painted his portrait;
and Andrea Navagero, ambassador from the Seign-
iory of Venice, was a third. The last brings us to a
definite point of departure.

Navagero traveled through Spain in 1525, and has
left a tolerably readable account of his travels. By
listening to his complaints of customhouses and
customs dues, the reader gets to understand what an
almost insuperable obstacle the division of Spain into
half a dozen little self-sufficient provinces interposed
to national unity. Stops, delays, examinations, ex-
actions on every boundary line, lay like lions in the

path of trade and mutual good-understanding; ambassadors were searched and taxed, and it is said that
even the royal suite fared no better. Spain was less a
nation, in any strict sense, than a collection of separate states that held together because their several
crowns were on the head of one king. Even a hundred
years later, an Englishman, Henry Peacham, writes:

Spain being divided into many Kingdoms or Provinces,
you are allowed to carry about you, only but an hundred
reals [about 6s. 3d]; what you have above that is forfeited;
and for that purpose, at every bridge or passage where the
Countries part, you are to be searched.

Navagero also, like every traveler before him and
since, until after George Borrow's day, complains of
the inns (*posadas malventuradas*); and a city inn was
much better equipped than the village *venta*. What a
posada was like may still be seen in the *Posada della
Sangre* at Toledo, and what a *venta* was like you will
find in the first part of *Don Quixote*. In the *posada*
the guest was greeted by four walls hung with pots
and pans, and furnished with a bare bedstead; he was
obliged to bring or procure his food and bedding,
make his own fire, and cook his own food. Peacham
(1621) reports:

It is a country for Travaile very combersome in respect
of lodging and dyet except when you come into the walled
Townes, where you shall according to their meanes be
accommodated well enough.

But apart from inns and customhouses, Navagero
enjoyed himself. He visited various cities. Like
everybody else, he found Barcelona most delightful
with its gardens of oranges, lemons, and flowers; at

Burgos he liked the people especially; at Alcalá de Henares he remarks that the lectures at the college were still given in Latin, whereas at Salamanca and elsewhere they were given in Spanish; at Toledo he found that the clergy ruled everybody, especially the women, *"dandose la mejor vida del mundo, sin que nadie les vaya a la mano"*; at Seville he saw some American Indians. But the diary displays no real enthusiasm until he reaches Granada; there he indulges in an elaborate account of the Alhambra, the Generalife, and other sights. What delighted him most, however, were the little Moorish houses round about the city, hidden among musk roses and myrtle and gay with fountains. He noticed, as Guicciardini had done, the sharp contrast between the industry of the Moors and the idleness of the Spaniards: "The Spaniards in the kingdom of Granada are not very industrious, they do not care to till the soil, or cultivate grain, but take to soldiering or go to the Indies to get rich." But I must leave the journal and come to my point. The real matter of interest in Navagero's visit to Granada lies in his meeting with Boscán.

Juan Boscán (1495–1542), by birth a Catalan, was a poet who, after studying under Lucio Marineo, had become tutor to young Alva, afterward known as the Great Duke (1507–1583). At this time, I think, he was still connected with the ducal household. Boscán and Navagero met and fell into a conversation about literature, of which Boscán has left an account:

I talked with him about literature and genius and the individuality of different languages; he asked me why I did not try to compose sonnets, and other sorts of poetry in Spanish, according to the metres in vogue among good Italian poets; and after conversing in a general way, he went on to urge me to do so. A few days after that I started out for home. The road was long and lonely, and my mind wandered over various things, and often went back to what Navagero had said to me. From that dates my attempt at this kind of versification. In the beginning I found some difficulty, as the Italian style is highly artificial and very different from our way of doing in many particulars. But afterwards it seemed to me (perhaps from the affection one has for one's own handiwork) that I was doing pretty well, and I went on, by degrees warming to my work as I went. Nevertheless, that would not have been enough to make me proceed very far, if I had not consulted Garcilaso and been fortified by his approval, for his opinion is a safe criterion, not only to my thinking but in the judgment of all the world. He often praised my undertaking, and supplemented his approbation with his own example, and so finally induced me to spend all my leisure time over this Italian manner.

It is agreed on all hands that Boscán is not a great poet. He holds his place in the history of Spanish literature because he introduced Italian forms and measures — whether for good or ill is a matter of dispute — and because he was a friend of Garcilaso de la Vega. The friendship between these two men is very charming:

> For we were nursed upon the self-same hill,
> Fed the same flock, by fountain, shade, and rill;
> Together both, ere the high lawns appear'd
> Under the opening eyelids of the morn,
> We drove afield.

I think that he has a third title to fame. He is the only Spanish poet I can think of — and the only

poet except Ovid, until recently — who sings the
praises of his wife:

que es principio y fin del alma mia.

She gave him, he says, new life, and filled his heart
and mind with felicity.

Boscán's friend, Garcilaso de la Vega (1501–1536),
occupies a position in Spanish literature and history
such as Sir Philip Sidney holds in English. There is
no need to cite authorities; all readers of Spanish
poetry are agreed. Garcilaso came of an ancient
house; the Marquis of Santillana was his great uncle
and Pérez de Guzmán his great-grandfather. He was
born and educated in Toledo, and then joined the
court of the young King, Charles V. His life, like that
of Jorge Manrique and of so many other Spanish
notables, was devoted both to literature and to war,

tomando ora la espada, ora la pluma.

He saw considerable service: he fought against the
comuneros (1520–1521) although his elder brother,
a friend of Juan de Padilla, was one of their leaders;
he took part, together with Boscán, in the unsuccessful attempt to relieve the island of Rhodes, besieged
by the Turks (1522); he served with the forces that
recaptured Fuenterrabia from the French (1523); he
was with the Emperor at the taking of Tunis (1535),
and finally in the unsuccessful campaign in Provence
(1536), where he was killed while scaling a tower in
an attempt to dislodge some French peasants. As
with other courtiers, his place in the sunshine of
prosperity depended upon the Emperor's favor, and
Garcilaso was imprudent enough to abet a marriage
of a near kinsman in the teeth of the Emperor's

disapproval. For this he suffered confinement on an island in the Danube (1532), where he wrote one of his most charming poems, and the further punishment of a mild exile in Naples. His gallantry at Tunis, a few years later, seems to have restored him to the Emperor's good graces, and but for his premature death he might have risen to a high political position.

The collected poems of Garcilaso, such of them as could then be found, were published together with Boscán's by the latter's widow, a year after Boscán's death (1543). They are not very numerous: three eclogues, two elegies, verses to Boscán, five odes, thirty-eight sonnets, and some fugitive pieces. The sonnets and odes are composed after Petrarch's models, and contain a good deal concerning his passion for an unnamed lady or ladies. His statements are accepted as biographical, but the emotions of imitative poets are sometimes imitations themselves. If a poet sets out to write in Petrarchian fashion, what can he do but recount in mournful numbers devotion, desire, admiration, and despair? It is difficult, too, not to suspect that Garcilaso's love of nature — *flores* and *ruiseñores* — was learned rather from the pastoral poets of Naples, Sannazaro and others, than from nature. The ode to the "Flower of Gnido" is usually regarded as the best of his minor poems; it was written, according to tradition, to further the suit of a friend, and reminds the lady how a scornful nymph was turned into marble by the just gods because her rejected lover was found dead by his own doing outside her door.

But Garcilaso's reputation in its fullness depends

upon the eclogues, in which, according to an American
scholar, "he found a perfect medium for the expression of the characteristic qualities of his genius, a
certain atmosphere of melancholy regret at the crud-
ities and cruelties of life, and a splendid mastery of
the forms of harmony." To-day, the classical poetry of the sixteenth century requires considerable
scholarship and a broadly cultivated taste; and it
would be grossly disrespectful to the accepted judgment of a dozen generations not to take the blame
wholly upon one's self for a failure of sympathy. But
when a shepherd steps forward, pipe in hand, to
bewail the death of a friend self-murdered for love of
a fair cruel maid, it is difficult for the Philistine to
continue. An Englishman, Jeremiah Holme Wiffen,
a hundred years ago, attempted to translate Garcilaso's poems, and did but confirm the lesson of common experience that poetry, since its essence lies in
the order of words, cannot be translated from one
language into another. Other English translators
have added superfluous testimony to this well-
settled principle. The interested reader must go to
the original Spanish.

Garcilaso and Boscán address themselves to a
cultivated class, and their poetry is the poetry of
men accustomed to polite society. But just about the
time that Boscán's widow was publishing her husband's and his friend's poems, a book of poetry was
published in Antwerp of a very different category,
entitled the *Cancionero de romances*, the first important collection of Spanish ballads. The special
excellencies of Spanish literature, *Don Quixote* apart,
are its ballads, plays, proverbs, and mystical litera-

ture; and the ballads, I suppose, are superior in both number and quality to those of any country, unless it be Great Britain.

After the first collection, published at Antwerp, others soon followed. In 1600 there came the *Romancero general* and a few years later the second part of it; and then collections of ballads upon the Cid, or upon the *Seven Nobles of Lara*, and so on. On a college shelf you will find for modern use the nineteenth-century collections of Depping, of Durán, of Wolf and Hoffmann, and translations by Lockhart, James Young Gibson, and others. The early collections contain most of the really old ballads, narrating an episode in the life of some hero, Don Roderick, or Bernardo del Carpio, Fernán González, for instance, that had been handed down anonymously, while the later collections are made up of recent ballads written by various poets in the manner of old ballads and usually on matters of heroic tradition, on fights with the Moors, on the love of a Castilian knight for a Moorish maiden, and suchlike.

There is not as yet complete agreement among scholars as to the origin of ballads. Were they originally written as ballads in the heroic days that they celebrate? Or are they the more striking passages of lost epics, out of which the duller connecting parts have dropped and been forgotten? And are some ballads based on the historical chronicles, and are the chronicles, in their turn, built up out of earlier ballads, or epics? And so on. Here is material for discussion; and happily a knowledge of the right answers to these questions is in no wise necessary to an enjoyment of the ballads themselves.

XXII

ARCHITECTURE UNDER ITALIAN INFLUENCES

In literature, as I have said, the famous conversation between the Venetian ambassador Navagero and the poet Boscán marks a definite turn in the road; in the other arts the influences of Italy, though quite as masterful, make no such theatrical entrance, but slip in quietly like schoolboys late for school. I begin with architecture.

The church of Santiago of Compostela, I repeat, the first great monument of the Romanesque style, testifies to the influence of Cluny; a hundred years later the abbey of Las Huelgas, with its transition into early Gothic, to that of Cîteaux; and in the thirteenth century the three cathedrals of Toledo, Burgos, and Leon proclaim the complete triumph of the Gothic style. Up to this time French influence dominates; but now comes a change, and we meet Flemish and German influences. I do not know of any one building that is wholly Flemish or German; these new foreign elements appear in additions and modifications. A cathedral is rarely built by one sustained effort, following out the plans of the original architect. It grows during generations. Workshops spring up about it, guilds of masons pass down their trade from father to son, sculptors hand on their craftsmanship, one master of the works succeeds another, and chapels, cloisters, steeples, lantern, and other additions, furnish labor for a hundred years. At Toledo we meet the Fleming, Annequin de Egas; at Burgos the German, Hans of Cologne, who put up the crocketed and perforated steeples; his son Simon, who built the Constable's Chapel; and his son Francisco, who designed the Puerta de la Pellejeria (1516). I say nothing of the cathedral of Seville (fifteenth century) because nobody knows who was the architect or whence he came. This mighty church, in spite of defects in details here and there, produces an impression of majesty, as if indeed Divinity were present; the pilgrim falls upon his knees. But I have no space to recount its magnificence, its chapels, its *coro*, its treasures of sculptor, painter, glazier, smith, and iron-worker; I hurry on to the subject of this chapter.

Italian influences appear plainly in the reign of Ferdinand and Isabella, but I shall begin about the time of the Queen's death (1504). Styles run into one another. A fashion is pure only at its height; in the beginning it blends with that which went before; at the end, with that which comes after. This new style has various names: some speak of the Italian or the Renaissance style; others of Græco-Roman architecture; the Spanish call it *obra del romano*. A common designation is the "Plateresque" style, which seems to me the most accurate, for it indicates that this style is a matter of ornament, not of structure; that it lays on decoration after the manner of silversmiths (*plateros*), working upon vessels of silver (*plata*).

The best analogy in architecture to Boscán in literature, is Enrique de Egas (*d.* 1534), son to Annequin de Egas, whose name in Flemish is said to be Jan van der Eyken, master of the works at Toledo. The great Cardinal, Don Pedro de Mendoza (1424–1495), wished to build a hospital at Toledo, their Majesties *los Reyes Católicos* proposed to build another at Santiago of Compostela, and Isabella a third at Granada. Enrique de Egas was appointed architect in each case. The plans for the hospital of Santa Cruz at Toledo were made first (1495?), but the hospital at Santiago was the first built (1501–1511). The original plans of all three were, I understand, on the same general pattern, a rectangular building divided into four quarters by a Greek cross, with patios between the arms. The façade at Santiago is long and low; a great doorway stands in the middle, originally flanked only by little windows. A rich, fanciful cornice gives weight and beauty to the line of the roof. The doorway has, on each side and above, mouldings, statues, and carvings of great variety. Nothing could be more charming than this flat surface set off by incrustations of imaginative ornament. But I must warn the beginner that conventional — or perhaps I should say well-educated — taste has not yet approved it wholly. Baedeker cautiously remarks, "This demands attention." Street says: "The detail of this hospital is extremely late and poor." It is "late," in that work done in 1501–1511 is later than the Pórtico de la Gloria across the square, which was carved in 1168–1188; but I think that the adjective "poor" proves that Street's taste was purely mediæval. The patios, he concedes, are "fine." So they are. If there were shrubs and rose bushes about the antique well in the centre, to set off the graceful Italian arcades that support the upper verandah, the convalescent patients could ask for no more attractive spot. The building is still used as a hospital. The condition of the wards is, I imagine, very much the same as it was in the days of Ferdinand and Isabella. At Toledo the Hospital de Santa Cruz lies to your left as you go from the Plaza de Zocodóver past the Posada de la Sangre. The whole was designed on a more magnificent scale than the hospital at Santiago, but it has never been finished.

Enrique de Egas also built the Colegio de Santa Cruz at Valladolid, which Baedeker boldly says is "a masterpiece of the Plateresque style." This is an earlier work, and to me appears to lack the elegance of proportion and the brilliant handling of ornament that mark the hospital at Santiago. He also built the Capella Real at Granada (1506–1511), which contains the tombs of Ferdinand and Isabella and of Philip the Handsome and Mad Joan; and he made the ground plan for the cathedral there. In the latter he followed the plan of the cathedral at Toledo; but for some reason or other he was dismissed, and his successors built the present temple. Egas was a man of genius and rare taste; the Plateresque style is a happy blending of the exuberant forms of late Gothic with the elegant, classical fashions of the Italian Renaissance, and withal it is amazingly original, and strikes the beholder as the first and also the most characteristically Spanish style in the whole history of Spanish architecture.

Enrique de Egas

Toledo

HOSPITAL DE SANTA CRUZ

(Old print)

The next famous architect of the Plateresque style is Alonso de Covarrubias, who married a daughter of Enrique de Egas and succeeded to the latter's position as master of the works upon the cathedral at Toledo. The sacristan will point out his hand there in various chapels; but his most conspicuous memorial is the west wing of the archiepiscopal palace at Alcalá de Henares. Another great architect of the time is also associated with Alcalá de Henares, Rodrigo Gil de Ontañon. He designed the new façade for the university building that Cardinal Ximénez had founded. Part of our interest in the fanciful lines of his elaborate Renaissance ornament lies in the thought that very likely a little barefoot boy, Miguel, son to Rodrigo de Cervantes, a modest surgeon of the town, played about the materials before they were put in place, and watched, with bright, tender, observant eyes, the busy architect directing the workmen.

Although Rodrigo executed this Plateresque masterpiece, he was by training — as Egas was, and Covarrubias too — a Gothic architect, and built, in collaboration with his father, the last two Gothic cathedrals in Spain, at Salamanca and Segovia.

Two other names I must mention. Diego de Riaño (*d.* 1533), who designed the *sacristiá mayor* and other parts of the cathedral at Seville, and the south wing of the Ayuntamiento (town hall), "*insuperable de elegancia y de buen gusto,*" as Señor Lámperez very truly says. Riaño is the chief Plateresque architect at Seville. Diego de Siloe (*d.* 1563) holds a similar place at Granada. His principal work there is the cathedral, which he built upon the ground

plan drawn by Enrique de Egas. This cathedral
has been dubbed the eighth wonder of the world,
and Baedeker, planting his feet on the testimony of
German experts, drops all the caution that he showed
at Santiago and declares that this is "on the whole
the best Renaissance building in Spain." Fergusson
a little ambiguously says: "In respect to its plan,
it is one of the finest churches in Europe." Other
architects praise its amazing technical excellences.
But only craftsmen wholly absorbed in their craft
could be blind to its intolerable dreariness, its
spiritual dullness, its pagan indifference to the
Christian religion. It might just as well be a temple
to Dagon or Behemoth.

But Diego de Siloe erected a monument supreme
in its kind, which all the world, educated or not,
unites to admire — the *escalera dorada* in the north
transept of the cathedral at Burgos (1519). This
stairway is one of the most beautiful things in Spain.
It rises from the floor as a queen rises from her
throne, mounts with railing and banisters of marble
to the first landing, then divides right and left into
branches that flaunt glorious balustrades of forged
iron, and meet again, as if to the music of a minuet,
some twenty or thirty steps higher up, before the
portal that leads into the calle Fernán González.

Of course there are many other monuments of the
Renaissance scattered about Spain, often brilliant
and beautiful, and almost all — at least to the eye
of the uneducated — typically Spanish: at Burgos,
Salamanca, Jaen, Saragossa, Leon, Seville, and elsewhere. I should like to loiter over the Palacio de
Monterey at Salamanca, which usually serves for

Diego de Siloe

ESCALERA DORADA AT BURGOS

the model of the Spanish building at World's Fairs; over the upper storey of La Giralda, which Hernán Ruiz added (1568) to the ancient Moorish prayer-tower at Seville; over the Plateresque church thrust into the very middle of the Mezquita at Cordova, also designed by Hernán Ruiz; and over the palace of Charles V, built with arrogant insouciance right against the Alhambra, as Drake or Hawkins might lie alongside a Spanish galleon. But I must refer the reader, for all of these, to more learned books.

XXIII

SCULPTURE

This period is so full of all sorts of energy and achievement that I shall continue to linger over it. Spaniards conquered Naples and Milan, they garrisoned the Low Countries, they fought Frenchmen, German Lutherans, and Turks, they swarmed across the ocean and added a continent to the Spanish crown, while in their own land they were filling their cathedrals and churches with things of beauty to the glory of God and the honor of their kings. In this chapter I deal with sculpture.

Spanish sculpture begins — I mean, for elementary students — with the Pórtico de la Gloria in the cathedral at Compostela (1168–1188). The next great collection of statuary and carving is on the portals of the cathedral at Burgos, all the work of unknown thirteenth-century sculptors. The next is on the west and south fronts at Leon, at the end of the thirteenth century. The portals of the west front at Toledo belong to the first half of the fifteenth century (1418–1450); the Puerta de los Leones is a little later. At Seville, if you are to follow the development of this sort of ecclesiastical sculpture, you will find terra-cotta figures on the western portals, the Puerta del Bautismo, and that of San Miguel (1500).

But I leave portals and pass on to the tombs.

In Spain sculpture was a handmaid to the Church, and you will not find statues like Donatello's Saint George, or Verrocchio's Colleoni. You must visit chapels and cloisters.

The connoisseur will go to Cuenca and Sigüenza, and out-of-the-way places. But the Beginner had best go direct to Burgos: to the cloisters for statues of an ancient king and his wife; to the *coro*, where Bishop Maurice's tomb stands; to the Capilla de San Ildefonso, where there is a Gothic tomb to the memory of Cardinal Albornoz — he that is charged with having put the archpriest of Hita in prison — and to a chapel off the transept, which holds the tomb of Bishop Alonso of Cartagena, a prelate famous because on his way back from Germany he fetched Hans of Cologne to build the steeples of his cathedral. Bishop Alonso's effigy has a sweet, noble face, and lies in rich trappings, his crozier by his side. Some say that this tomb is the work of Gil de Siloe, father of Diego the architect; others say of Simon, son of Hans of Cologne. It is a work of great merit, rich, restrained, solemn. But Gil is the undisputed artist of the sculpture in the Charter-house church at Miraflores, a mile or two outside Burgos. There is a great gilded retablo behind the altar, with a crucifix in the centre, and about it statues, reliefs in medallions and niches, and all the pious ornaments you can think of. A retablo is as essential in a Spanish church as a silk hat at a wedding, but the taste for retablos is a special gift and all people do not possess it.

Before the altar stands the great sixteen-sided tomb of Juan II and Isabella of Portugal, father and mother of Isabella of Castile. The two effigies lie on a base that is adorned with all the resources of the sculptor's art. The cautious Baedeker, in a fine burst of admiration, nearly forgets himself, but recovers enough to slip in a "perhaps:" "This is, perhaps, the finest monument of its kind in Spain, perfect both in design and execution." In execution — perhaps; but the overwrought intricacy of the design detracts from the simple solemnity that should shroud a tomb. To the left, against the wall, is a tomb to the Infante Alfonso, Isabella's brother, who died at the age of sixteen and left his claim to the crown of Castile to his sister. The kneeling figure seems to me to suffer from the overemphasis of the setting. But a French critic says, "*Rien de plus fin, de plus délicat, de plus capricieux.*" These several works give Gil de Siloe a high rank among sculptors.

I have referred somewhere to the tombs of Don Álvaro de Luna, his wife, and his kinsmen in the chapel of Santiago, in the cathedral of Toledo. They are the work of Pablo Ortiz (1488). So much for the Gothic tombs. I pass on to those in the Italian manner.

The Italian influence came in as it did in literature. Among the Italian artists who went to Spain the most famous are Torrigiano, — who broke Michelangelo's nose — and Andrea da Sansovino; but I take up another, less widely known but a far greater artist. Domenico Fancelli (1469–1518) was a Florentine from Settignano, gifted with the delicate sense of beauty that marks his fellow townsman Desiderio and his neighbor Mino da Fiesole. He first appears at the top of his profession. He was chosen to design

Granada

TOMB OF FERDINAND AND ISABELLA (left)

Domenico Fancelli

TOMB OF PHILIP I AND MAD JOAN (right)

Bartolomé Ordóñez

the marble tomb in memory of the Infante Juan, the only son of Ferdinand and Isabella, who died at nineteen in all the beauty of adolescence (1497). Several years earlier his parents had founded the Dominican convent of Santo Tomás, outside the walls of Ávila; and there in the church, before the high altar, the tomb was placed in accordance with Isabella's dying request. Here in eternal beauty, as if carven out of the *Coplas* of Jorge Manrique, the young man's effigy lies in its marble sleep. The base is decorated in royal fashion with frieze, mouldings, medallions, figures in niches, gryphons at the corners, and all such; but here the decoration, though elegant and even exquisite, is subordinate to the recumbent effigy, and serves to heighten its dignity, nobility, and beauty. I doubt if there be another tomb so beautiful in the world.

Fancelli also made the more famous but less beautiful tomb with the effigies of Ferdinand and Isabella in the Capilla Real at Granada, of which Navagero says in his superior Venetian way, "*assai belle per Ispagna.*" He designed the tomb to Cardinal Ximénez, now in a church at Alcalá de Henares, but died before he had time to do more. His follower, Bartolomé Ordóñez of Burgos (*d.* 1520) executed this design, and also sculptured the tomb of Philip the Handsome and Mad Joan, which lies beside that of Ferdinand and Isabella in the Capilla Real at Granada. Bartolomé's tomb lacks the ripeness of his master's touch, but the face and figure of poor Joan are done with great tenderness, and if the comparison with Fancelli were not thrust upon him, the monument would be even more admired than it is. Another pupil of Fancelli's, Vasco de la Zarza (*d.* 1536), designed the handsome monument to Bishop Alfonso de Madrigal, *el Tostado* (*d.* 1455), that stands by the wall in the cathedral at Ávila.

Diego de Siloe, the architect, also achieved a distinguished reputation as a sculptor, as you will see by the tomb in the Capilla de Santa Anna in the cathedral at Burgos, which is fully worthy of his father's chisel at its best. He also carved the retablo in that chapel. Another famous artist is Daniel Forment, a native of Valencia (*d.* 1541). He carved the great retablos in the cathedral of the Vírgen del Pilar at Saragossa, another for the cathedral at Huesca, and possibly that for the monastery at Poblet. Felipe Vigarni (*d.* 1543), usually called Philip of Burgundy because he came from the diocese of Langres in Burgundy, has left a greater name than the others, perhaps because his retablos and stalls lie on the highroad of ordinary tourists. He was a most industrious man and one of the first to follow the Italian style. At Burgos he carved an incredible number of stalls (1507–1512), and half the upper row of stalls in the cathedral at Toledo (1539). Stalls, like retablos, are an acquired taste; you have five minutes to make the round of a hundred-odd pictures from the Bible in low relief, and you become confused and weary.

I now come to the greatest of all Spanish sculptors, Alonso Berruguete (1486?–1561), a man of prodigious energy and a temperament like young wine. Théophile Gautier says: "*Ce prodigieux Berruguete, qui vécut plus de quatre-vingts ans, couvrant sa patrie de chefs-d'œuvre d'un style varié et d'une perfec-*

TOMB OF INFANTE JUAN, SON OF FERDINAND AND ISABELLA

tion toujours égale."   A Spanish critic speaks of his
"fogosidad" as unparalleled in the whole history of
art. And indeed he possessed the fury, the *terribilità*,
of Michelangelo, but lacked his imaginative power
and his divine sense of beauty. On the other hand,
Street was oppressed by his "heavy, dull paganism."
But Street, who regarded all the art of the Renaissance as pagan, is surely wrong here; for Berruguete
expresses better than anyone else the passionate
Christian creed of his country. All his works are
allegories, or at least exposition and comment upon
the driving force that carried the banner of Spain
against heretics, infidels, and pagans. In his youth
he spent ten years or so in Italy and came under the
mighty influence of Michelangelo; possibly he was
one of the master's pupils. He also learned much
from the classical statues in Rome; for instance, he
entered into a competition for a bronze copy of the
Laocoön, then recently unearthed and the cynosure
of artistic eyes, and made a wax model; but the prize
was awarded — by Raphael, who acted as judge —
to Jacopo Sansovino. Bramante proposed the competition. So you see that Berruguete came into close
contact with the greatest artistic school since the
days of Praxiteles.

To lovers of repose in sculpture these two influences, the puissance of Michelangelo, the agony
of the Laocoön, seem unfortunate; they stimulated
Berruguete's high-wrought temperament, encouraged
his inclination to nervous excitement, and taught
him to prize sensational effects above dignity and
beauty. On the other hand, perhaps just such an
education was necessary to enable him to express

in sculptured form the passionate religion of Cardinal
Ximénez, Torquemada, Hernando Cortés, Ignatius
Loyola, Christopher Columbus — of all the most
daring spirits of that brilliant generation.

Berruguete was an indefatigable worker. You
will find statues in Valladolid, Salamanca, Toledo,
Cuenca, Ubeda, Cáceres, and elsewhere. Much ascribed to him must have been done by pupils and
assistants, but the salient strokes, the final touches,
are his; for instance, his contract for a retablo at
the monastery of San Benito, in Valladolid, specifies
what the master shall do himself: "Item: both the
painted scenes and the carved figures must be by
the master's own hand; in particular, the statues
shall be cut out of the rough by the master, and the
faces and hands shall be finished by his own hand."
The tourist is certain to see his stalls at Toledo,
and the tomb of Cardinal Tavera, the last work of
his old age, in the hospital of San Juan Bautista,
outside Toledo.

Berruguete is the greatest of Spanish sculptors
and, taking him all in all, among the foremost in
modern times. He is as necessary for an understanding of the reign of Charles V as Ignatius
Loyola, Garcilaso de la Vega, or Francisco Pizarro.
I quoted Gautier to the effect that his works are
"varied, but always of equal perfection"; yet I
hardly think that the ordinary tourist will share
his opinion. To me they are of very unequal merit.
Usually his figures express intense emotion. Catholic
art demanded that they should; so did the subjects
— the crucifixion, the sacrifice of Isaac, the Pietà,
Elijah in the fiery chariot, Isaiah's lips touched by

Berruguete

Toledo

TOMB OF CARDINAL TAVERA

the coal of fire, sorrowing Job, and so on. But other reliefs are full of beauty, dignity, and repose, such as the Juno-like Madonna in the retablo of the church of Santiago at Valladolid, and various panels in the coro at Toledo. These differences may be classified as his Spanish and Italian moods.

Contemporary opinion, however, is always the most interesting. It is spontaneous and natural; whereas well-settled authority in critical judgments always reminds one of policemen directing the traffic. A contemporary, a notable man of letters, Cristóbal de Villalón, who was at Salamanca studying and teaching in the university while Berruguete was working there, and who afterward followed Berruguete to Valladolid, writes to a friend:

Berruguete is living here in Valladolid; his figures lack only breath of life in order to speak. He has completed the altar screen (retablo) in San Benito that you must have seen many times. If Philip of Macedon and Alexander, who appreciated works of art in their day, were living now, they would not think all they possessed sufficient to pay him; but nowadays men are carried away by unconsidered opinions, and they criticize.

Cristóbal de Villalón admires what he deems to be extreme fidelity to nature, which quality later critics, both of art and literature, judge the greatest merit in Spanish paintings and books. But another contemporary took a different view of Berruguete's achievement:

Of late years [he says] a lot of cheap Jacks are going about Spain and elsewhere, giving themselves out as sculptors and painters. God forgive the man that introduced this way of doing to Spain. Without reckoning the works he himself did, he was the cause that a thousand men of talent took the wrong road, did not follow nature and the ancients.

In other words, this critic, I take it, accuses Berruguete of introducing the baroque style, somewhat as Bernini did in Italy — of which charge it would be difficult to exculpate him.

XXIV

THE REIGN OF PHILIP II

In 1556 Charles V laid down his crowns and his son Philip II reigned in his stead. Outwardly the power and condition of Spain appeared much the same, but a great inward change was taking place. Philip himself is the best index of the change, the figurehead of the new spirit.

Americans, as a rule, bred upon Motley's *Dutch Republic* and warped by conventional English Protestant traditions, are inclined to think meanly of Philip, as a cruel, dull, contemptible bigot; but to Spaniards, even to-day, he looms up as an heroic figure, a colossus. The Europe of his own time looked upon him as the Great King, very much as the ancient Greeks, with mingled fear and reverence, looked upon the King of Persia. To me Philip II, with this great burden of an empire on which the sun never set upon his un-Atlantean shoulders, is one of the tragic figures of history. From his grandmother, Mad Joan, he seems to have inherited some constitutional taint, for two brothers died in infancy of epilepsy, and his oldest son, Don Carlos, was defective both physically and mentally. Philip's intelligence was mediocre; he was cautious, reserved, hesitating, dilatory, procrastinating, stubborn, suspicious, melancholy; and yet he was patient, persevering, laborious, and conscientious to an unusual degree. His early education strengthened his natural traits; his father taught him to suspect the motives of his ministers, to pit one against another, to lend a ready ear but to keep his own counsel. You can see the effect of this counsel in the young portraits by Titian and Antony Moro — a cold, measuring, distrustful face, always on guard. Though slow of mind, he was intelligent and in a measure cultivated; and he had his own taste in painting and in architecture. He was very popular with his Spanish subjects, dearly beloved by his various wives, and he bore disappointment, bitter sorrow, broken ambitions, and grievous physical pain with the calm courage of a Roman Stoic. He was very religious. He looked upon himself as a servant of the Almighty, the captain general of God's forces upon earth, charged with a duty to overthrow and trample down whatever might intrude between God's will and its accomplishment. To this conception of his duty he was nobly faithful. He honored the Church, but insisted on his right to exercise sovereign supervision over it in his own dominions, and felt in his heart that he should unite — in substance if not in show — regal and sacerdotal functions, not for his own glory but to ensure the truimph of true faith. This childlike sense of theocratic duty ennobles his plain and repellent figure with a tragic pathos.

The deeds of his reign that occupy so great a space in European history may be traced back, however devious the course, to this theocratic root. His brief war with Pope Paul IV, the fiery old Caraffa, in which the Duke of Alva seemed likely to repeat Bourbon's action in 1527 and sack the city of Rome,

was due to the Pope's fear and resentment at what
he regarded as Philip's usurpation. The war with
Henry II of France, though primarily an inheritance
from the lifelong struggle between Charles V and
Francis I, had its origin in Philip's purpose to make
Europe Catholic. His subsequent alliance with the
rebel House of Guise and the Catholic League against
Henry of Navarre was due to the same cause. Bigoted
religious persecution goaded the Moors in Granada
to rebel (1568–1571). The wars with Turkey and the
Mohammedan states of North Africa were primarily
religious. The attempt to crush heresy in the Low
Countries was a matter of conscience. Royal support
of the Inquisition, the marriage with Mary Tudor
(1554), and the expedition of the Invincible Armada
(1588), were acts of religious policy. The only important event of his reign that was purely secular was
the acquisition of Portugal, which he obtained under
a claim of next-of-kin and by virtue of asserted military power (1580). Of all these great doings I shall
speak only of the revolt in the Netherlands and of
the Invincible Armada.

Ill will between the Netherlands and Spain had begun in Charles's time, when the young King brought
a crowd of hungry Flemings with him into Spain and
gave them rich offices. Then the Spaniards were
indignant. When Philip turned the tables and appointed foreigners to high office in the Netherlands,
the Flemings forgot that they had had their innings
and became as angry as the Spaniards had been. Far
worse than this, in the course of a generation large
parts of the Low Countries had become Protestant.
The situation was big with danger. The natives

wished for local self-government; Philip pursued a policy of centralization. They wished to garrison their towns; Philip introduced Spanish soldiers. They had their notions of just taxes; Philip had his. Serious trouble began when Philip attempted to enforce some rigorous edicts against heresy. "If necessary," he said, "I will send sixty thousand men to the stake." Many Protestants emigrated to England. The chief nobles, Orange, Egmont, and Horn, became malcontent; a conspiracy was formed (1556) and riots broke out. The Duke of Alva was sent with an army (1567), and his bloody assizes condemned five hundred persons in a single day. William of Orange escaped, but Egmont and Horn were trapped and beheaded (1568). A few years later (1572) the Dutch provinces were in open rebellion. Alva adopted a system of terror, but it failed. Philip changed his method, removed Alva, and tried conciliation.

Nothing succeeded. His purse was empty, his unpaid troops mutinied, France and England openly or secretly assisted the rebels. Philip held firm. "Though I should lose the Netherlands, I will not yield one jot or tittle in matters of the Holy Catholic Faith." Holland and Zealand declared their independence (1574). Philip tried new governors. His half-brother, Don John of Austria, young, charming, decked out with the laurels of the glorious victory of Lepanto, came first. He was full of imaginative ambitions, now to marry Queen Elizabeth, now to conquer England by force, but accomplished little or nothing. On his death (1578) the distinguished soldier Alessandro Farnese took his place.

By this time it became obvious that English aid

must be cut off, or Spanish rule would be at an end.
This consideration led to the Invincible Armada.
Months were spent in collecting ships, equipment,
stores, arms, sailors, and soldiers. Philip, as usual,
scrutinized every item of expense; he got up early in
the morning and went to bed late at night, consider-
ing, consulting, adopting, rejecting, amending, praying, wasting time and effort, until opportunity had
kicked up its heels and was off. The old sea-dog the
Marquis of Santa Cruz died, and the King appointed
a landlubber, the Duke of Medina Sidonia, in his
place. The poor duke tried hard to refuse:

I am not well enough to go to sea [he wrote to the King]
and from my little experience of the sea I know that I get
seasick. I can't in conscience undertake the job. The
enterprise is so important, the preparations so great, that
it would not be right for a man with no experience either
of sea or war to accept it; and I have had no experience at
all. . . . Besides, to go aboard the Armada wholly green,
with no knowledge of it, nor of the captains or officers, nor
of the reports about England and the English ports, nor
any acquaintance with the despatches that the Marquis
of Santa Cruz has been handling for years, would be to go
into it blindfold . . . and without a doubt, after groping
my way blindfold, I should have a bad account to render.

But go he had to. The orders issued to the fleet
read:

Let every man from highest to lowest know that the
chief motive that has induced His Majesty to undertake
this expedition has been, and is, to serve the Lord God and
bring back to His Bosom and His Church many peoples
and souls now persecuted by heretical enemies of our Holy
Catholic Faith. . . . Keep your eyes upon this mark. . . .

Let every man, in sincere repentance, confess his sins and be shriven before embarkation. . . . Let no soldier, sailor, or other person aboard the fleet utter any blasphemy, nor show disrespect to Our Lord, Our Lady, or the Saints. . . . Every day, at dawn, let the sailors call out Hail Mary, at the foot of the mainmast, and at night the Ave Maria.

Alas for piety! Everybody knows the story: how tempests broke the Spanish line, and how the English ships, the Bull, the Bear, the Revenge, the Dauntless, the Black Dog, and their fellows, with greater speed and longer range of guns, bore down on Nuestra Señora, Santa María, La Trinidad, La Concepcion, La Magdalena, San Márcos, San Luis, San Mateo, and the rest (1588). Many great galleons, galleasses, and galleys were sunk in the Channel; the rest fled up the North Sea, rounding the top of Scotland. A pitiable remnant of the Invincible Armada reached home at last. Philip behaved generously, accepting defeat as part of the inscrutable designs of Providence.

The necessary consequence of this defeat was the ultimate triumph of the Dutch rebels; but I shall leave that story of battles, sieges, opened dikes, of victories and defeats, and pass on to other matters.

XXV

THE RELIGIOUS WRITERS OF THE SIXTEENTH CENTURY

THE story of Philip II's reign, coupled with that of the Inquisition, presents a perplexing mixture of deep beliefs, high purposes, fanaticism, and political expediency. It shows us one aspect of the religious character of the Spanish people; but it is fair to hurry by that aspect with judgment suspended, and pass on to the deeper, nobler, and more permanent aspect of that same character as it revealed itself in a religious literature that, so far as I know, has no equal in the Western world. It is only through this literature of lyrical outbursts, ethical exhortations, and mystical revelations that we can come to any real understanding of the Spain of Charles V and Philip II, so alien in many respects to our modern North American ideas.

Spanish moral and mystical writing, as a branch of literature, rivals the Spanish theatre at its height. I have read that the number of Spanish mystics exceeds two thousand; of all these ardent spirits but few are familiarly remembered, and I shall speak only of the half-dozen most celebrated. The first great Spanish mystic — I pass over the strange mediæval philosopher, the Catalan, Raymond Lull, as outside the current of Castilian literature — is Ignatius Loyola. But his only book, the *Spiritual Exercises,*

is not intended for general reading, but as a guide
to spiritual directors, and so I pass him by. Next
comes Juan de Ávila (1500–1569). His book of
Spiritual Letters is reckoned among the Spanish
classics; yet he is not a true mystic, but rather a
director of souls, and only now and again, in speaking
of prayer, touches the borderland where reason stops
and religious yearning unfolds its wings. Even this
borderland came dangerously near the doctrine of the
Illuminati, for a soul that mounts into immediate
communion with God needs neither priest nor sacrament, and Juan de Ávila was denounced to the
Inquisition and spent some months in its prison
(1532–1533). The same experience had happened
to Loyola twice, in Alcalá de Henares and at Salamanca, while he was seeking to save souls at street
corners.

Luis de Granada (1504–1588), who for his eloquence has been called *el Tullio español*, was a disciple
of Juan de Ávila, and wrote his biography. He became a Dominican monk at the age of sixteen, and
gained great renown as a preacher. The fourteen
volumes of his collected works make a handsome
show on the shelf. His most famous book, the *Guide
for Sinners*, achieved a European reputation; more
than a dozen editions of the English translation were
published in Queen Elizabeth's time. E. Mérimée
says he is "*l'une des figures les plus nobles, les plus
parfaites et les plus sympathiques du xvii*ᵉ *siècle.*" He
is too much of a Ciceronian for modern taste; his
language flows on like a river from chapter to chapter,
from volume to volume. But he is eloquent, and his
exhortation to prayer, for instance, could proceed

only from the personal experience of a pure heart.
As with so many of the mystical writers, his higher
reaches of metaphysical yearning take their start in
the Biblical Song of Songs, which, according to the
interpretation of the Church, expresses the love and
mystical marriage of the soul and Christ.

Of all these religious writers, not even excepting
Loyola himself, Saint Teresa (1515–1582) is the most
universally known. Her union of shrewdness, common-sense, childlike simplicity, energy, perseverance,
courage, and administrative talents, together with
her poetical imagination, hungry mysticism, and
feminine charm, captivated her fellow countrymen,
and many others as well: for instance, the English
poet, Richard Crashaw. In Spain, admiration and
reverence for her reached such a point that a widespread popular movement endeavored to set her by
the side of Santiago, as a co-patron saint. There is
but one unfriendly criticism that can be made upon
her, and perhaps that will affect only Protestants;
I refer to her renunciation of home and of her old
father, a lonely widower, for the grilled seclusion of a
nunnery, when she was but eighteen. She writes:
"My father's love for me was so great that I could
never obtain his consent, nor were the prayers of
others, whom I persuaded to ask him, of any avail.
The utmost I could get from him was that I might
do as I pleased after his death." But she had heard
the call, from Heaven, as she believed, and obeyed
the words of her Lord: "He that loveth father and
mother more than me is not worthy of me." And
in time, so she says, her father was glad that she had
put her pious purpose into effect.

Teresa rose to be Mother Superior, and founded seventeen convents and fifteen monasteries, all according to the stricter rule of the reformed Barefoot Carmelite Order. Her energy was prodigious; so was her bravery. She herself says: "They say of me that my courage is not slight; and it is true that God has given me a courage beyond that of women; but I have made poor use of it."

Her energy displayed itself in whatever she did. She wrote with extraordinary rapidity; "her hand went so quickly that it seemed impossible that anyone could naturally write so fast." And yet her style is said to be of the very best. Fray Luis de Leon, a great authority, says:

In the form of her language, the purity and facility of her style, the grace and perfect order of her words, in the delightful quality of unadorned grace, I doubt if there be any Spanish writer that can compare with her.

She had the gift of depicting her own soul and, by the general consent of Spanish critics, her soul "is one of the greatest souls known to history . . . its beauty binds all who read her books."

Her most celebrated works are the *Autobiography*, — written at the command of her confessor, — the *Inner Castle*, and the *Book of Foundations*. Of all these Father Walter Elliott says: "Given a reader with any degree of devout receptivity and Saint Teresa's writings are quickly established among his master books, to be used occasionally all through life, and in many cases to be used unceasingly." The *Inner Castle* is nearly as autobiographical as the autobiography itself, for even there she says little of outward events, reckoning them as nothing in comparison with the growth of the soul.

A good specimen of her didactic manner is her parable of watering the garden entrusted to each one of us (that is, the soul), and of the four ways of obtaining water. The first way is to draw up water from a well: this means that beginners must strive to meditate on the life of Christ, although the understanding is wearied thereby. The second is to employ a windlass ("I have drawn water in this way myself sometimes"): this means the prayer of quietude, in which the soul is gathered in upon itself and touches the supernatural. Here understanding and memory aid the will; "O my Jesus, O my Lord, how Thy love presses in upon me!" The third stage is where the garden is watered by a brook: here the soul is in communion with God, but the faculties are still conscious, while the will abides in a great peace, although at the same time the understanding and memory may be occupied in works of charity. In the fourth stage rain falls direct from heaven: this is union with God.

How this, which we call union, is effected and what it is, I cannot tell. Mystical theology explains it, and I am ignorant of that science; nor can I understand what the mind is, nor how it differs from the soul, or the spirit either, for all these seem to me but one; though I do know that the soul leaps forth out of itself, like a fire that burns and becomes a flame, and occasionally this fire increases violently — the flame ascends high above the fire; and yet it does not become a different thing; it is still the same flame of the same fire. . . . What union is, is plain enough, two distinct things becoming one. O my Lord, how good Thou art! He that has had raptures will, I am sure, understand this well; to him who has not had that experience it will be but folly. . . . It seemed to me, when I tried to make some resistance, as if a great force beneath my feet lifted me up. I know of nothing to compare it with; but it was much more violent than any other spiritual visitation, and therefore, I was as one ground to pieces.

The greatness of Saint Teresa's reputation has obliged me to encroach upon the space I should like to have given to the next representative of Spanish mysticism, the great poet Fray Luis de Leon (1527–1591), who, in his way, is as remarkable as she. Cervantes says: *"Fray Luys de Leon . . . á quien yo reverencio, adoro y sigo."* He was a scholar, a theologian as well as a poet. The Beginner is likely to find his theology out of date; for instance, I find *Los Nombres de Dios*, a treatise on the mystical significance of the names given to Christ in the Bible, far beyond the horizon of my interest. But his poems, *La Noche Serena* or *La Vida Retirada*, are, if I may make what might seem a paradoxical comparison, as beautiful as Leopardi's, and with something of a kindred spirit. They and others have been translated by Longfellow, by Arthur Symonds, by Churton, and also by Thomas Walsh. When the tourist goes to the university of Salamanca he will enter the room where Fray Luis used to lecture, and see the very desk at which, tradition poetically says, he uttered his famous words, on his return from nearly five years in the Inquisition prison: ". . . As I was saying." The Inquisition was always shy of mysticism; it held back Saint Teresa's autobiography for years.

The last on my list, Juan de la Cruz (1542–1591),

is as a mystic second to none; and, to my thinking,
he is the most charming by far and the most sympathetic of them all — a creature that should have been
born into a more spiritual world than this. His life,
it is said, "was rather that of an angel than a man."
His long poem, *El Cántico Espiritual*, composed in
confinement, — not the doing of the Inquisition, but
of some unascetic monks, — is the most celebrated
of his books. It is closely modeled upon the Song of
Songs, and consists of a series of poems between the
soul and her Spouse. Each stanza is accompanied
by an elaborate — and, I may add, very necessary —
explanation of its allegorical meaning. It is the story
of the soul that passes through darkness and purification to ultimate union with God, a holy but passionate epithalamium, and is accounted to be one
of the books that belong to the literature of the
whole Christian world. Menéndez y Pelayo says,
"One cannot doubt that the Holy Spirit guided
the writer's pen."

XXVI

MINOR ASPECTS OF PHILIP'S REIGN

You cannot draw an indictment against a nation, neither can you draw its portrait in outline. The best I can do is to offer the reader some random aspects, embodied in artists, men of letters, or statesmen, with the warning that very likely another man would offer him quite a different collection. Philip's Spain was complex; Philip himself was not so simple as English-speaking Protestants have been taught to believe. So I will ask the reader please to enlarge his idea of Philip's Spain enough to include the following items.

In part, at least, there seem to be two distinct currents or tendencies, such as we noticed in Berruguete's work, one of violence and extravagant expression, the other of dignity and noble calm. For instance, in sculpture there is Becerra (1520–1570), whose "chief merits are an ideal beauty and dignity," and there is Juan de Juni (*d.* 1586), of whom Cean Bermúdez says: "Juan de Juni, in order to give life to his figures, adopted an extravagant fashion of contortions, even for quiet attitudes, and such an arrangement of eyes, arms, muscles, that instead of arousing devout emotions they just scare you." You will think that Bermúdez understated the case when you see Juni's statues in the museum at Valladolid. On the other hand, the poet Fernando de Herrera el

Divino (1534–1597) wrote patriotic odes of a noble, stately grandeur. A favorite painter of the time is Hieronymus Bosch, the Fleming. Every visitor to the Prado knows his Walpurgisnacht pictures, where a not unkindly but rather vulgar imagination — as if Sancho Panza had had a talent for painting — heaps together the most curious distortions of human, animal, and insect life in bewilderingly comic situations. Don Felipe de Guevara, a grandee who acpanied Charles V in his expedition to Tunis, wrote a book on painting in which he speaks of Bosch's great celebrity in Spain, so great that there were numerous imitations and forgeries. On Guevara's death Philip bought of his estate six of Bosch's pictures and tried to get elsewhere all he could. Five he took to Madrid, nine to the Escorial, some half-dozen more to his hunting-palace of the Prado. How do you account for a taste for Hieronymus Bosch in the builder of the Escorial?

The Escorial stands on a spur of the Guadarrama about thirty miles northwest of Madrid. Philip desired to express in a form worthy of Spain's greatness and of his own nobler self the stern ascetic creed of Castile, and he succeeded. The mighty edifice of ashen-gray granite stands cold, hard, solid, and magnificent, a corporeal mate to the cold, hard, solid, and magnificent spiritual edifice which at that very time — obedient to Philip's will — the Fathers of the Holy Catholic Church, Roman and Apostolic, assembled at Trent in universal council, were embodying, piling dogma on dogma, in a vast spiritual Escorial.

The original architect, Juan Bautista de Toledo,

had received his training in Italy under Michel-angelo, at that time master of the works upon St. Peter's Church. Juan Bautista designed an immense quadrangle, 675 by 530 feet. A square tower, sur-mounted by a small turret, stands at each corner. Within, the church, with dome and towers, sets its back against the eastern wall. The corner stone was laid in 1563. Four years later Juan Bautista died, and Juan de Herrera, his chief assistant, succeeded to his office and completed the building in 1584. There have been many different opinions upon it. Théophile Gautier (although he was driven there by four mules in a *voiture chamarré d'amours à la grisaille et d'autres ornaments pompadour*) found "*l'Escurial le plus ennuyeux et le plus maussade monument que puissent rêver, pour la mortification de leurs semblables, un moine morose et un tyran soupçonneux.*" But then, perhaps King Philip would have passed an equally unfavorable judgment on *Mademoiselle de Maupin* and *Le Capitaine Fracasse*. Richard Ford, in his racy English, expresses the same general idea as Gautier. Others, especially architects who understand the problems and difficulties of building, admire the whole or parts of it, according to their particular interest; for instance, Mr. Arthur Byne says: "The dome in its structural perfection far surpasses that of Michelangelo." To the lazy tourist, however, the interest of the Escorial lies in its testimony to Philip's spiritual conception of life and its values.

To me it appears profoundly religious, but of an ascetic religion, in which there are no glad animal movements, no voices of children, no kindly miracle to add innocent gayety to a marriage feast. It is a

religion that withdraws from sunlight, blue sky, and
flying clouds, for these things do not yield themselves
to dogma, and it has chosen dogma for better, for
worse, and it abides by its vow. But the Escorial
does not do Spanish Catholicism justice — as is plain
enough to anyone who will read Saint John of the
Cross, for instance.

These things that I have enumerated are contradictory, and yet there is a man of genius who com-
bines in himself elements of the dogmatism of the
Escorial, the extravagance of Juan de Juni, the intense interest in life of Berruguete, a touch of Bosch's
waywardness, and more than Becerra's noble dignity. I refer to Domenico Theotocópuli (1547–1614),
commonly called El Greco. This great painter was
born in Crete, went to Venice, where he studied
Tintoretto and Titian, then stayed for a time in
Rome. A painter writes (1570): "There has come to
Rome from Candia a young pupil of Titian's, who in
my judgment is an extraordinary painter. Among
other things he has done a portrait of himself that
has dumfounded all the painters in Rome." Six or
seven years later he went to Spain and settled in
Toledo. He lived in an apartment in a palace, since
pulled down, close to the house now called after him,
where in the dark cellars — so it was whispered —
our culinary friend, Enrique de Villena, long years
before had studied the black art and sold his soul to
the Devil. Mystery and mysticism hung about the
place, and turned the painter's thoughts to a world
that can be depicted only by arbitrary symbols.
You will find a room of his pictures in the Prado;
and Toledo is full of them. There are others in the

Escorial and at Illescas. In 1586 he painted his masterpiece, the Burial of Count Orgaz, for the church of Santo Tomé, where it still is.

This picture is very large, measuring about fifteen feet by eleven. It is divided into two parts: below, the scene on earth, where, thanks to heavenly intervention, Saint Augustine and Saint Stephen, come back to earth, are holding the dead body of the Count in the presence of a goodly company of Spanish gentlemen; and above, the scene in Heaven, where Christ and the Virgin, attended by a heavenly host, receive the Count's soul. The contrast between the faces of the Spanish dons on earth, admirable portraits of grave, melancholy, serious-minded, high-bred gentlemen, and the fantastic shapes of the figures in Heaven is very striking. As a portrait painter El Greco is of the first rank; dignity, courtesy, and a religious joylessness, such as Philip II embodied so effectually in the Escorial, are stamped upon each face. On the other hand, the scene in Heaven is charged with symbolism. El Greco strove to represent, by painting the essential traits of Spanish mysticism, a mingling of yearning, dogma, passion, and peace. The two figures of Count Orgaz represent the change wrought in the twinkling of an eye, by which his corporeal body has become a spiritual body. At the top, from the abode of the souls of the righteous, Christ's gesture is plainly an invitation to enter into the joy of the Lord; while the keys of Paradise, that hang listless in the long emaciated hand of Saint Peter, testify that their use has been superseded by the rapture of spirit that will not be stayed on its flight to union with its God.

El Greco   Escorial

SAN MAURICIO

I do not wish to mislead the Beginner. There are many views concerning El Greco's art. Pacheco, the painter, Velásquez's father-in-law, says that "he was as peculiar in everything else as in his paintings," and the general voice repeated the same thing: "extravagant, like his paintings." But how could anybody with whom Velásquez was in sympathy comprehend a mystical attempt to symbolize the soul? Since then opinions have ranged widely. Some say that El Greco is wayward and peculiar; some, that he was mentally deranged, a little cracked; others, that his eyesight was defective. But I believe that he strove to express a mystical conception of spiritual realities, and so I have brought him into this chapter to help explain that strange, passionate, misunderstood Spain of Philip's time.

XXVII

MIGUEL DE CERVANTES

PHILIP the Second's last injunction to his son
Philip the Third bade him rule with justice and be
true to the Holy Catholic Faith. I shall not dwell
upon the political events of the latter's reign (1598–
1621). The war with Holland was interrupted for
a time by a truce, and that with England ended
on the accession of James I. But, war or peace,
there were always Dutch and English privateers,
pirates one might call them, hovering about the
Spanish Main, looking for a town to sack or a
galleon to scuttle. Peace was made with France;
the heir apparent married a French princess, and
Louis XIII a Spanish infanta. There was some
fighting with the Turks, there were some acts of
piracy committed against the Venetians, but nothing
of any great note. I proceed at once to the memorable glory of Philip III's reign, the publication of
Don Quixote.

Of Cervantes (1547–1616) all the world may be
proud. He is the most lovable among the great
men of literature. Shakespeare's disposition was
serene and his apprehension godlike, but we know
little about him. Dante was a sort of archangel,
proud and stern; Molière was lovable and not without a touch of the heroic; but Cervantes, serene,
heroic, not free from faults, and of uneven genius,

inspires every reader of *Don Quixote* with a sense of personal devotion, such as a first-year fag at Rugby might feel for Tom Brown, after Tom had got to the top of the school. He was born in Alcalá de Henares, but his family moved to Valladolid, and from there to Madrid in 1561, the year in which that city became the capital of Spain. Little is known of these years. In 1569 he went to Rome in the train of a great prelate; there he enlisted in the *tercio* of Miguel de Moncada, a Spanish officer who served under Marcantonio Colonna, commander of the papal contingent of the allied Christian forces in the war against the Turks. He fought on board the galley Marquesa in the glorious victory of Lepanto (1571).

Cervantes was badly wounded. After his recovery he embarked for Spain, seeking promotion, but was captured by Barbary pirates and taken to Algiers, where he remained a prisoner for five years. The tale of "The Captive" in the first part of *Don Quixote*, as well as the plot of his play, *Prisoners in Algiers*, tells, in a more or less imaginative setting, the story of his experiences. After several vain attempts to escape, in which he behaved with honor and distinguished courage, he was ransomed and, on his return to Spain, took to a literary life, writing poems and plays. He had but moderate success on the stage. He gave it up, and in 1587 was employed by the government as a commissioner in its preparations for the Invincible Armada. He spent the following years for the most part in Seville, collecting — or trying to collect — taxes and various dues. He was ill suited to the work; and these years tell a story of mismanagement, of slovenly bookkeeping, of negligence perhaps, of incompetence almost certainly. Twice he was arrested for malfeasance or neglect and put in prison, and finally he was dismissed from his employment, all lost except honor. He returned to literature and lived in shabby quarters at Valladolid with his daughter, his sisters, and a niece. Here some night-wandering gallant was inconsiderately murdered directly in front of the house. Cervantes was accused of complicity, and the good name of the ladies of the family was questioned; but for this there seems to have been no ground.

In money-making Cervantes had no success; he was, I suspect, very happy-go-lucky, and he liked to amuse himself with games of chance. One can see him look up with a smile, and say, "*Paciencia y barrajar*" (patience and shuffle the cards). But Fame has made up for what Fortune denied. The first part of *Don Quixote* was published in 1605. Before that he had written sonnets, lyrics, comedies, tragedies, long poems, and what not. Once he won three silver spoons as a prize. But none of these writings, not even the highly patriotic tragedy, *Numancia*, praised by Shelley, would be remembered, had it not been for *Don Quixote*. In 1613, at the age of sixty-five, he published his *Novelas ejemplares*—a collection of short stories, one of which is delightful, "Rinconete y Cortadillo," a tale of a school for thieves, the prototype of Fagin and his pupils.

In the preface (1613) Cervantes describes his own personal appearance:

Of aquiline features, chestnut hair, smooth unruffled brow, merry eyes, a Roman nose well proportioned, a silvered beard that twenty years syne was golden, large moustachios, little mouth, teeth not to boast of, for he has only six, and those in bad condition and worse placed, for they are not opposite each other; his body between extremes, neither big nor little; bright complexion, rather light than dark, shoulders somewhat rounded. Such is the author of *Galatea* and *Don Quixote* . . . known generally as Miguel de Cervantes Saavedra; for many years he was a soldier, then five and a half in captivity, where he learned patience in adversity. At the naval battle of Lepanto he lost his left hand by the shot of a musket, a wound that has an ugly appearance, but he deems it beautiful, as he got it on the noblest and most memorable occasion that past centuries have seen, and such as centuries to come may never hope to see, fighting under the flag of that thunderbolt of war, Charles V. [And then he adds] One thing I make bold to say, that if in any way these stories could excite any evil thoughts or desires in the reader, I had rather cut off the hand with which I write than publish them.

The first part of *Don Quixote* had been a great success, but the happy-go-lucky author preferred to write short stories, to make poor rhymes, to play cards, or to sit about and watch the shabby pageant of life that passed through the poor quarters where he lived, rather than set to work to write the second part that he had promised. Fortunately, some impudent fellow, trying to steal the book's popularity, published a false Part Two. At this Cervantes lost his temper, sat down, and finished the great book (1615). By this time he was an old man, and life was drawing to a close, but poverty still pressed him; he wrote a fantastic romance, *Los Trabajos de Pérsiles y Sigismunda*, read by scholars or idolaters of Cervantes, but to unliterary pleasure-lovers quite unreadable, except for this bit of the dedication to the Conde de Lemos, from whom he hoped for more patronage:

Our old ballad, once so much in vogue, that begins, "One foot already in the stirrup," might with a few changes be put at the head of this dedication; for, do what I can, I remain in a condition to say,

> One foot already in the stirrup
> Into another world to ride,
> I dip my pen in ink, to write
> (If my heart's wish be not denied)
> Upon these sheets of paper white
> The love for you I cannot hide.

Yesterday I received extreme unction; to-day I write to you. The crises of my mortal disease follow one another fast, the next may be the last; I regret nothing in this life except the pleasure I had so greatly hoped for, of seeing Your Excellency, once more, happy and content. I think that this pleasure, alone, would have prolonged my life, but Heaven has ordered otherwise; its will be done.

He died four days later, the same year, the same month, and, according to English reckoning (for Protestant England refused to accept a correct but papistical calendar), the same day, April 23, 1616, that Shakespeare died in Stratford-on-Avon. It was really twelve days later; but Shakespeare's soul tarried a while, and the two noble gentlemen went together to the Happy Isles.

Of Cervantes' masterpiece there is little need for me to speak here. In the preface he expresses a wish that he might write "*el más hermoso, gallardo y discreto*" (the most wise, delightful, and merry) book in the world. The wish was granted. Don Quixote and Sancho Panza are as wonderful and immortal as Falstaff, Hamlet, Faust, or Odysseus. Of his other books I have not much to say. The Beginner will certainly read *Don Quixote*, and he must read it in Spanish, for the book, like poetry, has qualities that are lost in a translation. Cervantes himself has used a good simile; a translation, he says, is like the wrong side of a carpet. The *Novelas ejemplares*, the first short stories in Spanish, were admirable in their day, but modern readers, with a wealth of short stories to choose from, — Paul Heyse, Maupassant, Verga, Bret Harte, O. Henry, Mrs. Wharton, and scores of others, — make greater demands upon the art. *Galatea* is a pastoral romance (1584). I do not believe that any reader who reads merely for pleasure will ever read it; its virtues, of a mediocre order according to the critics, belong to a fashion long past. Don Quixote, after he has been unhorsed by Samson Carrasco and pledged his honor to forgo the life of a knight errant, suggests to Sancho that they should become shepherds. If Don Quixote had piped and Sancho had herded with a beribboned crook, that would have been another story, but without them Teolinda, Damon, Carino, Crisalvo, Erastro, Lidia, and the other shepherds and shepherdesses have no attractions. Cervantes simply took up without success a contemporary fashion in literature, introduced from Italy by Montemayor. The *Viaje del Parnaso* (1614) is a long sequence of indiscriminate eulogies upon his contemporaries; its one merit is that it reveals a kind, generous heart, free from envy, hatred, and malice. *Ocho Comedias y Ocho Entremeses nunca representados* are not for Beginners. The comedies, all agree, are poor; and the *entremeses*, little farces, which are said to display "vivid realism," are not very much better. *Pérsiles y Sigismunda* has been read "by many students with interest." Personally I cannot understand going further than turning over the pages. If after reading *Don Quixote* I am hungry for more Cervantes, I read *Don Quixote* again; and that I commend as the better way.

XXVIII

LOPE DE VEGA

WE think of Philip III's reign as the epoch of *Don Quixote*, but Spaniards speak of it as the epoch of Lope de Vega.

I suppose that Lope was the most prolific writer who ever lived. He wrote verse and prose of all sorts: sonnets, odes, lays, madrigals, ballads, epics, pastorals, hymns, stories, a novel, and what not, beside eighteen hundred plays and four hundred and fifty autos. It is said that he put on the stage seventeen thousand characters or more. A Spanish critic says that the reason why Lope, with intellectual genius equal to Shakespeare's, is inferior, is that Shakespeare always aimed before he shot, but that Lope fired before taking aim.

Lope de Vega (1562–1635) was born in Madrid, of parents in humble circumstances. He was as precocious as he was prolific; at the age of ten he translated Claudian's verses into Spanish, and at twelve wrote his first comedy. In 1583 he served in a naval expedition against the Azores, under the Marquis of Santa Cruz, and a few years later he enlisted in the Invincible Armada. But prior to this enlistment, while he was composing comedies for the director of a company of players, he fell in love with the director's daughter. For four years she was his mistress and then, it seems, he got tired of her; at any rate, he wrote and circulated foul and false charges against her and all her family. When accused, he denied that he had done it; then to bolster up his lies he forged an infamous letter in the girl's name, and lied about that. Her father prosecuted him. Lope was adjudged guilty and banished from Madrid for eight years. His American biographer, Mr. Rennert, says, "Lope would seem to have been a foppish young libertine devoid of all moral sense"; this is as gentle a phrase as could well be selected, and Mr. Rennert seems to have felt its inadequacy, for he says, further on: "To have wronged the woman he had loved . . . was an act base and despicable enough. In attempting, after his arrest, to blacken her character and ruin her reputation still more effectually by means of a forged letter, Lope sank to the lowest depth of turpitude." This is a more reasonable statement. It has been suggested in Lope's defense, by an ingenious application of some intimations to that effect in his own ballads, that the girl had already accepted another lover; but unfortunately for that theory (which a second time assails the girl's reputation) Lope swore at the trial that he "held her to be a very reputable woman"; and at that time he propounded, as the reason why her father prosecuted him, that he no longer supplied the father with plays, but had entered into dealings with another manager.

I shall not follow the long story of his amours — it is like walking through a cow paddock; Cervantes refers ironically to his *"occupacion contínua y virtuosa."* An American scholar, more liberal-minded, says: "Lope drank deep of life." Before his amours were concluded he became a familiar of the Inquisition (1608), a member of the Congregation of Slaves of the Holy Sacrament (1609), a member of the Third Order of St. Francis (1611), and also a priest (1614). It seems that he took holy orders in order to qualify himself to receive a benefice from his patron, the Duke of Sessa, whom he served in disreputable love-affairs. So much for my office of *avocatus diaboli*.

Now for Lope's good side. He had great talents and various virtues. He loved his children and he loved his garden. He writes:

Nature, which as you know is content with little, has been so gracious to me that with a few books, a half-dozen pictures, and a garden with a flower or two, I pass my time free from envy, desire, fear, or hope, victorious over Fortune, disillusioned of greatness, cloistered in the midst of confusion, and cheerful in want; and I do not fear the end that is both so certain and so uncertain. Wrapped about with philosophy, I keep as far as I can from ignorance, and I avoid the slings of calumny and the traps of envy.

In his lifetime he completely dominated the Spanish stage, and marked out the path that later playwrights should tread. His industry, his fancy, his fertility, his command of versification, are prodigious; his contemporaries admired his *inundaciones de armonía*, his *océano de obras*. Tirso de Molina calls him *honra de Manzanares, Tulio de Castilla y Fénix de nuestra nación*. Cervantes writes of his early career:

Then came that prodigy of Nature, the great Lope de Vega, mounted the dramatic throne, and subjected all theatrical managers to his authority. He crowded the world with good, sensible, successful plays, in such numbers

that they fill more than ten thousand written pages. . . .
Many have tried to share his glory, nevertheless, all
of them together, with all they have written, have not
achieved one half as much as he did single-handed.

Lope was able to write his incredible number of
plays because verses flowed from his pen as if from
the fountain Helicon itself. A friend has recorded
this anecdote:

Lope wrote a play in two days, though the mere writing
would have been no easy task even for a skillful scrivener.
Once in Toledo, while staying at a private house, he wrote
fifteen acts — that is, five plays — in fifteen consecutive
days, and read them aloud as he went; Senor José de Val-
divielso, who was also there, was witness to this. And as
stories about him vary, I will relate what I know of my
own personal experience. Roque de Figueroa, the theatre-
manager at Madrid, was so short of plays in carnival time
that the Theatre of the Cross was closed; he was so pressed
that Lope and I sat down to write a play together as fast
as we could, entitled *The Third Order of St. Francis*, in
which Arias played the Saint's part more to the life than
it has ever been played before. Lope took the first act, I
the second, which we wrote in two days, and we shared the
third — eight pages apiece. The weather was bad and I
spent the night at his house. Seeing that I could n't keep
his pace, I hoped to catch up by extra diligence, got up at
two o'clock in the morning, and finished my half by
eleven. Then I went to look for him and found him in the
garden busy over an orange tree that had been frostbitten.
I asked him how his verses had gone, and he answered, "I
began to write at five o'clock and finished the act about
an hour ago; had a rasher of bacon for breakfast, wrote
fifty tercets, and now I am pretty tired with watering the
garden." And taking out his sheets of paper, he read me

the eight pages and the tercets. I should have been dumfounded if I had not known his extraordinary fertility and
his mastery of verse.

Lope's public life was one long success; he became
a great celebrity, his picture was to be seen everywhere, he was pointed out to strangers, followed in
the streets by an admiring throng, and women leaned
from windows and blessed him as he passed. Nevertheless, Fate took more than Fortune gave; his fire-
side held many a vacant chair. He says, "*Mis deseos,
morir* (my one wish is to die.)"

In the half page at my command it would be impossible to do justice to this amazing genius. I will
quote an American admirer: "Of the prominent
themes of love and jealousy little need be said. No
other poet of the world's literature has sounded their
sombre depths more skillfully; no one has given them
more graceful, witty or humorous terms and defini-
tions, or presented them in more different moods."
Be this as it may, there can be no doubt of Lope's
unparalleled versatility; he knew the stage, its traditions, its formulæ, its conventions; he knew also
how to depict real life, and he poured forth verses as
a canary sings. No sane person will compare Lope de
Vega to Shakespeare; as a usual thing Spaniards —
and I have in mind a cultivated living Spaniard who
was born in Guatemala and bred upon French literature and appears to be singularly free from national
prejudices — rank him above Molière. I do not understand this judgment; but certainly Lope, though
lacking in the splendid passages that mark the
Elizabethans, is far more readable to-day than any
English dramatist from Shakespeare to Sheridan.

XXIX

GÓNGORA AND QUEVEDO

BEFORE I take up other men of great name in literature, who won their chief laurels during the reign of
Philip III, I must say a word or two of the Duke of
Lerma, for he and not Philip was the real sovereign.
Not since the days of Don Álvaro de Luna had a
subject ruled the king, and now Lerma begins again
a shameful list of Spanish favorites. Philip himself
was a poor creature, timid, lazy, superstitious (*el
Piadoso*), and a wastrel. The one praise vouchsafed
him is that he was a good dancer. Too slothful to
attend to business, he handed over the government
to the Duke of Lerma, whose deficiencies, though of a
different sort, were as great as his own. The Duke,
a man of very agreeable manners, was avaricious,
incapable, and corrupt. His only care was to make
parade of his power, and to fill his own pockets and
those of his followers. Although the kingdom was
exhausted by foreign wars, the Duke squandered
money in fêtes, in gifts, in superfluous salaries; and
worse than his wastefulness were the financial measures he devised to counteract the waste. He first
had a plan to lay hold of all the silver vessels in
the country, but the outcry from the Church frightened him off. He then went begging from door to
door for alms to replenish the King's treasury; I speak
literally — every parish was assigned to royal so-

licitors. This measure aroused much scorn and contempt, but brought in little money. He decreed that copper money should have twice its value, that one penny should be worth two — with the result that prices doubled and copper flowed in from everywhere. He transferred the Court from Madrid to Valladolid, and thereby upset all business in Madrid and every sort of civic life in Valladolid. But everything else he did to harm the kingdom sinks into insignificance in comparison with the expulsion of the Moriscos. He laid the project before the King, and his Majesty replied, "That is a grand plan, Duke; go ahead with it." An exception was made in favor of those condemned to take their places in an auto-de-fe, and also of some other categories; otherwise all Moriscos were ordered to go. It is said that over five hundred thousand went.

The motives behind this measure sprung from popular prejudice. Rumor reported, and in part truthfully, that there was always danger of an insurrection, and that the Moriscos gave aid to foreign enemies, to Turks, to the French, and especially to raiders and pirates from the Barbary coast. This fear was quickened by their rapid growth in numbers. In Valencia, for instance, the Moorish population had increased during twenty-five years above forty per cent; they married young, they never became monks, they did not emigrate to America, none were killed in war. The expulsion caused a very serious economic loss. The historian Lafuente says that the Moriscos were virtually in control of agriculture and commerce, of the mechanical occupations and useful arts; that they were economical, sober, excessively

frugal, and consequently much better off, in spite of
the enormous taxes laid on them, than the Spaniards
who were less laborious and greater spenders. He
quotes Cardinal Richelieu, who said that it was the
most rash and barbarous measure known to history.
No wonder that it is the custom among Spanish
historians to lay much of the blame for Spanish decadence upon bad government. So much for the
Duke of Lerma's statesmanship. I now return to
literature.

The chief poet of this period is Don Luis de Góngora y Argote (1561–1627), a native of Cordova.
When but a youth of four and twenty, Cervantes,
who to be sure is generously prodigal of praise, called
him a *raro ingenio sin segundo*. After studying law at
Salamanca, Góngora entered upon an ecclesiastical
career, without displaying any qualifications for it.
His bishop complained that he neglected the customary services, prayed with scant devotion, attended bullfights, frequented the society of players,
and so forth; nevertheless, thanks to the powerful influence of the Duke of Lerma, he finally rose
to be chaplain to the King. Velásquez painted his
picture; but it is doubtful whether the portrait of
Góngora now exhibited in the Prado with this attribution is really that very picture. The portrait is
not sympathetic; it shows a grim, austere face with
an unamiable mouth, straight nose, and high, dome-
like forehead: on the whole, an intellectual, self-
contained, cold-blooded man.

It is said that Góngora began his poetical career
with imitations of Herrera el Divino. Apart from
this he had two distinct manners, an early and a late

manner. In the early manner his poems are *de una sencillez y naturalidad encantadoras*, clear, simple, charming, with something of the charm of Robert Burns. Of this the selections given in the *Oxford Book of Spanish Verse* are evidence enough:

> *Las flores del romero,*
> *niña Isabel,*
> *hoy son flores azules,*
> *mañana serán miel.*

Spanish critics say that Góngora is a master of *nuances*, of exquisite expression, of pure elegance, of aristocratic distinction, in short, that he is the greatest poet of his time. They also agree that his second manner is bad. Góngora turns his back on the general public and addresses himself to persons of culture; he piles up affectations, twists his phrases wrong side before, adopts far-fetched words, delights in antithesis and metaphor. Gil Blas said, "*C'est l'obscurité qui en fait tout le mérite.*" This style is called *culteranismo* from its extreme affectation of refined culture, or *Góngorismo* after the poet; and a great ado was made over it, literary men spending much energy in arguments on this side or that. It is the same sort of thing that is called euphuism in English and *Marinismo* in Italian.

A much more important general figure is Don Francisco de Quevedo (1580–1645), who fills a great place in Spanish literature, comparable, I am told, to that occupied by Swift in English literature. Velásquez painted a portrait of him, with big-rimmed spectacles; the original, or a copy, is at Apsley House, London. Quevedo was born in Madrid; he studied theology at Alcalá de Henares, where it is fair to suspect that his conduct as an undergraduate rather befitted a young guardsman than a theological student. In 1601 he followed the court to Valladolid, and then to Madrid. Having money enough in his pocket, he took up no definite occupation; he wrote poetry and satires, and attached himself to a political grandee, the Duke of Osuna. In 1611 Quevedo, who is described as a *pundonoroso caballero* with various duels and honorable scars to his credit, killed a man in a quarrel; he was obliged to fly from Madrid, and took refuge with the Duke, then Viceroy of Sicily. During his sojourn in Italy he was concerned in the piratical conspiracy against Venice to which I have alluded. Venice, alarmed by the dominating power of Spain in Italy, had entered into some agreement with Holland. The circumstances are obscure; but it seems that the Duke of Osuna — then Viceroy of Naples — and the Spanish Governor of Milan put their heads together and planned a *coup de main* against Venice. Quevedo entered the city as a sort of spy. His presence was discovered, but he escaped in the disguise of a beggar, and the Council of Ten were obliged to content themselves with burning him and the Duke of Osuna in effigy. Quevedo continued to attend the Duke at Naples where, according to his nephew, "he had many adventures." One gets the impression that Quevedo was ready to do anything that the Duke asked. He took a shameful part in removing an obstacle to the marriage of the Duke's son with the granddaughter of the Duke of Lerma. He also went to Madrid on behalf of the Duke's ambition for higher office, and, to use his own expression, "greased the wheels." But political lobbying of this character was not looked upon as a fault. Everybody did it, for everybody knew that it was necessary: *No ay que acabar nada si no es con untarlos muy bien las manos.* Spanish politics were not only corrupt, they were also uncertain; both the Duke of Osuna and Quevedo came to grief. Philip III died soon afterward, and Philip IV succeeded him; or rather, the Conde Duque Olivares reigned in place of the Duke of Lerma. Quevedo did his best to stand well in the good graces of the new favorite, but he did not succeed very well. After various vicissitudes, it happened one day that a satire upon Olivares was found under the King's plate; Quevedo was suspected of writing it and was imprisoned in the monastery of San Marcos in Leon. There he stayed over three years and a half, and after his release, broken in health, he lived but two years.

Quevedo wrote a great deal and of many sorts — political brochures, moral, philosophical, and religious treatises; he translated Epictetus, Seneca, Saint François de Sales; he composed poetry, and wrote a picaresque novel, *El Buscón,* called also *El gran Tacaño.* I found this novel hard to understand, — Mérimée says of it, *"rien de plus difficile à entendre,"* — and what I did understand bored me, but then it might not bore others more discriminating. Fashions change; for most readers classical satire has a musty savor. *El Buscón* seemed to me like the cruel temper of Jonathan Swift expressed in the comic style of Tobias Smollett. Quevedo's most famous satire is *Los Sueños,* a visit to Hades, where he sees all sorts of types of Spanish society. The scenes are somewhat of the same sort as Goya's Caprichos.

"*Rien de plus amusant*," according to Monsieur Mérimée. Anybody that wishes to acquaint himself with Spanish literature must read *Los Sueños*, but unless his sense of humor jumps with that of Mérimée, I think he will get more instruction than pleasure. But of Quevedo's rank in literature there is no question. Cejador says: "*Es Quevedo el sátiro más terrible, desenvuelto, duro, seco y desvergonzado de España;* he did not spare the frailty of ladies, the seclusion of nuns, the high-mightiness of favorites, or the sacred character of friars or priests." But in spite of all his apparent freedom of thought, this savage, cynical, gross satirist, who had no intention of forsaking the society he belabored, enrolled himself among *los indignos esclavos del Santísimo Sacramento.* His style has been greatly praised, but at the same time he is the head and front of *conceptismo.* This is a literary habit allied to *culteranismo*, only it deals with the affectation of thoughts rather than an affectation of words (so far as the two may be separated), with conceits, whimsies, and so forth, such as we associate with the heroines of *Les Femmes Savantes* and *Les Précieuses Ridicules.* Of what I have read of his, I like best his ballad on Don Dinero:

> *Poderoso caballero*
> *es don Dinero.*

XXX
GUILLÉN DE CASTRO, TIRSO DE MOLINA, ALARCÓN

But although ballad poetry (*romances*) and picaresque novels constitute famous departments of Spanish literature, they are not of equal consequence to the Spanish drama. Voltaire says: "*Lorsque Corneille donna le Cid* (1637), *les espagnols avaient sur tous les théâtres de l'Europe la même influence que dans les affaires publiques; leur goût dominait ainsi que leur politique.*" This reference to the *Cid* brings me at once to a dramatist but a few years younger than Lope de Vega. Guillén de Castro (1569–1631) was born in Valencia, where his family belonged to the *sociedad elegante* of the town; and he had enough leisure and means to make poetry his chief occupation. Cervantes speaks of his *suavidad y dulzura* (his sweet and pleasing numbers). At Valencia he probably became acquainted with Lope de Vega, who sojourned there during the period of his banishment from Madrid. At any rate, in later years the two were good friends; Lope dedicated a play to Don Guillén, and he, in return, dedicated a book to Lope's daughter Marcela. Somewhat later he commanded a troop of coast patrol that watched for the coming of Barbary pirates. He went to Italy, — no one knows why, — held office under the Viceroy of Naples, and lived a life of dissipation, adventure, and intrigue. On his return from Italy he settled in Madrid, where he passed the last years of his life in poverty and distress, comforted, however, by the society of Lope and other men of letters, such as Tirso de Molina, Alarcón, Góngora, and Quevedo. His claim upon our memory is due to Corneille, who took the plot for his great play, *Le Cid*, from Castro's *Las Mocedades del Cid*. Ever since then, Spanish and French men of letters have been at loggerheads as to how much the fame of the Frenchman's play is due to his borrowings from the Spaniard. The controversy still continues; it is always highly emotional, full of dramatic give-and-take. The ordinary Philistine, dipping in anywhere, will find it more stimulating than *Las Mocedades del Cid* and more entertaining than *Le Cid*.

Another disciple of Lope de Vega, Gabriel Téllez (1571–1648), better known by his nom de plume, Tirso de Molina, had a fate curiously similar in one respect to that of Guillén de Castro, in that he too is known out of Spain solely because Molière, Mozart, Byron, and others took directly or indirectly from his play, the *Burlador de Seville*, the character of Don Juan, who in consequence has become as much of a cosmopolitan personage as Faust. Oddly enough, as it seems to us, Tirso was a monk, and rose to high position in the Order of Mercy. He wrote several hundred plays, of which about eighty survive. One play deserves to be read, *El Condenado por desconfiado*, not merely for the rank it holds in Spanish estimation, but also (whatever the original source of the questions raised), for the light it throws on the religion of the Spaniards of that time. The plot turns on the doctrine of grace as opposed to good works. A saintly hermit is tricked by false statements, made by the Devil in disguise, into a belief that he will be damned. He despairs of God's grace; that is, he doubts that God will save him at the last moment. Such doubt is a damnable sin, and the hermit is damned for it. On the other hand, an arrant scoundrel who has committed all the offenses known to man, from the mere fact that he always believes that God's grace will save his soul in the end, is saved. The hermit's soul goes to Hell, and the scoundrel's to Paradise. This divorce of religion from ethics perplexes Protestants. But the Spanish creed is justified by the one possible analogy, that between grace and the workings of Nature; for Nature grants her salvation, not to the man of good purposes, but to the man that knows her formulæ.

El Vergonzoso en Palacio is a delightful play in which a maiden contrives to cure her lover of his bashfulness. I venture to commend it to Beginners and Philistines. After this mild praise, it is but right to quote the opinions of those competent to judge. Fitzmaurice-Kelly puts Tirso "among the great creators of all time"; Menéndez y Pelayo calls him *nuestro Terencio castellano* and says that all the world, except the French, agree that he is a better poet than Molière. Señora de los Rios de Lámperez says that "in strict æsthetic judgment Tirso, beyond dispute, is entitled not only to a leading place among our dramatists but also to a glorious place in the front rank of the dramatists of the world."

Another playwright of the first rank is Juan Ruiz

de Alarcón (1581–1639), a proud, sensitive little humpback whom Lope de Vega mocked for his deformity — and also, to their shame be it said, Góngora and Quevedo as well. Alarcón was born in Mexico, but he was educated in Spain and passed most of his life there. He too contributed to the creation of the French drama, for Corneille in *Le Menteur* imitated his *La Verdad sospechosa*. Critics say that his characters are well drawn and his ethical purpose high, his taste perfect, his language sober, his dialogue animated, his versification excellent; and that, although he lacks the power and creative imagination of Lope or Tirso, he is freer than they from faults. Spanish scholars are apt to lay on rich colors when they praise the Spanish theatre and Spanish playwrights, very much as English critics praise the Elizabethans: "*el gigantesco edificio de nuestro teatro . . . la gloriosa procesion de nuestros escritores.*" Therefore perhaps I may venture to disclose, in the interest of those unscholarly readers for whom I write, although at the risk of impertinence, some of the impressions concerning Alarcón's plays that I find jotted down in the privacy of my notebook: "*Gañar amigos* — complicated and dull"; "*Los Pechos privilegiados* — the services of a wet nurse receive high recognition; very flat"; "*No hay mal que por bien no venga* — both entertaining and instructive." But I am told that *El Tejedor de Segovia*, *Las Paredes oyen*, and *La Verdad sospechosa* are admirable plays, much better than those I have mentioned.

XXXI

PAINTING PRIOR TO THE GREAT
MASTERS

IT would not be right to start in upon the great
Spanish painters without some sort of prologue. I
shall not attempt to speak of the earliest stages of
pictorial art, nor of the primitives. Lovers of such
things will find delicate miniatures on codices in
the Escorial, such as those of the *Cantigas* of Alfonso
el Sabio; they betray, I am told — and as one would
expect to find — the influence of French art. Old
frescoes are scattered about in churches here and
there, in which connoisseurs detect Byzantine,
French, or Tuscan influences; and there are many
paintings of the fifteenth century, for instance, such
as the altar screens by *cuatrocentistas catalanes*, well
worth a leisurely study. But no real notability appears in the story of Spanish painting until the
famous journey of Jan Van Eyck, who came in the
train of the Burgundian ambassador (1428–29) for
the express purpose of painting a Portuguese princess, — "*peindre bien au vif la figure de madite dame
l'Infante,*" — in order to enable his master, the Duke
of Burgundy, to decide whether he should like to
marry her. Van Eyck painted the princess, who
was charming, and probably traveled through Spain
from Santiago of Compostela to Granada. What
painters he saw and what his influence may have

been is a matter of conjecture; but it is certain that admiration for Flemish art soon became a powerful influence in the peninsula. Enrique IV (1454–1475) presented to a monastery in Segovia a picture, the Fountain of Life, now in the Prado, painted in the Van Eyck manner. The eminent Flemish masters, Petrus Christus, Roger van der Weyden, Dierick Bouts, Gheeraert David, Joachim Patinir, as well as Jerome Bosch, were very much the fashion. You will find paintings by Flemings, or in the Flemish manner, in various places from Barcelona to Seville.

By the time of Ferdinand and Isabella, Italian painting, which all through that century had been instilling its influence, became dominant. Charles V and Philip II brought to Spain the great collection of Titians, Tintorettos, and Veroneses, now lodged in the Prado. Charles met Titian for the first time at Bologna in 1533, and at once conceived a great admiration for him. In Philip's time Antony Moro (1519–1576) was the chief court painter. Moro came from Utrecht and was presented to the young Prince by Cardinal Granville, whom Motley has belabored in a most partisan fashion in the *Rise of the Dutch Republic*. Moro found favor, and painted portraits of Philip, his wife Mary Tudor, the great Duke of Alva, Ruz Gómez de Silva, Prince of Eboli, Alva's political rival, and various other members of the royal court. On Moro's departure, the Spaniard, Alonso Sánchez Coello (1513–1590), succeeded to his post. Coello painted a number of historical personages, among others the Princess of Eboli, wife of Ruiz Gómez, renowned in the licentious

Titian   *Madrid*

CHARLES V

society of her time, the gay and gallant Don John of Austria, hero of Lepanto, the poor little odious, deformed Don Carlos, on whom legend, seeking to make up for the niggardliness of Nature, has poured a prodigal portion of perverted romance; and many others. A Spanish critic says that Coello's style is *pulido y perfecto en su tecnica*, and in his own day Lope de Vega sang his praises:

El noble Alonso Sánchez . . .
de quien hoy han quedado
honrando su memoria
eternos cuadros de divina historia.

After Coello, Pantoja de la Cruz, one of his pupils, held the position of court painter. But besides having members of the royal family painted, Philip was much concerned to furnish the Escorial with pictures to his taste. He employed Luis Morales (1509–1586), but did not like his paintings and dismissed him; nevertheless, other people did, especially his pictures of the Saviour crowned with thorns, and nicknamed him, because of his Christs and Madonnas, *el Divino*. Philip preferred Fernández Navarrete (1526–1579), who is known as *el Mudo* (the dumb man) and also as *el Tiziano español*, and employed him to paint over forty pictures for the Escorial.

Apart from the court, the Church was the great patron of art; the cathedrals needed pictures as well as *sillería*, retablos, grilles, tombs, and windows. If you look about you in the cathedral of Seville, you will see painted statues, and the sacristan will say, "*Pintado por Alejo Fernández*," and you will answer: "Oh, yes." In another picture he will point out the leg of Adam, "*La Gamba,*" which is a conspicuously beautiful leg, and in the guidebook you will read that it was painted by Luis de Vargas (1502–1568). In the sacristy you will find a fine picture by a naturalized Fleming, Pedro Campana; and so on.

But I will leave these lesser men and go to the painter who first refused to imitate Raphael and the Roman painters, and started out on the true Spanish path of going straight to nature. Such at least is the reputation of Juan de las Roelas (1560–1625). Nevertheless, a man can rarely escape the influence of the great contemporary masters of his craft; their fame shapes and moulds public taste and sets the standard of beauty and technique. Roelas was influenced by Tintoretto, and when he was forty years old went to Venice for several years in order to study the great Venetian masters. Spanish viceroys issued orders in the kingdom of Naples and the province of Lombardy, but Italian poets and Italian painters of the sixteenth century gave their commands throughout the Spanish peninsula. However, Roelas is a remarkable painter. You will see his pictures in the museum at Seville and in the hospital, as well as in the cathedral. In a chapel there is his Santiago. The laborious German critic, Herr August L. Mayer, is unable to contain his enthusiasm for this painting, its "perfect composition," its "magnificent color," its chiaroscuro, the "extraordinary handling of mass." In order to liberate his fine Teutonic enthusiasm he is obliged to use words twenty-three and thirty-one letters long; and *ausgezeichnets* are peppered over the page. Others admire other pictures. It is said that Murillo used to linger in admiration before Roelas's Death of Saint Isidore. And Richard Ford, whose opinions usually square with uneducated taste better than the judgments of professional critics, says: "No one ever painted the Jesuit like Roelas . . . he is a very great master, much less known and appreciated than he should be."

Roelas's reputation in Spain, however, seems to be inferior to that of Francisco de Herrera el Viejo (1576–1650), another Sevillian painter. Sentenach calls Herrera a "veritable Titan" and says that he accomplished "a revolution in technique." Ford calls him a "bold, dashing" master. Herrera is sometimes regarded as having been the first pioneer in the great naturalistic movement, but Carl Justi says that he got his style from Roelas. Everybody agrees that he had passion and power. Mayer calls him *"umgestüm und aufbrausend"*; and indeed German adjectives are appropriate to his rough, vigorous manner. The ordinary pilgrim gets tired of Saint Ildefonsos, Saint Isidores, and Purísimas, so I should counsel him, if it be in his way, to look up the Blind Musician in Vienna, and the Fishmonger in Berlin. Herrera possessed great skill as an engraver, and at one time ill-advisedly employed his dexterity in counterfeiting coin. He fled for refuge to the Jesuit college of San Hermengild, and painted there a picture of the Saint. Philip IV happened to see it (1624), and for the sake of the painter pardoned the counterfeiter. But the crown of his glory is that he was master to Velásquez.

Roelas and Herrera el Viejo are so vigorous, so full of energy and originality, that they do not fit with any propriety into the reign of Philip III. Pacheco (1571–1654) does; he was a mediocre painter, a bad painter one might say, who among other things decorated the ceiling in the reception room in the Casa de Pilatos. I should add, however, that portraits of his father and mother in the Museum at Seville were greatly to my taste, and I find that critics now and again praise his portraits. Pacheco owes his fame to two circumstances: He was father-in-law to Velásquez, and he compiled a Book of Portraits, drawn with black or red chalk, a quarter the size of life, which included many of the celebrities of his time, beginning with Philip II. He also painted numerous portraits, among others, it is said, that of Doña Catalina de Erauso. This lady seems to me half mythical — perhaps wholly. In early life, when fourteen or fifteen years of age, as her alleged autobiography says, she escaped from a nunnery, dressed as a man, underwent various adventures, enlisted as a soldier, and led a wild life for more than twenty years among the Spanish conquistadores in Peru and elsewhere, undiscovered until, thinking that she was going to die, she confessed her sins to a bishop.

One other painter I shall mention here, Juan de Jáuregui (1583–1641), a pupil of Luis de Vargas, the painter of The Leg, not because of his skill in the art of painting but because Cervantes, in an obscure and much discussed passage, says that Jáuregui had, may have, might or should have, painted his portrait. Some people, Sentenach for

instance, think that Jáuregui did paint it, and that
the supposed portrait that now hangs on the wall
of the Spanish Academy is the very one. To judge
from the photograph, the face might well belong to
the author of *Don Quixote;* but there is small probability in the attribution.

XXXII

RUBENS IN SPAIN, RIBALTA, RIBERA

PHILIP III has an elusive personality. I cannot find
that he was interested in anything but building monasteries and, I believe, in hunting. But the conventions of royalty required that artists should attend
his court, and also that his effigy, with drawn sword,
on a prancing charger, should adorn some public
square. John of Bologna was employed to cast such
a monument in bronze for the Plaza Mayor in
Madrid; and Pantoja de la Cruz painted an eques-
trian portrait to serve the sculptor as a guide. A
king also must fill his palaces with bric-a-brac; and
Juan de Arphe (1523–1605), a member of the famous
family of gold- and silver-smiths that filled Spanish
sacristies with pyxes and monstrances, wrought a
lavabo in classical style, encrusted with gold, silver,
and enamel. But there is one circumstance of real
interest connected with this reign: a visit of Peter
Paul Rubens in 1603.

Gonzaga, Duke of Mantua, wished for Spanish
support, so he sent Rubens, then in his service, to the
Spanish court with presents for the King and for the
Duke of Lerma. To His Majesty Gonzaga sent a
carriage and horses and eleven arquebuses; to the
Duke, who enjoyed the reputation of an amateur
patron of art, he sent copies of twelve famous portraits; and to a lesser favorite, Rodrigo Calderón, two

dozen less important pictures. Although more dignified, this mission was not unlike that performed by
Quevedo some ten years later for the Duke of Osuna.
Dádivas quebrantan peñas. On unpacking, the pictures were found to be sadly damaged by rain. Gonzaga's ambassador to Spain, Signor Iberti, wished
Rubens to get some Spanish painters to repaint the
damaged canvases offhand. Rubens declined to do
this "on account of the incredible incapacity and
carelessness of these painters"; he did not wish to
have their work attributed to him. He managed to
do himself what was necessary, and he also painted
two smaller pictures, a Heraclitus and a Democritus,
which he included in the donation with the others.
The presentation was duly made. Rubens wrote to
Gonzaga: "As to the Duke of Lerma, I had the
satisfaction of hearing and marking the judicious
admiration that he felt for what was good; and his
satisfaction was not feigned, for, so far as I could
judge, he appreciated the worth of the presents. So
I hope that some time the donator will be repaid
for his gifts." And to Gonzaga's secretary he wrote:
"They put me near the Duke. . . . His pleasure over
the excellence and the number of the pictures was
very plain; and, thanks to the damage and the
touching up, they all had a certain ancient air. He
took them all for originals, at least most of them,
without any questioning on his part or any suggestion
on ours to make him think so." Don Rodrigo Calderón and his wife were no less delighted with the
pictures given to them, and expressed themselves
as under an everlasting obligation to his Grace of
Mantua. I may add that in earlier days the Duke of

Lerma preferred pictures of more liberal subjects; but just at this time his duchess had died and "he was all for devotion, religion, and withdrawal from worldly things." He put away his profane pictures and substituted those presented by Gonzaga. A Spanish scholar has taken umbrage at this disparagement of Lerma as a connoisseur; I regret that I have no space for the niceties of international irritations. Rubens painted a portrait of the Duke of Lerma on horseback, and various other pictures. He says that he was astonished by the quantity and quality of the Italian pictures, by Titian, Raphael, and others, at the Escorial and in the palace at Madrid; "but there are no modern pictures there worth anything." With that I leave him, and go to two painters of Valencia.

Francisco Ribalta (1555–1628) studied in Italy. His manner is said to show the influences of Raphael, Sebastiano del Piombo, and Correggio. Nevertheless he is regarded as one of the leaders in the realistic movement of national painting. The most conspicuous of his pictures in the Prado is a Vision of Saint Francis. It is a very odd picture. The figure of the Saint, shrinking in alarm and reverence from an oncoming angel, is true to nature, a well-studied portrait, but the oncoming angel is neither more nor less than a comic figure; he comes prancing through the air, holding his guitar as if he were blowing a bellows. Even for Mayer he is "*eine höchst eigenartige Gestalt.*" It creates an unfair impression of the master. Carl Justi says that his art is "rude, coarse, and somewhat tasteless," where it is not violent. But photographs of his pictures at Valencia (which I have not seen) convey another impression; of these Richard Ford says, that his San Vicente de Ferrer, "one of his masterpieces," is "painted in a style between Titian and Van Dyck"; and that in a grand Last Supper the head of an apostle "is equal to anything painted by the old Venetians." He also comments upon a "charming" Holy Family in which "the child is painted like Titian." These pictures were, as I understand, painted about 1605.

But when all is said, Ribalta is best remembered as the master of the great Ribera (1588–1652). Ribera's career belongs perhaps to the reign of Philip IV (1621–1665) rather than to that of Philip III; but as his first patron was our acquaintance, the Duke of Osuna, and as throughout the later reign he lived in Naples and became wholly identified with Italy, where he acquired the sobriquet *Lo Spagnoletto*, I put him in here. Ribalta told him that he must go to Italy; so he went, with empty pockets. In Italy he wandered in the north, where he conceived a great admiration for Correggio; afterward he fell in with Caravaggio's work and adopted much of Caravaggio's mannerisms, which he found well suited to express his own outlook upon life. Caravaggio (1569–1609) was a revolutionist, who despised the fashionable schools of Bologna and Rome and betook himself to a study of nature. From the time of his acquaintance with Caravaggio's pictures, Ribera always painted from a model. From Caravaggio, too, he learned to look upon nature not as a Raphael or a Corot might see it, but somewhat as Zola did, as ugly and brutal; and yet Ribera has "two soul-sides," one violent, the other tender. He experimented with sharp contrasts of light and darkness, and hit upon a startling way of throwing his figures into high relief. Critics praise his drawing and his color: "Spain possesses a few of those masterpieces in which he rivals Titian in beauty and brilliancy of coloring and shows himself to be the greatest colorist of Italy in the seventeenth century." The uncultivated spectator admires most his religious passion and his dramatic power.

At Naples the Duke of Osuna, the Viceroy, made Ribera his court painter (1616). He married a girl of fifteen, became a Neapolitan, enjoyed a high renown, and never, I think, went back to Spain. A Spanish painter once asked him why he did not return. He answered:

My dear fellow, I have a great desire, but from what truthful people of good sense tell me, there is an objection; that is, the first year I should be welcomed as a great painter, but the second year, being there, I should lose prestige and no one would pay any attention to me. I am confirmed in this view because I have seen some works by excellent masters of the Spanish kingdom that are held in little repute. In Naples I am well thought of. I am satisfied by the prices paid for my paintings, so I act on the adage, "He that is well off had better stay still."

There is little further to tell of his life. Many of the best-known people in Spain must have been going frequently to Naples. Quevedo was there on and off from 1616 to 1619. Guillén de Castro, we know, was there a few years earlier. Velásquez came in 1629 and again twenty years later, and of course went to see him. In 1648 occurred the sorrow of his life. The year before, a revolt had broken out in Naples; the

Spanish Viceroy was hated, taxes were high, riots in Sicily were contagious. French *agents provocateurs* were at work, and so on. The brilliant fisherman Masaniello, famed in opera, was the ringleader. Young Don John of Austria (Second), bastard son of Philip IV, a youth of nineteen, came with a fleet to suppress the insurrection. Don John's mother was a celebrated actress, la Calderona, who had attracted the King's attention while acting in Lope's plays. The insurrection was put down, and Don John, gifted and charming, became the cynosure of all eyes. Ribera, as court painter, lodged in the Viceroy's palace. The painter's daughter Anna was seventeen and very beautiful. Don John sat for an etching. The girl eloped with the Prince. The poor father hid his head in Posilipo; it is said that he was only able to finish an Adoration of the Shepherds (now in the Louvre) and painted no more. In the convent of the Agustinas Descalzas at Salamanca, over the high altar, hangs one of the loveliest pictures in the world. The Virgin, maiden and goddess, wrapped in her free-flowing mantle, stands in mid-air, her hands crossed on her breast, her feet upon the crescent moon, and garlands of cherubs, bathed in light divine, flutter below and above in a hurly-burly of religious joy. Here is the ecstasy of innocence, a soul created by the hand of God pure as true love. Legend says, quite untruthfully, that the Virgin is a portrait of the beautiful girl that loved the fascinating prince. Twenty or thirty years afterward the door of the convent of the Descalzas in Madrid opened to receive the Excelentisima Señora Doña Marguerita de Austria, a granddaughter of the great painter.

The number of pictures that issued from Ribera's atelier at Naples and are now scattered over Europe is so enormous that his assistants must have worked on many of them; but you will see in the Prado a dozen of such excellence that you may be sure that they were painted by the master's own hand. There is the wonderfully drawn and modeled Martyrdom of Saint Bartholomew, violent, dramatic, and beautiful; Saint Francis of Assisi in ecstasy; a Trinity, with God the Father most carefully coiffured and a strangely beautiful Christ (better befitting an illustration to "La Belle Dame sans Merci"); and various other pictures of brilliantly painted old saints. The Betrothal of Saint Catherine in Lord Northbrook's collection, Saint Agnes (in Dresden), and many others must be beautiful pictures, to judge from what the critics say and from photographs. For the uneducated pilgrim, Ribera will take rank among Spanish painters only lower than Velásquez, even perhaps above El Greco and Murillo. Sit down before Saint Bartholomew in the Prado; look at Le Pied Bot and the Adoration of the Shepherds in the Louvre; go back to gaze at the Immaculate Virgin in Salamanca; and you will feel that here is a Spaniard of ten talents, a puissant genius.

XXXIII

THE REIGN OF PHILIP IV

On March 28, 1621, King Philip III lay dying in his palace at Madrid. The holy image of Our Lady of Atocha was brought to the convent of Las Descalzas Reales and "a great number of penitents scourged themselves cruelly." The King would be succeeded by the young Prince of Asturias, then sixteen years of age, but the sequence of rulers was less certain. The Duke of Lerma had been superseded by a scurvy, intriguing knave who had contrived to displace him, to wit, the Duke of Uceda, his own son. But though the favorite ruled, it lay with the King to appoint the favorite, and nobody could be sure what the Prince would do. On the twenty-ninth the dying King summoned the Prince and begged him to retain his counselors, especially the Duke of Uceda. On the thirtieth he had the body of Saint Isidore placed by his bed, and vowed to build him a chapel. The next day he died. The Duke of Uceda went to the Prince's chamber, fell on his knees and kissed the Prince's hand. A few days later the old King's body was borne to the Escorial accompanied by "*un assés chetif convoy pour un sy grand roi,*" and there, in the sombre crypt, a fit dwelling-place for corporal death, his ashes lie. On April 12 Count Olivares was created a grandee of Spain. On April 15 the new King declared that in pursuance of his father's testament he revoked the 1,400,000 crowns that his father had paid to the Duke of Lerma under an old agreement. A day or two later the Duke of Uceda was removed from office.

Between the lines of this brief chronicle, which I take from the journal of M. Bassompierre, the French ambassador, you may read the story of ferocious intrigues. The old favorites had fallen with a vengeance. Rodrigo de Calderón (who received the second-best pictures) was beheaded, the Duke of Uceda died in prison, and the Duke of Lerma owed his head to the prudence of having put on a Cardinal's hat. The new grandee, the Conde-duque de Olivares, who did not relish rivals, ruled in their stead. So the downward course of the kingdom passed into the hands of a new favorite, and Philip IV, after some feeble efforts, renewed now and again, to do his royal duty, gave himself over to women and hunting.

Of all the kings of Spain Philip IV, styled by his admiring subjects *Don Phelipe el Grande*, *sobre todos los Reyes máximo monarca*, is most familiar to us. We know how he looked at stages all through his life. At eighteen or nineteen, his dull, whopper-jawed, melancholy, irresolute face shows a dim consciousness of royal dignity and a feeble purpose to be king. A little later he wears budding moustachios, while marks about the eyes tell how he has passed the intervening years. Another decade, and the foolish countenance has become listless, and yet kingly; the eyes look out wearily; one hand rests irresolute on his sword hilt, the other hangs irresolute by his side. Next, the Conde-duque thought that Philip IV should follow the custom of his ancestors and be

painted on horseback, — or perhaps the great painter
wished to paint a horse, — and so the listless King of
fatuous face, with a bâton in his irresolute right hand,
rides a melodramatic charger. Then Velásquez
wished to paint a dog, and the blasé, dull-eyed hunter,
content to exchange the ennui of hunting for the
ennui of posing, holds a gun. Finally the heavy, up-
late-o'-nights, half-sick, half-dissolute face presents
its pitiful record of feebleness and failure, yet nevertheless kingly in its mien. Is it ethical that a painter
should gain so great renown by so ruthless a denunciation of his king? R. M. S. Stevenson, ignoring
ethics, says:

His slow transformation of this face, through a hard
realism of feature and detail to the suavity of impressional
beauty, seems comparable to that tireless climb of the
Greek sculptor through so many stiffly studied athletes,
to the breadth of Phidias's gods or the suppleness of the
serene Hermes of Praxiteles.

It is not necessary to read the tragic story of bad
finance, of huge taxation, of official corruption, of
universal self-seeking, of idleness, bigotry, and
ignorance. There in the Prado you divine in the sad,
melancholy eyes all the sickening prospect of national decadence that the King looked out upon.

Velásquez has also told a good deal more about the
royal court, and far more vividly than the historians.
You see the clever, crafty, astute, shallow Conde-
duque de Olivares, conscious of his own astuteness
but not of his shallowness. There he hangs forever
on the telltale walls of the Prado, accompanying the
feeble King down the road of life, with his long

moustachios upturned, his little fantailed beard, and his general air of a successful Bowery merchant. He too in a cuirass, with a broad-brimmed, beplumed sombrero and uplifted bâton, bestrides a melodramatic horse, which holds up its fair round belly and sturdy flanks on two hind hoofs, forever. As years go by, the Conde-duque's fantail beard moults, his front teeth go, the fat jowl has become a schemer's mask, while his greedy little eyes twinkle craftily. There is the King's brother Don Carlos, sad, gentle, pathetic, resembling the King, only more likable; his other brother, Don Fernando; the King's wife-niece, Mariana of Austria, thirty years younger than himself, a masque-faced doll fourteen or fifteen years old, tragically subdued to clothes, coiffure, ceremony, and all the social tyranny of the Spanish court; the charming and delightful boy, Don Carlos Baltasar, soon to be taken from the sorrows and degradations of life; the exquisite little daughter Margarita and her maids of honor; and the little dwarfs, tragic creatures that bear their sorry testimony to the inhumanity of the Spanish court.

Philip's reign is only less sad than his face. I shall not linger over politics. The war with Holland continued until Spain was at last forced to recognize Dutch independence. One Spanish triumph (1625) is immortal because Velásquez painted the Spanish general — an Italian, the Marquis of Spinola — receiving the keys of Breda from the Dutch commander, while his spearmen hold their cluster of lances in pictorial parallels. The dignified courtesy in this gallant gentleman is as fine as a noble passage in Shakespeare, and serves to remind us that the heroic

Velasquez   St. Petersburg

CONDE-DUQUE DE OLIVARES

tone in Spanish plays was not without its counterpart in actual life. There was war with France, because Philip supported the Austrian branch of the House of Hapsburg, and Richelieu had vowed to abase it. At least that seems to have been the reason. Voltaire says: "*Il est difficile de dire précisément pourquoi l'on fesait cette guerre.*" The most memorable occurrence in it was the field of Rocroi (1643), where le Grand Condé at twenty-one destroyed the reputation of the long-dreaded Spanish infantry. But far more memorable is the capture of Jamaica by the English (1657), for that was the beginning of the long process of disintegration and loss that continued fitfully but steadily, until Spanish incapacity, corruption, ignorance, and exhaustion bore its necessary fruit, and with the loss of the Philippines, Cuba, and Porto Rico, the once glorious Spanish Empire came to its end.

One more record of political failure and I shall have done. Fomented by Richelieu, the individualistic tendency of Catalonia broke out into a rebellion for the avowed purpose of establishing a republic. This revolt was suppressed, but on the other hand the spirit of independence triumphed in Portugal (1637–1668), where the union with Spain had never been acceptable to the people. After nearly thirty years of fighting, the battle of Villaviciosa (1665) restored to Portugal, under the House of Braganza, both her lost independence and her old empire.

XXXIV

COURT LIFE UNDER PHILIP IV

WHILE these great affairs were enacted in the distant background of Philip's stage, quite different matters went on in front. What these were, we learn from a *Court Gazette*, published in 1636–1637. The park in Madrid, or that part of it known as *el Buen Retiro*, was originally laid out by the orders of the Conde-duque. It soon became a fashionable place of resort, and many of Lope de Vega's scenes take place there, or near by. Gallants, young ladies and duennas, old noblemen, ecclesiasts, ambassadors, officers of the guards, poets, and so forth, made it a place of sauntering and rendezvous. I now quote from the *Gazette*:

In the evening there was a sort of festa [in *el Buen Retiro*] such as never was seen in Spain before. The poet Atellano, who has just come back from the Indies, may be justly called a *monstruo de naturaleza*, for such he showed himself. His poetic inspiration is so great that he will pour forth on the spot a torrent of verses on any subject proposed and withal in suitable style, spiced with appropriate quotations from Holy Writ and the classics, with comparisons, emphases, digressions, and poetical figures that fill the audience with admiration and astonishment. It seems like the black art, for his verses never drop a foot, nor omit a syllable, nor make a mistake, whatever the metre. After him came another poet; then dwarfs performed, and a black clown. There was a masked ball, and all ended with a banquet that the Countess Duchess Olivares gave to their Majesties. . . .

For the benefit of the revenue the exemption of the tax on sales [the *alcabala*, one tenth of the value] was removed from certain classes: the household of the King, Queen, and Prince; booksellers; and painters (except on pictures of saints).

Diego Velásquez has been created a valet of His Majesty's wardrobe. This carries with it the hope of becoming a valet de chambre some day and of wearing the dress, as Titian did. . . .

In consequence of a street fray, an order has been issued forbidding carrying firearms, or laying hand on sword, dagger, or knife, under penalty of two hundred ducats and exile in the case of nobles, and two hundred lashes and the galleys for plebeians. . . .

Don Francisco de Quevedo is at court. He is publishing the career of the Duke of Osuna in Flanders and Sicily. In this lucubration the reader is at a loss whether to admire most the energy and wit in what the Duke did and said, or the comments on each that Don Francisco makes with admirable skill. . . .

The Duke of Medinaceli is valiantly studying the Hebrew tongue, and keeps a rabbi in his house for that purpose, and has made such great progress that he knows how to read without points. . . .

Juan Gómez de Mora has lost his post of curator of the pictures in the Palace. . . . He pays dearly for having presented to Don Lorenzo Ramirez a picture by Titian that belonged to His Majesty, and putting a copy in its place. Criticism is directed against Don Lorenzo for accepting it. . . .

His Majesty has issued a decree granting permission to the Grandees to enter his apartment at certain hours; and if His Majesty should be getting up, his gentlemen will

hand them the towel, and the Grandees may call them
You or by their surnames only. . . .

Don Luis de Narvaez [a poet] has been arrested and
locked up for having published a comedy which is an
atrocious satire on Don Francisco de Quevedo. Don Luis
might have got out of his trouble, for there are various
persons to whom he might have ascribed the play; nevertheless he would not, but proclaimed himself the author,
like a proud father. It is believed that Don Francisco
secretly contrived to have him arrested, although he
denies it loudly and, full of spirit, swears that when Don
Luis gets out of jail he will challenge and kill him, though
he be a famous fencer. . . .

The festival at *el Buen Retiro* had been postponed, although they are making all possible haste to complete the
new square. . . . The *corregidor* has set up stocks there to
punish the workmen who do not complete their tasks, and
as a warning to the others. . . .

A public challenge has been posted in Madrid and in
many other cities by Don Juan de Herrera, Knight of the
Order of Santiago, in which he alleges at length an offense
committed against him by the Marquis de Águila and
challenges the latter to fight him in Germany, because for
good reasons a duel is impossible in Spain. Over this there
has been much discussion as to the Marquis's duty, some
caballeros castizos hold that he need not go, saying that
Don Juan is inferior in birth, that the only road to Germany lies through enemy country, etc., and allege a precedent of the Prince de Condé. Others think differently and
allege the precedent of the Cid and the Infantes of
Carrión. . . .

Don Juan Pacheco has been imprisoned in the convent
of Calatrava for having given orders to have Tomás Fernández, a playwright, slashed in the face with a knife,
because the playwright declined to write a new play when
the young lady whom Don Juan Pacheco was courting

recovered from a fever. While the assault was taking place, Don Juan was strolling up and down in a cemetery awaiting the result. . . .

To-day, Friday, the poets' Academy will meet in the presence of His Majesty. The poets will improvise on subjects to be proposed. It is said that one of the subjects is: "Why is Judas painted with a red beard?" It is hoped that Luis Vélez and Don Pedro Calderón will distinguish themselves. . . . [This is Luis Vélez de Guevara (1570–1644) known out of Spain mainly because Le Sage imitated his *Diablo Cojuelo* (*Le Diable Boiteux*). Don Pedro Calderón is the great dramatist.]

El Conde-duque [N.B. I interpolate: The French are close to the Spanish border and threaten an invasion], in accordance with his customary piety, has withdrawn for Holy Week to the dormitory of San Jerónimo el Real to give better attention to spiritual matters. . . . His Eminence heard sermons by the best preachers of the court, and the attendance was very large; but there was some scandal because the preachers did not all confine themselves to preaching Christ crucified. Some thought of nothing but how to win fame as eloquent masters of profane rhetoric. . . .

The body of glorious Saint Isidore has been shown to Father Victoriano, the Minorite, who has come from France to see it. The body was perfect, but they cut off a finger to give to the friar to carry to the Queen of France, who asked for it. . . .

Three young noblemen have been exiled from the Palace for having scaled the walls. . . . It is most scandalous and insufferable that married men should be allowed to go courting ladies publicly, with no better excuse than that such is the custom. . . .

Madame Marie de Rohan, Duchesse de Chevreuse, the celebrated beauty, has arrived. . . . All Madrid turned out to see her. Their Majesties peeped out of

the curtain as the cavalcade passed the *Buen Retiro* . . .
[condensed].

Diego Velásquez is now painting the Duchess's portrait
in her French toilette.

There are records of brawls, intrigues, and of much
else quite unedifying. I need only add that the
reign of Philip IV was the heyday of bullfighting.
It is said that the festivals in honor of the canonization of Saint Ignatius Loyola and of Saint Francis
Xavier were celebrated by *corridas*.

XXXV

VELÁSQUEZ AND CALDERÓN

The whirligig of Time brings its revenges. In Philip's reign Velásquez was proud to be *ayuda de guardaropa* and then *ayuda de cámara;* he also was given a reserved seat at the bullfights and finally had the honor of membership in the Order of Santiago. To-day King, Queen, the Conde-duque, Infantes and Infantas, even Ambrogio Spinola, "famoused for fight," are best remembered, with a rank scarcely higher than the sad-eyed dwarfs or the merry topers, because of his canvas and palette.

Diego Velásquez (1599–1660) was born in Seville. He studied under old Pacheco, the painter and pictorial chronicler, married his master's daughter, and moved to Madrid in hopes of royal patronage. There was some hitch. At Pacheco's suggestion he painted a celebrity, the poet Góngora. In 1623 he painted his first portrait of the King. That was the year that the Prince of Wales and the Duke of Buckingham ("Baby Charles" and "Steenie") came on a wild project of wooing, to be borne in hand by the crafty Conde-duque, gloriously fêted, and sent back empty-handed. In 1628, Peter Paul Rubens, then the most distinguished painter in Europe, came for the second time to Spain. His errand was political: Pacheco says, "He had little to do with painters; he made friends with no one except my son-in-law, with whom he had been in correspondence. He made much account of his work, because of his modesty, and the two went together to see the Escorial." Critics dispute as to whether or not Rubens exercised an influence upon Velásquez's art. Some say Los Borrachos (1629) shows that he did; others say it shows that he did not. At any rate Rubens encouraged Velásquez to go to Italy. Velásquez went in the train of the great Marqués de Spinola. He landed in Genoa and hurried on to Venice, where he studied Titian and Tintoretto, then on to Rome, where he sketched and painted in the gardens of the Villa Medici, and to Naples, where he paid his respects to Ribera. I have no space for his career as court painter or as master of festivities; and of his art it would be impertinent in me to speak. His keen cold eye, untroubled by any disturbing affections, saw an object as light presented it, and his power of expression with brush and pigment have never been surpassed. But was he a great man? In high human qualities, in depth of sentiment, in power of admiration, in passion for spiritual adventure, was he as great as Cervantes, as Ignatius Loyola, or, I will ask, as Ribera?

I now proceed to the second great glory of Philip IV's reign, Calderón de la Barca, whose genius seems to me as unlike that of Velásquez as is possible between two contemporaries of the same nation; for Velásquez professed allegiance to nature, whereas Calderón is of imagination all compact. Pedro Calderón de la Barca (1600–1681) was born in

Madrid. His fame was announced by the unusual circumstance that he wept before he was born, "*Pues ante de abrir (como nuevo sol) las orientales puertas, lloró en el materno seno.*" His ancestors were *antiguos hijosdalgo* and his father *ilustríssimo.* He went to a Jesuit school and then to the university of Salamanca, *madre gloriosíssima de todas las Sciencias, y de los mas vehementes Ingenios que han ilustrado las edades.* He served in the army in Lombardy and Flanders (1625–1628), being present, it is said, at the siege of Breda, on which subject he wrote a play; and again ten years afterward, against the Catalan rebels (1640). He won the King's favor, and received the habit of Santiago (1636) twenty-three years before Velásquez did. In 1651 he became a priest and chaplain to the King. He lived to an honored old age. He is said to have written over a hundred plays, and nearly as many of the religious mysteries known as autos.

Of his character his biographer, Don Juan de Vera Tassis, says:

He was the oracle of the Court, the cynosure of strangers, the father of the Muses, the lynx of learning, the light of the theatre, the admiration of mankind; his virtues were singularly shining; his house was the general shelter of the weak; his common-sense was very wise, his humanity very profound, his modesty very elevated, his courtesy very solicitous, his friendship very trusty and benevolent, his speech very frank and honest, his pen the most well-bred of his age; he never hurt any man's reputation with unkind comment nor spoke ill of backbiters, nor did he give ear to the malice of envy.

Calderón was the prince of Castilian poets.

This is the Spanish equivalent for our English "a jolly good fellow," and such Calderón undoubtedly was.

Calderón wrote all sorts of plays, — historical, tragic, comic, religious, — and in his own day was immensely popular. In the next century forgetfulness drew its curtain over his fame until August Wilhelm von Schlegel and other Germans of the romantic school raised a hue and cry. You will find their eulogies in the textbooks. First let me say, that while translation may, when it is good, convey to foreigners a fair likeness of a drama, it must of necessity destroy such poetry as consists — as most poetry does — in the order of words; therefore translation is disastrous with the dramatists of *el Siglo de Oro*, and with Calderón more than any other, for he was the greatest lyrical poet of them all.

His plays are in verse. Sometimes the verses are in *redondillas*, lines of seven or eight syllables, rhyming, *abba;* or in quintillas, *abbab;* or in the Italian fashions of *ottava rima* and *terza rima*. Usually they are assonants, that is, short tripping verses of eight syllables, where every other line, in complete disregard of what the accompanying consonants may be, secures a certain suggestion of rhyme by a repetition of the same final vowel, or, if the line ends in an unaccented vowel, of the same last two vowels. Such Spanish verse is untranslatable. I have looked at German, French, and English translations, but I do not find any resemblance whatever to Calderón's iridescent verses that wing their fantastic way from conceit to conceit like tropical birds. James Russell Lowell speaks of

Calderón's "Arab soul in Spanish feathers"; and one feels that the same spirit that built the thousand arches in the Mezquita at Cordova inspired Calderón's genius.

Various attempts have been made to translate him into English. Denis Florence MacCarthy's imitative measures are but a sieve, to my mind, though others disagree; the poetry slips through. Such passages as Shelley rendered of *The Mighty Magician* may be finer than the original, but they are different. Edward Fitzgerald, who called Calderón "one of the great men of the world," translated six plays. Four of these, he says in his preface :

may be lookt on as a better kind of what we call melodramas; [and adds] I do not believe an exact translation of this poet can be very successful . . . so much is still bombast to English ears. . . . Conceits that were a fashion of the day; idioms . . . violations of the probable, nay, possible, that shock even healthy romantic license; repetitions of thoughts and images that Calderón used (and smiled at) as so much stage properties — these are insuperable obstacles.

And in his letters he says:

I think you can hardly make Calderón interesting to English readers unless with a large latitude of interpretation (1853). [The difficulty lies in the] forms of verse and thought, irreconcilable with the English language and English ways of thinking.

From the earlier translations he proceeds to what he calls "a great man's masterpiece," *The Mighty Magician*, and *Such Stuff as Dreams are Made of*. But Fitzgerald's verses, though brilliant, are not

translations in any usual acceptance of the word;
they are adaptations.

Shelley began his acquaintance with our poet in
1819:

A kind of Shakespeare is this Calderón. . . . I have
been reading Calderón . . . some of craggy and mountainous magnificence, some clothed with moss and flowers
and radiant with fountains, some barren deserts. . . .
Some of the ideal dramas of Calderón (with which I have
lately and with inexpressible wonder and delight become
acquainted) are perpetually tempting me to throw over
their perfect and glowing forms the grey veil of my own
words. . . . I am bathing myself in the light and odor of
the flowery and starry autos. . . . Plato and Calderón
have been my gods. . . . Some of them [the religious
plays] certainly deserve to be ranked among the grandest
and most perfect productions of the human mind. He ex-
cels all modern dramatists with the exception of Shakespeare, whom he resembles, however, in the depth of
thought and subtlety of imagination of his writings, and
in the one rare power of interweaving delicate and powerful comic traits with the most tragic situations, without
diminishing their interest.

XXXVI

REIGN OF CHARLES II (1665-1700)

Velásquez has handed Philip IV down to posterity as a tragedy, kingly though in ruin. But before I pass on to the unkingly tragedy of his son, Carlos el Hechizado, I will mention two aspects of Philip's character. As a French lady delicately expressed it, "*Ce prince si froid et si sérieux en apparence, que l'on ne voyait jamais rire, était en effet le plus galant et le plus tendre de tous les hommes.*" But the King was ashamed of his loose life, and his most sympathetic trait is his seeking for spiritual absolution. From the time of the disgrace and fall of Olivarez to his own death, Philip corresponded with a cloistered nun, Sor María de Agreda. He asked for counsel and she gave it. The correspondence is pitiful. The poor, ashamed King drops his royal mask, and reveals a passionate desire to do his best for his kingdom, to lead a higher life — and yet he clings to his gross pleasures. In one letter (November 26, 1649), Sor María says: "I beg you, my Lord, to propitiate the Almighty by an amended life. Fix all your inclination and will upon the Queen, [his fourteen-year-old niece, Mariana, married within a week or two] and do not turn your eyes upon outside objects [*otros objetos peregrinos y extraños*, a prudish phrase]. This will please God, and you shall find less blame in His eyes." At other times she comforted him about the affairs of the kingdom, bade him be of good courage; "for this ship of Spain, even if the flood rises to the neck, shall never sink"; advised him what to do and how. He must ask God's help, but not omit human means; he must perform his royal office, govern of his own will, otherwise he shall not save his soul, no matter how pious a believer he may be.

When Philip IV died, poor little Charles was but four years old. Nobody could have been worse equipped for the business of reigning than this puny, feeble, underwitted boy. His life is dreadfully pathetic; he wanders down his allotted years like a harmless patient along the corridor of a lunatic asylum. And after his death, the apparent blessing that he left no child to carry on the degenerate inheritance of the Hapsburg blood brought years of war upon his poor kingdom. His mother Mariana, the little lady painted in monstrous coiffure and *guardainfante* by Velásquez, acted as Regent during his infancy. Madame d'Aulnoy, the French traveler, saw her in 1679: "She is very pale, her face a little long and flat, her eyes gentle, her countenance pleasant, her figure of medium size, her hands little, thin, and white. She is dressed, as are all Spanish widows, in a nun's dress, not a hair visible." But Juan Carreño de Miranda (1614–1685), who succeeded Velásquez as court painter, has left a more vivid portrait. There she sits in her nun's dress, with her dull, sad, ugly Hapsburg face that, though expressionless, could express so well the unpalatableness of life. Good cause she had to look so, with such an uncle-husband and such a son. And to add to her troubles, her bastard stepson, the capable and ambitious Don John of Austria (the Second) headed an opposing political party and disputed the government with her. Don John, you remember, seduced Ribera's daughter. Madame d'Aulnoy describes him as of middle height, well made, with regular features, lively black eyes, a handsome head, good manners, generous and valiant; he spoke five languages, was well read in history, knew how to paint and to play several musical instruments. The French Ambassador, the Marquis de Villars, agrees to this description, but adds a qualifying phrase: "*Tous les dehors du mérite, sans mérite même.*" Don John prevailed (1677). He packed off the Queen's advisers and carried the day in favor of his French candidate for the young King's wife against the Queen's German candidate. Little Marie Louise d'Orléans, the young Queen, could not speak Spanish nor Charles French, but the Marquis of Villars acted as interpreter: "*Il leur fit dire de part et d'autre, ce qu'ils avaient pu penser de plus honnête.*" But Don John did not live to see the wedding; he died in 1679.

Meanwhile the decadence continued faster and faster. Both Spaniards and foreigners have recorded their explanations: war, emigration, monopoly, incompetence of the government, bad roads, no waterways, taxes and tolls at frontiers and bridges, the pride and idleness of the nobles, — for nearly half the people regarded themselves as hidalgos and despised all handicrafts as beneath them, — guilds of artisans aping the upper class, apprentices cramped and kept under, bigotry concerning *limpieza de sangre*, general ignorance, and so on. Fields were left uncultivated, towns were depopulated. Where there had been one thousand inhabitants there were but five hundred; where there had been five hundred there were scarce one hundred. Seville was reduced to a quarter of its population. Not one twentieth of the rural land round about was tilled. Trade dwindled away. Imposts were tripled, but receipts fell to one third. Food was scarce; innumerable families had little but herbs to live on. "*La pobreza era terrible, espantable.*" The royal treasury was empty; soldiers got no pay. Even the King's household went hungry. In Madrid, in 1699, a rabble shouted, "Bread! Bread!" under the King's windows. The birth rate dropped; baptisms fell off one half. Pests swept over great stretches of country.

I will digress here for the sake of quoting some observations on the state of the country by a lively French lady, Madame d'Aulnoy, who was in Spain for several years at this time (1679–1682). Like all travelers, as I have said, she complains of the provincial customhouses and of the octroi on entering the towns. She had been furnished with a passport from the King, but it did not protect her from dues. "What good does it do me then?" she asked; "None." And the inns were always wretched. The stairs were like a bad ladder; the walls were plastered with religious daubs; the beds had no curtains; the coverlets were fairly clean, but the sheets were the size of a napkin, and the napkins that of a handkerchief. There was but one cup in the whole inn, and that was always in the hands of muleteers. There were no chimneys. There was a fire in the middle of the kitchen, with a hole in the roof above, but the smoke prevented you from going near. The people in the kitchen were ragamuffins, and dirty as pigs; a fiddler was always strumming, and someone else singing like a sick cat. The kitchen, in fact, was damnable. The innkeeper provided no food; the traveler was obliged to send out and get it, and then cook it, even at midnight. The cooking was all done with oil; partridges were done to death; the bread lay like lead on one's stomach. However, the wine was fair and the fruit good. At midday her party always preferred to picnic.

As I have mentioned autos several times, — for all the great dramatists wrote hundreds of them to meet the popular demand, — I will give the plot of one that Madame d'Aulnoy saw in Madrid:

Our Lord goes to the Knights of Santiago and asks to be admitted to the Order; they demur to taking in a member whose father is a carpenter and whose mother plies the needle, and refuse. Thereupon the Order of Christ is founded, and everybody is happy.

The city of Madrid was not to her taste. "Strangers come less to Madrid than to any place in the world — and they are right." It was hard to get lodgings; there were but two hotels and both small. The city was wretchedly paved; the streets were all mud and trickling rivulets. It was difficult to drive a carriage; there were plenty of sedan chairs, but only the old or sick ever used them. Besides these ills, some street customs remained the same that they had been in the reign of Charles V: "*Les maisons n'ayant pas de certains endroits commodes, on jette toute la nuit, par les fenêtres, ce que je n'ose vous nommer."* Dead animals were left in the streets.

And the morals of the aristocracy were like the street manners. The great amusement was courting. Young gentlemen of quality, with money, began at twelve or thirteen to keep a mistress for whom they neglected their studies, and took everything in the paternal mansion that they could lay hands on. During their young manhood, they passed the time in pitiable idleness, sauntering on the public promenade, bowing, smirking, and ogling the ladies. They were most self-satisfied, convinced that no class of men in the world were so worthy of admiration as themselves. When a man married, he did not dream of leaving his mistress. The double relation was more than a custom; it was the fashion. The Marquis of Elche used to say that in order to be the happiest of men he needed only a charming wife as well as a charming mistress. The young swells, at sixteen or seventeen, married girls younger than themselves, and either continued a life of debauchery or sat at the corner of the hearth like old men. Some were sent as viceroys or proconsuls to govern provinces that suffered under their ignorance. *"Ces animaux,"* she says, "pillage their subjects and come back very rich. But one thing must be said for Spaniards: they are very sober and drink healths in water."

Lord Bacon remarks: "Let States that aim at greatness take heed how their nobility and gentlemen do multiply too fast . . . if the gentlemen be too many, the commons will be base." This was certainly true of Spain. Madame d'Aulnoy reports:

"Every other person you meet is an hidalgo. Even when you refuse a beggar you must say, '*Caballero, perdone usted, no tengo moneda.*'" And among this multitudinous nobility the code was highly artificial; neglect or breach led to serious consequences:

En ce pays-ci, il est assez ordinaire d'assassiner pour plusieurs sujets; a blow, a slap with a glove, the word *ivrogne* or *certains termes qui intéressent la vertu de son épouse* can be avenged only by assassination. . . . They say, quite rightly, that there is no sense in risking one's life in a duel with unequal skill in weapons, for the injured man might be the one to be killed. . . . When they go about an assassination they carry relics with them and, as an act of charity, order Masses to be said for souls in Purgatory.

I have made this digression into details to help explain the decline and fall of Spain. I now return to general matters on the same subject. The government acted with folly at home and with folly abroad. The colonies were treated outrageously. They were forbidden to manufacture wool or silk, they were forbidden to grow vines or plant olive trees. Their industry was scotched right and left, in the supposed interest of the mother country. In Europe the fatal Hapsburg foreign policy oiled the wheels of political ruin. Louis XIV, bristling with arrogance, kept launching attacks on Flanders, and although most of Europe banded together against him, it was Spain that got the knocks. The French invaded Flanders, Franche Comté, and Catalonia. French fleets, and also English and Dutch pirates, attacked Spanish ships on the high seas and pillaged Spanish colonies everywhere. And the worst of it was that

Europe was already quarreling as to what foreign prince should become King of Spain on Charles's death, and how the Spanish empire should be divided up. The two main claimants were Philip of Anjou, grandson of Louis XIV, and the Archduke Charles, son to the Emperor. The French claim came through an infanta who on marrying the French king had renounced all claims to the throne of Spain, but only upon the condition that her dowry should be paid. The dowry, however, had never been paid. The Archduke's claim seems to have come by the nearer relationship.

Such claims, however, are not settled by Blackstone's table of inheritance, but by the sword.

XXXVII

CERTAIN ASPECTS OF SPANISH CATHOLICISM

THE decline of Spain has been a favorite theme for preaching statesmen and political speculators. The causes usually assigned — exhaustive wars, emigration, false pride, political folly, and economic ignorance, were no doubt factors. But one aspect of this decline, religious superstition, whether it was a cause or an effect, appears so prominently in the daily life of this people, in the monastic establishments, in ecclesiastical art, that I will say something more of it.

King Ferdinand of Aragon was not trammeled by his conscience, but Isabella was very pious. Charles V ended his life as a bigoted adherent of the old order; Philip II squandered and spilt the riches of his empire in the same cause. Philip III is known as *el Piadoso*. Philip IV sought lessons in statecraft from a cloistered nun. These kings represented the national spirit. Columbus was primarily governed by religious ambition. Many of the conquistadores fought their way through Mexico and Peru from a desire to save the souls of the heathen. Loyola spent his genius *ad majorem Dei gloriam*. At home, men most distinguished for intellectual attainments — Cervantes, Lope, Tirso de Molina, Góngora — turned naturally to the outward badges of a higher life, and either took orders or joined a religious confraternity. As for Quevedo, the intellectual, cynical satirist, let me quote. In his *Life of Saint Paul* he relates this: The Sicilians say that, under the influence of Saint Paul's preaching the citizens of Messina sent an embassy to the Virgin Mary and that —

the Mother of God answered them by a letter, which is on file in the archives to-day in these words that are a faithful rendering of the Latin:

THE VIRGIN MARY, DAUGHTER OF JOACHIM, MOTHER OF CHRIST
CRUCIFIED, TO THE PEOPLE OF MESSINA
[I omit the letter]
Dated, Jerusalem, the twelfth year of Our Son: Indiction I., 3.
The Nones of June, twenty-seventh of the month.
(*Signed*) VIRGIN MARY (*who approved from on high*)

Quevedo admits that critics with *palabras rigurosas* pointed out difficulties in the document, but, he says, "I refrain from a critical examination of this ancient relic, and give my attention to admiring the piety that it produces." The matter of historical interest, to me, at least, is not that Quevedo, the most intellectual and inquiring spirit in Spain, believed in this letter, but that he abstained from criticism of it.

In 1622, at the proceedings for the canonization of Saint Ignatius Loyola, hundreds of miracles were adduced, some of which are not edifying. Voltaire is never tired of referring to the lobster that fetched from the bottom of the sea the crook that Saint Francis Xavier had dropped into the water. Credulity was rampant, and credulity was encouraged like a hothouse plant.

I have already spoken of the plot of *El Condenado por desconfiado*, the strange religious play by Tirso de Molina. Nothing could show better how waywardly, according to Protestant thinking, religious doctrine had gone on its own way, regardless of common ethics. A play by Calderón, *La Devoción de la Cruz* (1634), emphasizes this same waywardness. Some people think that it is his most brilliant play. In it the hero, Eusebio, becomes the chief of a robber band and commits "the oldest crimes in the newest kind of ways"; he bursts into a convent to ravish a nun; he murders; he spreads havoc over the countryside. But, owing to a strange circumstance, he has always felt a deep, overpowering reverence for the Holy Cross. Wherever he sees a cross, or the sign of a cross, he unbonnets, falls to his knees, says his prayers, and desists from evil. In the convent cell he spies a cross on the nun's breast, and turns back in horror. In the last act, having been desperately wounded in a fight, he crawls to the foot of a cross and there dies. (Stage direction: "*muere*"). Under ordinary circumstances a sinner who dies unshriven is damned forever; but "after Eusebio had died, Heaven put his soul back into his dead body until he had been shriven." This miraculous act of grace was conferred upon him because of his "*devoción de la Cruz.*" His soul was assoiled and went to Paradise. A Protestant critic has found fault with this plot as "the very sublime of antinomianism"; and it is difficult to see how it can escape such censure.

Evidence of various kinds could be adduced to show that in certain respects Spaniards of this time accepted the dogmas and rites of their Church as means to a higher life or to an escape from punishment hereafter, although the operation of those means might be unintelligible to human reason, or even contrary to the teachings of ethics. Clever observers thought them hypocrites. Guicciardini thought so, you remember. A Spanish gentleman told Madame d'Aulnoy that his fellow countrymen were *"superstitieux, fort catholiques, du moins en apparence."* I do not think them hypocrites; I think that they believed in what they called a spiritual world which overruled the laws of the natural world — including the laws of ethics.

Their superstitions were abominable. Take, for instance, the practices of the flagellants, which were considered both purifying and coquettish. Madame d'Aulnoy says:

The first time I saw them I almost swooned. I was taken quite unawares by this sight that can't but frighten one. Imagine a man coming so near you that he spatters his own blood on you; *c'est là un de leurs tours de galanterie.* There are rules for performing flagellation in the correct way; masters teach the art as they would dancing or fencing. The penitents are oddly dressed. They wear skirts, tall sugarloaf hats, masks, and shirts that leave great patches of the back bare. They scourge the bare spots until the blood runs down in streams. They walk slowly through the streets till they come to the house of the lady whom a penitent wishes to honor, and then he scourges himself while she peeps through a hole and contrives to give him a sign of her gratification.

Worship was largely a matter of penance, of wonder-working rites and words; in other respects it was pagan. Priests blessed the fields, rivers, winds; the disciples of Ignatius Loyola used to pray to the local saint, the pagan *genius loci;* processions carrying holy relics wound along the roads to bring rain, to put out a fire, or to quell a riot. Innumerable masses were said; lamps were kept burning, gifts and offerings made in pathetic prodigality. The days consecrated by the Church to commemoration of the mysteries of the faith were the gayest and rowdiest of the year. The Venetian ambassador said: "The faith of the nobles is pure hypocrisy, that of the common people mere superstition." A French witness reports:

> Nothing is more laughable than to see people at mass, great rosaries hanging down, telling their beads, and all the time paying heed to what may be going on about them, with little thought of God. . . . Any man that blasphemes or speaks disrespectfully of the saints or of the holy mysteries is punished severely, for, as they say, he must be a fool to commit an offense that has no pleasure in it; but such matters as frequenting shameless places, eating meat on Fridays, keeping thirty mistresses always about in public, does not arouse a scruple.

As I say, religion was divorced from commonsense. At a ball in the palace in Philip IV's time, a lady in waiting chatted and danced, and in between told her beads with paternosters and Ave Marias. Saint-Simon tells this anecdote: The Duke of Alva was forsaken by his mistress; he had masses said in order to soften her heart and bring her back. The masses were ineffectual. He then made a vow to lie in his bed on his right side, and never to get up or shift his position till she returned. She never came back, and the Duke lay on his right side in a bed — never made — until he died. No doubt this is a pleasantry; but it is not an exaggeration, as you will see from the following story that Señor Juderias says is taken from a document in the National Library (*Biblioteca Nacional*, G. 61).

Poor Charles II was approaching his end. The English envoy, the Honorable Alexander Stanhope, said that he "looked like a ghost and moved like a clockwork image" (July 9, 1698). The people believed that he was bewitched, and the physicians, unable to benefit him, agreed that "his ailment must certainly be witchcraft" (*do.*, July 15, 1699). The Inquisitor-General Rocaberti took the matter up. He sent instructions to the Cura de Cangas — a priest reputed to be possessed of special gifts in such cases — that he should ask the Devil himself if the ill were witchcraft; he assured the priest that there would be no sin in such dealings with the Devil and that he might go about it "*con toda seguridad de consciencia.*" The priest summoned the Devil. The Devil "made oath by God" that the King had been bewitched, and prescribed exorcisms and olive oil, that the King should masticate slowly and walk much, and that all his food and drink should be blessed. After hearing this the Inquisitor bade the priest bind the Devil "*por medio de estrechos y fuertes conjuros, en nombre de Dios,*" and ask for some other remedy more suitable to the King's corporeal condition, since olive oil was more likely to kill than to cure. The Inquisitor also wished for more light on the prescribed exorcisms: What exorcism is the most appropriate? Where should it be made? At what o'clock? How often? Was it to affect the whole royal body or only a part? If there was really witchcraft, what was the bargain that accompanied it? Is the bargain a continuing one? Who made it? Where? Are the infecting agencies in or out of the palace? How are the infected places to be purified? Is the Queen bewitched, too? And if Lucifer refuses to answer, press him in God's name, since he knows the hurt, to disclose the readiest remedies. . . . In no case must he be allowed to reveal the wrong and hide the remedy. If the Devil put forward excuses, the priest must laugh at them and the priest has him; for the Devil himself admits that God and His Mother are on our side.

The priest persevered, and the Devil finally admitted that the witch was well known, lived on Calle Mayor, was a married woman, had children, and her name was Mary. The Inquisitor wrote back that to look for a "Mary" in the Calle Mayor was like looking for a needle in a haystack. On the other hand the Emperor Leopold, the King's cousin, wrote to his ambassador at Madrid that he had authentic information that the witch's name was Isabella and she lived in Calle de Silva.

Unfortunately the Inquisitor died before the whole process of extracting the truth from the Devil could be completed, and the information as to who had bewitched the King, where, and how, and why, was so multifarious and contradictory and became so involved with the question of royal succession, that the truth never was learned.

This is a sorry picture of a once great nation, but

the Honorable Alexander Stanhope writes (January 6, 1699): "How wretched soever the present state of Spain may seem to others, they are in their own conceit very happy, believing themselves still the greatest nation in the world, and are now as proud and haughty as in the days of Charles the Fifth."

XXXVIII

MURILLO

LET us turn to a pleasanter prospect. Out from this political and moral bog one figure stands forth with a dignity worthy of the great traditions of *el Siglo de Oro*. Murillo was primarily a craftsman; he painted for painting's sake; but he was also profoundly religious, and he strove to express his religious sentiment by means of his art, so far as the naturalism dominant in Spanish painting would permit.

The passionate religion of earlier generations had passed; the yearning of Saint Teresa and Saint John of the Cross, the mad attempts of El Greco to portray such ecstasy as theirs, to compel the pictured image of a house of clay to body forth the thrill of the soul within, were out of date. Like mariners come to port after stormy seas, religious spirits sought rest and peace. They worshiped the God that abides in tranquillity.

As I am hurried, I pass by Zurbarán (1598–1662), another great painter of Seville, who though he painted monks and religious pictures, seems to me a master of light and luminous effects, of bluish whites and yellow ochres, a man primarily interested in his craft and not in things of the spirit. I also pass by Alonso Cano (1601–1667), whose stormy, quarrelsome life adds an interest to his paintings in the choir of the cathedral at Granada, and to his carving of Saint Francis at Seville (for he was as good a sculptor as a painter), I pass by the sculptor Montañés (*d.* 1649), whose picture Velásquez painted, and return to the greatest — Velásquez apart — of the school of Seville.

Murillo (1617–1682) was born in Seville, Andalusia. A German critic says that Murillo is the embodiment of *die andalusische Seele*, but the habit of German critics to give to each painter a cartouche and assign him to his regiment, company, platoon, and so forth, is too methodical for wandering pilgrims. Andalusia is a soft, languid, rich, luxuriant land of sunshine and color; it has been profoundly affected by Moorish blood and Moorish tradition, and Murillo shared in these qualities; but Andalusia is lazy and pleasure-loving; Murillo was hardworking and serious. Andalusia is sensual; Murillo was a man of self-discipline and refinement. Andalusia accepted religion in terms of magic; Murillo believed in spiritual mystery. It is safer to limit this epithet, "Andalusian," to mean that Murillo lived in Seville, was vastly admired by Seville in his lifetime, and has been its pride ever since. Théophile Gautier (1843) says:

Everybody in Seville offers you cigarettes and Murillos. You hear no other name mentioned but his. The humblest householder, the least prosperous abbé, possesses at least three hundred Murillos of the best period. You ask, What is that *croûte?* That is a Murillo in his misty manner. And that? A Murillo in his warm manner. And that over there? A Murillo in his cold manner. Murillo has three styles, so that every kind of picture may be ascribed to

him, and gives a glorious scope to picture-collectors. . . .
This does not prevent Murillo from being one of the best
painters of Spain or of the world.

Murillo's parents were in humble circumstances
and died while he was young. He had a hard time,
and we hear that he was obliged to paint rough
pictures on bits of sacking for indigent customers
at fairs, for priests, or friars, or adventurers off for
America. It chanced that at the age of twenty-four
he saw some copies of Van Dyck that a friend
brought back from Flanders. Convinced by this
new kind of excellence that he must enlarge his
experience, he managed to get to Madrid, where
the great Velásquez received him most kindly,
lodged him in his own house, procured him admission
to the royal galleries, and gave him counsel. After
two years spent in studying — the Italian and
Flemish masters, as well as Velásquez, Ribera, and
others — he returned to Seville, a new painter. His
merits were at once appreciated, and he received
more orders than he could fill. Altogether he painted
a great quantity of pictures. The main collections
are in the Museum and the Hospital de la Caridad
at Seville, and in the Prado at Madrid; but every
famous gallery in the world possesses some examples
of the master.

As Gautier indicated, critics assign to him three
manners: first, the *estilo frio*, where the outlines are
sharp and a little hard, the contrast between light
and shade strongly marked, and the tone cold;
second, the *estilo cálido*, where the painting is softer,
the color more tender and luminous, the flesh tints
like those of princesses in fairy stories, with cheeks

as red as blood and white as milk, and the whole tone warmer, as the name betokens; third, the *estilo vaporoso*, in which the chiaroscuro is more subtle, tints melt into one another, and a transparent misty loveliness covers the canvas. But I shall not attempt to classify or give a chronology, or tell how critics find in one picture the influence of the Venetians, in another of Ribera, in a third of Van Dyck, in a fourth of Velásquez, and so on. The pilgrim must procure such knowledge elsewhere. I shall merely indicate by some quotations, gathered together more or less at random, that the shepherds of pictorial opinion have not yet herded their flock into one fold, so that the Beginner is still at liberty to acknowledge his own likings.

Everybody delights in Murillo's little ragamuffins that munch grapes or melons, and everybody admires his portraits, for they are drawn after life. It is his religious pictures that call out differences of taste:

J. M. Hoppin (1892):

I claim for Murillo that he is a great religious painter. He is absolutely so in respect of religious feeling. He is a true interpreter of divine things. . . . He was a genuinely religious man, with the holy fire of devotion consuming what was base and earthly in him.

F. Madox Brown (1893):

Were there ever two great painters as wanting in the sacred feeling as Velásquez and Murillo?

Juan José Bueno (1863) [condensed]:

God wished to give mankind an understanding of His majesty and tenderness, of the beauty of celestial light, of the happiness of the elect, so He decreed: *Fiat Murillo*.

James Huneker (1910):

False sentiment . . . eye to the appeal popular . . . a magnet for the public. . . . The saccharine Murillo . . . a heavenly saraband among woolly clouds . . . prettiness idealized. . . . To be quite fair, it may be admitted that Murillo could make a good portrait.

George Borrow (1835), on the Guardian Angel in the cathedral of Seville:

Of all the pictures of this extraordinary man, one of the least celebrated is that which has always wrought on me the most profound impression. I allude to the Guardian Angel (*el Angel de la Guardia*), a small picture which stands at the bottom of the church. The angel, holding a flaming sword in his right hand, is conducting the child; this child is, in my opinion, the most wonderful of all the creations of Murillo. The form is that of an infant about five years of age, and the expression of his countenance is quite infantine, but the head is the head of a conqueror, of a God, of the Creator of the universe; and the earthly globe appears to tremble beneath its majesty.

Théophile Gautier (1843), on the Vision of Saint Anthony of Padua, in the same cathedral:

The magic of painting has never been pushed further. The saint is kneeling in ecstasy in the middle of his cell, in which all the little details are rendered with a vigorous realism. . . . The upper part of the picture is bathed in transparent, vaporous light, and occupied by groups of cherubs of an ideal beauty. The Infant Jesus, drawn down by the power of prayer, descends from cloud to cloud on his way to the arms of the Saint, whose head, luminous in the divine radiance, is thrown back in heavenly joy. I rate this picture higher than his Saint Elizabeth of Hungary, higher than all his Virgins and Christ Childs, beautiful as they are. It is necessary to see this Saint Anthony of Padua in order to know the last word concerning Murillo.

Richard Ford (1833):

Never has . . . heavenly beatitude past utterance . . . been more exquisitely portrayed.

Murillo himself judged Saint Thomas of Villanueva Giving Alms to be his best picture; but other pictures hanging very near Saint Thomas in the gallery at Seville are masterpieces also. To my mind the Immaculate Conceptions, of which there are some twenty, are the least interesting.

Murillo is the last great Spanish figure, the last of European stature, for a hundred years in any of the arts. His contemporaries, Valdés Leál and Claudio Coello, are far inferior. Of Valdés Leál (1622–1691), though there are many in Seville, the only interesting painting is in the church of El Carmen, a large canvas with ramping horses, hung so high that you cannot make it out. He is a great colorist, but he is by no means religious. And Claudio Coello (1642–1693), who painted the poor bewitched King, his tragically insipid mother, Queen Mariana, and also his wife, is best remembered for an amazingly clever picture that covers a wall of the sacristy in the Escorial, Santa Forma, the Host. Like Molinos among mystical writers, like Calderón in drama, like Charles II of the House of Hapsburg, Coello in painting marks the end of an era.

XXXIX
THE EIGHTEENTH CENTURY

WHILE poor Charles II, foully bewitched if ever a man was, lay dying, the rival partisans of France and Austria manœuvred and plotted. Where the carcass is, there shall the eagles be also. Stanhope, the English envoy that I have quoted, was there busily intriguing against the French. But finally the King decided in favor of Louis of Anjou, and then died (October, 1700). The French were jubilant; "The Pyrenees have disappeared!" The young King Philip V, only seventeen years old, and his spirited bride, Maria Louisa of Savoy, a girl of thirteen, came down to take possession of their kingdom. But Europe took alarm at this overthrow of the balance of power; Austria decided to fight for her claim, and the War of the Spanish Succession was on.

> Great praise the Duke of Marlborough won,
> And our good Prince Eugene.

And, besides fighting in Flanders, there was fighting in Italy, in Catalonia, on the high seas — all over. After ten or a dozen years of war, peace was made among the various combatants (1711–1715). The Treaties of Utrecht and Rastatt carved up the Spanish empire in Europe; Philip V was acknowledged King, but the crowns of France and Spain

were to be always separate; Gibraltar should belong
to England; Sicily go to Savoy; the other Spanish
possessions in Italy, together with Flanders, Luxembourg, and Sardinia, were handed over to Austria.
Catalonia, which had espoused the Archduke's
cause, was left to its fate.

Past politics are like yesterday's broken meats;
I shall not delay over them. Philip V was addicted
to hunting, always subject to some stronger will,
of little ability, very devout, but in his youth a man
of spirit — on the whole, not a bad fellow. During
the period of his first marriage (1702–1714) old
Louis XIV kept interfering, often to Philip's extreme vexation; a clever French lady married to an
Italian, the Princess Orsini, was sent to see that the
Queen exercised her influence in favor of France.
But Philip's second wife, Isabella Farnese, Princess
of Parma, an energetic, ambitious woman, gave
politics a very different turn. By the first marriage
there was a Prince of Asturias, so her concern was
to find kingdoms or, at worst, dukedoms, for her
two sons. She was ready to turn Europe upside
down if only she could drive the Austrians out of
the Italian provinces that Spain had lost and put
Italian crowns or coronets on the heads of her royal
darlings. In the end she succeeded. Charles, the
elder, became King of the Two Sicilies, and the
younger son, Duke of Parma. But for the rest of
Philip's reign, Spain's foreign policy necessitated
war and did not concern Spain's welfare at all. At
home there was a series of ministers — the Italian
adventurer, Cardinal Alberoni, the Dutch adventurer, Ripperdá, then a Spaniard, José Patiño;

there was a temporary abdication by the disgusted King, who was beset by a sort of religious melancholy; and what not.

Let us turn to other matters.

There is nothing in letters or art of first-class interest in Philip V's reign. In architecture, the only name that travelers know is that of Churriguera (1660?–1725), the great apostle of the baroque. Baroque has a grand manner of its own, and Churriguera had perhaps genius, but the present fashion is not disposed to do justice to either. Carl Justi states that in Germany Churriguera is regarded as "a mystagogue of the delirium of ornament"; but allowance must be made for German taste in phraseology. You will find one of his performances on the highroad of travel at Burgos, the chapel of Saint Tecla, in the cathedral. Worse even than this is the work of a pupil, the "fricassee of marble," as Ford calls it, that adorns *el Trasparente*, a hole cut through the roof at the back of the Capilla Mayor in the cathedral of Toledo; and there is a similar structure at Leon, where (I am quoting Richard Ford) "in both cases marble is tortured into every possible form into which it ought not to be." Beginners must be wary in following studious critics, even the delightful Ford, for their taste is pure and refined, and if we were to follow them blindly, we should hardly glance at *el Obradoiro*, the western façade of the cathedral at Santiago de Compostela (1738), which, though in "the most extravagant baroque style," seems to the Philistine (as I have tried to express) one of the most delightful achievements of exuberant fancy that there is to be seen.

In sculpture the same sort of taste prevailed. In painting, you may remember, if you like, the name of Palomino (1653–1726), partly because he painted a good picture for the cathedral outrageously thrust into the middle of the Mezquita at Cordova, and partly because he wrote lives of the Spanish painters. In Church music, which in earlier days had produced noble pieces for the organ, there was nothing. As to poetry, the *Oxford Book of Spanish Verse* quotes nothing between 1690 and 1750. Padre Feijóo, of whom I shall soon speak, says (1743), "Poetry is in a pitiful condition." According to Emilia Pardo Bazán, "It lay on its deathbed." The drama was no better. The universities were in a degraded condition. Torres Villarroel (1696–1770?), who was a professor at Salamanca at this time, says in his reminiscences:

Spain was a country of the blind; it suffered a darkness so ignominious that there was not a single man in any college or university who was able to light a candle to aid anybody curious about natural science. [And he adds that, when he took his chair at Salamanca he] found in this mother of learning the study of mathematics in an awful state of abasement and neglect, due to the folly of the majority of the students. . . . Some said that mathematics were mere trickery and divination, others that they savored of devils and witches.

As to the course in rhetoric, the professor lost his textbook and then was unable to continue, so the students always spent that hour chatting among themselves. As to the art of medicine, Villarroel says:

In one illness, when I was too sick to resist, they bled
me one hundred and one times. . . . In another, under
the idea that my troubles were hypochondriacal, they first
set themselves to sweep away the peccant humours with
the besom of some good stiff purges, in order to prepare
the way for antihypochondriacal and contrascorbutic
medicines. . . . The first purge was the usual mixture of
rhubarb, gum of the ash, tartar crystals, and chicory
water, a compound known on the comic stage as angelic
water. On top of that followed four hundred *catholic* pills,
and, a few days later, as they still thought that my stomach
had not got rid of its misdemeanors, they gave me *escro-
dero* water, whose efficacy or deviltry is of such double
effect that the doctors call it ambidexter. From this I
suffered agony. . . . To sum up: in twenty days I
swallowed thirty-seven purges. . . .

Altogether, Spain was very ill.

Philip had come from the civilized city of Paris,
and as soon as the war was over, vigorous French
influences made themselves felt. In 1711 a Royal
Academy was founded in Madrid, others in Barcelona and elsewhere; in 1738 an Academy of History
at Madrid; a little later, after the fashion of the
Hotel de Rambouillet, an *Academia de Buen Gusto;*
in 1757 the Academy of Fine Arts of San Fernando;
and so on. Literature, so far as it existed, accepted
French ideas of good taste and imitated French
models. Of such men of letters Don Ignacio de
Luzán (1702–1754) is the best exemplar. As a young
man he sojourned abroad for a long time, partly in
Naples, partly in Paris, where he was secretary to
the Spanish embassy. He acquired foreign languages
and a cosmopolitan point of view. He wrote an

Ars Poetica (1737) in which, after stating that his object is "to put Spanish poetry under the rules that obtain among cultured nations," he sets forth rules which he took from Boileau, as well as from Italian sources. These ideas go back, in great part, to Horace and Aristotle. Luzán stands out as the champion of the pseudo-classical ideas fashionable in France — ideas of reason, common-sense, and academic taste.

Luzán, of course, regarded himself as a reformer. There was a far more important reformer, Padre Feijóo (1675–1764), a Benedictine monk who occupied a chair in theology in the University of Oviedo. When George Borrow went to Oviedo his cicerone said, "You have doubtless heard of Feijóo, the philosophic monk, whose writings have so much tended to remove the popular fallacies and superstitions so long cherished in Spain," and showed him Father Feijóo's portrait. "The countenance was large and massive but fine, the eyebrows knit, the eyes sharp and penetrating, nose aquiline." Father Feijóo set himself to perform single-handed, in an orthodox fashion, the work done by the encyclopædists in France. He wrote hundreds of little instructive essays, published as the *Teatro Crítico* (1726–1739) and *Cartas Eruditas* (1742–1760), which deal with a great variety of subjects, for example, *Vox Populi*, *Virtue and Vice*, *On Medicine*, *On Almanacks*, *On Eclipses*, *On Comets*, and so forth. I have dipped into a number of them, and perhaps the Beginner will take it from me that, though the erudition is almost entirely from classical sources and of scant value to-day, there is so much common sense and kindness that one thinks of *Poor Richard's Almanack*. Father Feijóo called himself a "free citizen in the Republic of Letters," and he deserved well of his country.

Another torch-bearer who carried on the work of reform is Francisco de Isla, S.J. (1703–1781). He wrote a book that was very famous in its day, *Fray Gerundio*, of which there is a very fair English translation (1772). It is a burlesque novel written, with touches of the picaresque manner, to make fun of fashionable preachers who larded their discourse, like Osric in *Hamlet*, with exaggerated affectations. Perhaps you will recollect the kind of sermons preached before the Conde-duque Olivares in his retreat, while the French were threatening the border. The book is long since out of mode, but it is a monument, so we salute it as we pass. Padre Isla's patriotism, however, carried him in another instance too far. He maintained that Le Sage had merely translated a Spanish original into French when he wrote *Gil Blas*, and he did what he called "restoring" it to its native Castilian. His confident assertions, though he had nothing but a wayward remark by Voltaire and the brilliant accuracy of Le Sage's descriptions to go upon, misled many people, and even put disinterested scholars to some trouble before the Frenchman was allowed to enjoy his own in peace.

Spaniards are usually inclined to resent any theory that attributes a national reawakening to French influences; but I think that we must ascribe this reforming spirit in Luzán, Feijóo, and Isla to the coming of the Bourbons.

Ferdinand VI (*r.* 1746–1759) succeeded his father, but there is nothing in his reign worth recording, so I pass on. Ferdinand was succeeded by his half-brother Charles III (*r.* 1759–1788), son to the ambitious and successful Isabella Farnese. Goya's portrait shows a clear-eyed, intelligent, alert-minded, abstemious man, got up in hunting-dress, rather in the style of Frederick the Great. With Charles we feel that a door has been opened, and the fresh intellectual wind sweeping over Europe blows in. He was what is usually called an enlightened prince. He accepted much that the French encyclopædists taught, entertained liberal ideas, and was acutely conscious of a duty toward his kingdom. His foreign policy, perhaps, was not wise, but it was natural. England's behavior had become intolerable; although she was fighting France for dominion in North America and India, she maintained her hectoring attitude toward Spain. She hampered Spanish trade; she crowded Spanish fishermen off the Banks of Newfoundland; she squatted on Spanish land in Honduras, and so forth. Sooner or later Spain must fight, and it was far more sensible not to fight single-handed. Charles made the "family agreement" with France (1761), by which the Bourbons bound themselves, as we say, to stick together, with the inevitable consequence that Spain and England fell to fighting. Matters turned out badly for the Allies; France lost Canada and Spain lost Florida. Again, when the American Colonies declared their independence, it became obvious that France's intervention was merely a question of time, and that her intervention would drag in Spain, too. The United

States, however, thought these nations were slow to act, and proposed to send Benjamin Franklin to Spain to ask for help, but Franklin was diverted to France and Arthur Lee took his place. By the treaty of peace, Spain recovered Florida.

It is in civil affairs that Charles III won his great renown. He employed high-minded ministers, Aranda, Floridablanca, Campomanes, and others. Madrid was made a much cleaner and more inhabitable city; highroads were improved; restraints upon trade were removed; education was fostered; piracy from Algiers was stopped. Perhaps the best-known act of reform, if it may be considered such, is the expulsion of the Jesuits (1767). Their Society, founded by Ignatius Loyola at Rome in 1540, had long been a mighty power in Europe; before the middle of the eighteenth century, however, envy and opposing interests raised up many enemies against them. The universities were jealous of their colleges, and partisans of liberal thought looked upon them as champions of darkness. It seems certain that success had made them arrogant; and arrogance, or zeal for what they held to be right, brought them into conflict with other orders and with the secular clergy. Detractors said that they justified the killing of kings who resisted their domination. France and Portugal had already expelled the order from those countries. Finally the Jesuits were accused of fomenting riots in Madrid. The King's ministers marshaled the counts against them: teachings contrary to royal ordinance and to canon law; a spirit of fanaticism and sedition; intrigue in politics; covert dealings with the King's enemies; overweening power in the colonies; plans to monopolize trade in America; pride; the doctrine of tyrannicide; and so forth. So the Jesuits were expelled from all their houses and colleges in Spain, some 2746 persons, put on board ship and sent to Italy. But the enemies of the order were not satisfied even then; and Pope Clement XIV, under pressure, dissolved the Society in 1773.

As to Charles III, I will quote from a funeral panegyric delivered by Don Gaspar Melchor de Jovellanos, of whom I shall speak hereafter, delivered before the Royal Society of Madrid on November 8, in 1788:

An enumeration of the policies put into operation, by which this beneficent Sovereign won our love and gratitude, have been the object of discourses more eloquent than mine. My present purpose barely permits me to recall them: foundation of new agricultural colonies; partition of common lands; diminution of the privileges of sheep-raisers; abolition of the tax on grain, and free interchange, by which agriculture has benefited; encouragement of industrial education; reform of trade guilds; multiplication of factories; a generous bestowal of franchises upon the arts that improve industry; breaking old shackles of international trade; opening of new markets abroad; peace in the Mediterranean; periodical posts and free communication with our colonies over the seas to the advantage of commerce.

And this eulogy was well deserved.

XL

THE NAPOLEONIC ERA

THE reign of the enlightened Charles III is like the lull before the storm, although this appearance of tranquillity is chiefly the effect of contrast, for Spain was at war with England nearly all the time. In Madrid, too, there were riots because the prime minister, the Marqués de Squillace, undertook, for the purpose of making murder and dueling more difficult, to forbid cloaks that muffled up the chin and hats that could be drawn down over the brows. But the general impression is one of calm.

In 1788, the year preceding the French Revolution, Charles III died and his son Charles IV succeeded to the crown. Of all Spanish kings from Philip IV until to-day, those that have visited the Prado know Charles IV (r. 1788–1808) the best. Philip IV, sensual, weak, distrustful, sad, is always kingly; but Charles IV is, both body and soul, a clodhopper yokel. Goya did for his sovereign what Velásquez had done for his. The envious Casca could not have dealt a worse stroke. The dull-witted, gross, self-complacent, slow, ponderous fool stands in the pillory of the painter's canvases. Alone, on foot or on horseback, or with his family, the miserable monarch renders the account that he will render on the Day of Judgment. The only good thing I have heard of Charles IV is that he was fond of music. That most delightful lady, Madame de la Tour du Pin, says that he liked to play, or rather to believe that he took part in a quartette, whereas in reality an attendant musician performed the part, "*en donnant au roi l'illusion que c'était lui qui jouait.*"

Contemptible though he was, it is doubtful if he deserved such a wife as Maria Luisa of Parma. There she stands in Goya's terrible portraits, cruel, rapacious, sly, sensual, like an ill-omened bird of the night. Separate and apart in their several frames, King and Queen are repulsive enough, but Goya was not satisfied with that. They deserved their fate. He has put the whole family in one great canvas (1799). The Queen, almost a creature of dignity, so wicked does she look, dominates the room and gathers her brood, like a hen vulture, under her wings. The King stands near, decked out with decorations, like a clotheshorse. The seemingly innocent young people shock you by their callous indifference to being near their monstrous mother. But it is youth, not innocence, that drapes them in decent looks. If you are curious to see what they will become, look at the face of the old beldame who peeps out at the left of the picture. The Crown Prince, Don Fernando, stands to your left. You will see in the portrait of him as King Ferdinand VII (1814) that, though more intelligent, he is as fatuous as his father and as wicked as his mother. History says of them what Goya does. In these Bourbons humanity sounds its lowest notes. Let us leave them hanging in ignominy on the walls of the Prado, and glance at politics.

The times were unsuited to mediocre capacities.

CHARLES IV, HIS WIFE AND YOUNGER SON

(The Infante Ferdinand and the old aunt are omitted)

The French Revolution shook all the thrones in Europe, and young Napoleon was profiting by the commotion. The Spanish ministers of state were quite unequal to their tasks. You will see by Goya's picture (1783) that Floridablanca is an upright, reforming, intelligent man, wholly incapable of sailing the ship of state in a hurricane. He had been bred under the old régime; of course he failed. Count Aranda, who had known Voltaire in Paris and had been a guest in Madame du Deffand's salon, who had patronized Moratín and the wits of Madrid, tried his hand. But the Queen had a lover, Manuel Godoy, a clever, self-seeking, climbing guardsman, and she put him at the helm. Goya has portrayed his sleek good looks of self-satisfied, self-indulgent, gross comeliness (1800). Lady Holland, wife of the English Ambassador, writes in her *Journal* (1803), "Godoy is a large, coarse, ruddy-complexioned man with a heavy, sleepy, voluptuous eye." Richard Ford calls him "a thing of avarice" and likens him to "a foul beast of prey, always craving and swallowing." But it would not be fair to leave his reputation at that, for I believe that he was a much better sort of person than Queen, King, or Prince. Lord Holland wrote after Godoy's fall:

His manner, though somewhat indolent, or as the French term it, nonchalant, was graceful and engaging. In spite of his education, which I presume was provincial and not of the best, his language appeared to me elegant, and equally exempt from vulgarity and affectation. Indeed his whole demeanor announced, more than that of any untraveled Spaniard I ever met with, a mixture of dignity and politeness, of propriety and ease. . . . He seemed born for a high station — without effort he would have passed in any mixed society for the first man in it.

While Godoy was in office, as the Court, the Church and the conservative classes were in strong sympathy with Louis XVI, Spain joined the coalition against France (1793–1795); but the revolutionary armies were too strong and Spain was obliged to accept disadvantageous terms. Nevertheless, the country was thankful for a respite, and Don Manuel Godoy received his sobriquet, "the Prince of peace." The respite was short. The boisterous current of politics swirled and eddied, and Spain soon found herself in alliance with France and at war with England. From then on the country was dragged this way and that by Napoleon's ambitions. On October 21, 1805, the battle of Trafalgar was fought. Admiral Villeneuve was Commander-in-Chief of the allied fleet. Gravina was the Spanish admiral. It is said that Napoleon obliged Villeneuve to fight although "half the Spanish fleet was manned by landsmen and soldiers." Nelson watched their ships come out. "They show a bold face," he said, "but I'll give them such a dressing as they never had before." Of fifteen Spanish ships of the line three were sunk, three captured, four dashed to pieces on the rocks, and the others disabled. Gravina and his comrades, Churruca and Galiano, died as gallantly as Nelson himself. Godoy says of Gravina, "No sailor ever gave better proof of presence of mind than Gravina, nor of steadfastness in danger, no one knew better how to command, or what to do, or how to dominate evil fortune." *La destrucción, aunque gloriosa, de la armada española* was complete, and the lordship of the seas

passed beyond dispute to Britannia. The novelist
Galdós in one of his *Episodios nacionales* adopts the
Spanish opinion of the battle and lays all the blame
on Villeneuve.

One consequence of the defeat was that Godoy's
enemies, the anti-French party, rallied round the
Infante Ferdinand, who posed as favoring England.
Godoy, not to be outdone, veered toward England.
But Napoleon won the battle of Jena. Ferdinand
veered back toward France; Godoy also veered back.
Then Napoleon decided to take the affairs of the
Peninsula into his own hands. He needed a screen.
He stated that Portugal must not be allowed to
harbor English ships and upon this excuse sent a
French army across the Alps. This step created great
apprehension in Spain; intrigues at court burned
fiercely. The Infante Ferdinand and Godoy struggled
for mastery. The Infante was accused of plotting
against the King. He was arrested. It is said that he
confessed and denounced his accomplices (1807).
More French troops came. The royal family of Portugal sailed for Brazil; and Charles IV, taking fright,
also thought of embarking for America. There was
the devil to pay. The people in and about Madrid
sided with Don Fernando. They laid hold of Godoy,
whose life seemed in danger. The King, who shared
his wife's partiality for Godoy, at his wit's end, abdi-
cated (March 19, 1808), and it was arranged that
Ferdinand should ascend the throne.

They all reckoned without their host. Maréchal
Murat entered Madrid. There was much false deal-
ing. It all ended as in Æsop's quarrel over the oyster.
Napoleon lured King, Queen, Ferdinand, and Godoy

to Bayonne in France. The King and Queen arrived first. Madame de la Tour du Pin saw them there:

L'infortuné roi n'avait pas eu l'air un seul instant de comprendre la tristesse de sa position. Son attitude manquait complètement de dignité et de gravité. . . . The queen, *son horrible femme,* had come away unprovided for, and borrowed gowns from the Empress Josephine. She was troubled by the non-arrival of Doña Josefa Tudo, mistress of the "Prince of peace," Manuelito, as the King called him, but she was glad that her two sons, Don Fernando and Don Carlos, were prisoners, for she said that no evil could ever befall them as great as they deserved, that both were monsters and the cause of all her misfortunes. . . . *Le pauvre bonhomme de roi* tried to shut her up. [Madame de la Tour du Pin also says] Godoy came. He passed rudely by us, without any salutation, and we all agreed that neither his face nor figure justified the scandalous gossip about him and the Queen.

Napoleon divided the shells between the others and ate the oyster. He obliged Don Fernando to renounce all his claims whether as King or Prince, and Charles IV to abdicate in favor of some king of Napoleon's choosing (May, 1808). Father and son were liberally pensioned. Madame de la Tour du Pin adds: "*Cela lui* [*à Napoleon*] *donnait bien d'embarras, comme je l'avais lu écrit de sa propre main.*"

Meanwhile orders had been given Murat at Madrid to send on the King's grandson, Don Francisco, a child of thirteen. Murat prepared to do so. It was the second of May. The carriage was ready, but before the boy was put in the people of Madrid cut the traces. The French soldiers fired on them, and a street battle began. The heat of the fighting at first was in the Puerta del Sol, a square in the centre of the town, then shifted to the artillery park where the two patriot leaders, Captain Luis Daoiz and Captain Pedro Velarde, were killed. A great statue in the Plaza de la Lealtad records their heroism. The French troops, of course, put down the mob. What happened then you can see in Goya's terrific picture, *Los Dos de Mayo*, civilians lined against a wall, a French firing squad, and so forth. That day is for Spain what the Fourth of July is for us. Uprisings against the French took place throughout the country. Spanish poets and painters are never tired of celebrating it. Gautier remarks, "*Le Dos de Mayo est un épisode héroïque et glorieux, dont les espagnols abusent légèrement.*"

Napoleon seated his brother Joseph on the throne. The Spaniards, beaten in pitched battles, scattered and betook themselves to guerrilla warfare. According to the English accounts, the Spanish officers of the regular army were incompetent, and the Spanish soldiers not pertinacious in fight. But there can be no doubt of the valiant defense of Saragossa (1808, 1809), where the citizens under General Palafox underwent two sieges which native writers compare to the defense of Saguntum against Hannibal or of Numantia against Scipio. Marshall Lannes said: "Women allow themselves to be killed in front of every breach; every house requires a separate assault."

The English expeditionary force under Sir John Moore was unsuccessful; whether by his fault or no, was a great controversy; he is now regarded in England as a hero. Sir Walter Scott blamed him, but if he was at fault, his gallant death atoned for it. At Corunna, where he was killed (1809), he lies "alone with his glory" in a little garden, solemn and beautiful, at the edge of the old town, on a height overlooking the sea. Sir Arthur Wellesley had a very different fate. In speaking of him his English contemporaries borrow some typically Castilian phraseology: "The very personification of eagle-eyed power, iron in mind and frame, of lightning decision." "His splendor appeared as a flaming beacon to warring nations." Certainly Wellesley proceeded from victory to victory. First at Talavera in Estremadura, where, he reports, "whole corps of the Spanish allies threw away their arms and ran off in my presence . . . frightened, I believe, by their own fire"; at Bussaco; at Torres Vedras (1810). Ciudad Rodrigo was captured in 1812, Badajoz also, where the English behaved very much as the Germans did in Belgium, — "sad events, deplorable but unavoidable," — Salamanca, Madrid, Vittoria (1813); and the French were wholly driven out. King Joseph himself fled by the pass of Roncevaux.

Meanwhile a collection of liberal-minded citizens assembled at Cadiz as the national Cortes (1810–1812), declared the rights of man, and enacted a constitution that — on paper — limited the royal power very greatly, granted manhood suffrage, imposed universal taxation, set up a single Chamber, abolished the Inquisition, and so forth, according to the more advanced ideas of that time. These liberal illusions did not last long. On Napoleon's fall, Ferdinand VII was restored to the throne (1814). Few kings have been worse; and yet he was very popular with the uneducated masses. Historians who write about him ransack the dictionary for opprobrious adjectives: incapable, narrow, brutish, bigoted, rancorous, cruel, disloyal, ungrateful, false. He swept the reformers and their constitution aside, recalled the Jesuits, reëstablished the Inquisition, imprisoned various leaders and frightened others into exile — in short, he restored the old régime in all its glory.

But liberal-minded officers controlled the army and would not endure so much. Under their leadership the army mutinied and demanded a liberal constitution. The King yielded. "Let us," he said, "advance frankly, myself leading the way, along the constitutional path"; and he convoked the Cortes (1820). But the mass of the people did not keep pace with these advanced ideas. They upheld the King; and the Holy Alliance of the Emperors of Russia and Austria and the King of Prussia took fright lest a liberal régime in Spain might tell against absolutism elsewhere. A French army crossed the border and reëstablished the old order (1823). The reaction was cruel; it is said, evidently with gross exaggeration, that forty thousand constitutionalists were put into prison. The consequence was a division into two parties, one headed by Don Carlos, the King's brother, a most bigoted zealot for absolute prerogatives, and the other by the Queen María Cristina, a Neapolitan princess, who became liberal-minded by the mere fact of opposition to Don Carlos. The cause of opposition was this: the Queen's two children were girls, and if the Salic law prevailed, Don Carlos would succeed to his brother's crown. In old times a woman was eligible, but Philip V, in order to prevent the union of the crowns of France and Spain, had introduced the Salic law. Charles IV had, however, repealed this law, but privily; now, under the Queen's influence, Ferdinand VII published the repeal and confirmed it. This was the issue that gave rise to the Carlist war upon the King's death (1833).

Ferdinand's reign, however pitiful at home, is marked by still greater calamities abroad. All the Spanish colonies on the mainland of America were lost. Florida was of necessity sold to the United States; Chile, Colombia, Peru, Mexico, which had long suffered under the incompetence and tyranny of the Spanish government, took advantage of Spain's distracted condition to declare their independence. Canning, then Prime Minister of England, supported them, and President Monroe proclaimed what became the Monroe Doctrine. And so the Spanish empire on the mainland of American came to its end.

XLI

THE ROMANTIC MOVEMENT

To the literary reader the phrase "the Romantic Movement" brings up recollections or hearsay of Götz von Berlichingen, stamping his steel-shod boots in reverberating halls; of young Werther killing himself for love; of Ivanhoe unhorsing Brian de Bois Guilbert; of Hernani winding his horn; of Giaours and Zuleikas; of colossal sentiments, of yearnings for death; of color, heat, passion, extravagance; of cathedrals, and mediæval armor. And a hodgepodge of all this, but in the vigor and freshness as of a world new born, swept over Spanish poets toward the end of Ferdinand's reign. Young men, who in the fervor of patriotism had plunged into liberal politics, and had been obliged to save their lives by flight, during their exile in Paris drank deep of literary enthusiasms. On Ferdinand's death they came back, and wrote plays and poems in high romantic vein.

The school had its chiefs, also its precursors; but first I will go back to Charles III's reign, in order to indicate the background against which this romantic passion sticks fiery forth. In art the great Tiepolo (1695–1770), having covered the ceilings of all the palaces in the Veneto with angels and other celestial beings, soaring, swimming, or diving through clouds and azure sky, came to exercise his marvelous ingenuity in palaces in Spain. Another foreigner, Raphael Mengs (1728–1779), whose academic correctness has become sadly insipid to modern eyes, painted Spanish royalty, occupied a commanding position as arbiter on all matters of pictorial taste, and taught pupils — among others, Goya's brother-in-law, Francisco Bayeu (1734–1797). Then came Goya (1746–1828), as revolutionary in his way as the most romantic playwrights.

In literature, Moratín the Elder (1737–1780) lectured at Madrid in support of Luzán's poetical theories, presided over a salon of *buen gusto*, where conversation was confined "to the theatre, bullfights, love, and poesy," and wrote plays impossible to act, and a poem, *Fiesta de Toros en Madrid*, which finds a place in every anthology. His son, Leandro Fernández de Moratín (1760–1828), wrote a play that ranks as a classic, *El Sí de las Niñas* (The Maiden's Yes). The point or moral of the play is that a girl should be consulted in the choice of a husband. The Beginner will surely read this. I should not compare Leandro Moratín to Goldoni or to Oliver Goldsmith; he is less gay and debonair than the first, less witty, less human than the latter; but his name may go in the same category. A much livelier playwright, Ramón de la Cruz (1731–1794), wrote innumerable little plays, without a plot or nearly so but humorous and realistic, the delight of his middle-class audience, somewhat on the order of Harrigan and Hart's plays of forty years ago. All this, you see, partakes of that eighteenth-century calm which I called, with reference to politics, the lull before the storm. Then came first the muttering and afterward the thunder of the French

Revolution. So I proceed to the forerunners of the romantic movement, who point the way and anticipate several characteristically romantic traits. This was natural enough, for Spanish literature from the first had had a romantic cast; see their ballads, their rogue-stories, Calderón's plays, Quevedo's *Sueños*, and so forth.

Of these forerunners José Cadalso is the first. This gallant soldier and man of letters was killed in 1782, at about the age of forty, in one of the vain attempts to dispossess the English of Gibraltar. Cadalso had been in love with a beautiful actress, and on her death he was so beside himself with grief that he went by night to her grave and tried to dig up her body. His poem, for so I should call it, though it is a dialogue in prose, *Noches Lúgubres*, is based upon this experience. It is very gruesome and presents the melodramatic extravagancies of the romantic manner. Cadalso lived in the reign of the enlightened Charles.

The next forerunner is a man of far greater historical consequence. Gaspar Melchor de Jovellanos (1744–1811), although a man of letters, was primarily interested in public affairs; he rose to hold high office, wrote grave treatises on economic questions, and, being a reformer, drew down on himself the dislike of the royal favorite Godoy. You can easily see a photograph of Goya's portrait of him (1798), seated in a thoughtful attitude, his cheek resting on his hand, the figure of intelligent and perplexed patriotism. Jovellanos was interested in art, corresponded with Bayeu, the painter, with Ceán Bermúdez, the chronicler of Spanish artists, and so on. But his claim to notice here rests mainly on his poem that describes a deserted monstery, *Descripción del Paular*, in which he sounds the familiar death-desiring note of romantic melancholy:

Busco paz y reposo, pero en vano
los busco

A third forerunner is Juan Meléndez Valdés (1754–1811). He, too, sounds a note that reminds one of Alfred de Musset: *Huyendo de todos, sin destino, perdido, extraviado.* Azorín says: "*Cadalso, Meléndez, Jovellanos: románticos, descabellados románticos, desapoderados románticos; románticos antes, mucho antes del estreno de Hernani en Paris.*" But these men of Charles IV's time, as I say, speak but the prologue. We reach the culmination of the movement when exiles returning from Paris to Madrid on the death of Ferdinand VII, like bees laden with pollen and nectar, people the theatres of Madrid with Hugoesque dramatis personæ.

Martínez de la Rosa (1787–1862), after living in Paris with other Spanish liberals from 1823 to 1833, where he came under the spell of Chateaubriand, Victor Hugo, and their ardent co-workers and disciples, returned to Madrid with the manuscript of *La Conjuración de Venecia* in his pocket. This play is full of tragedy, comedy, local color, and love, and was, I believe, the first of its kind to be acted.

His successor Ángel Saavedra, afterward Duque de Rivas (1791–1865), is the real protagonist of the romantic movement. Saavedra was a man of somewhat the same type as Martínez de la Rosa, but of a much more solid and imposing reputation. His position in Spain is comparable to that of Alessandro

Manzoni in Italy; he was the foremost man of letters
of the time in the country, a patriot, radical in youth,
and in his dignified old age a pillar of conservatism.
Saavedra was the son of a grandee, and at the age of
six months received the cross of *Caballero de Justicia*
of the Order of Malta. In early days he painted,
wrote poetry, fought against the French, and at
thirty was exiled for his liberal opinions. In London
he read Byron; in Paris he was borne aloft by the
romantic gale, and wrote *Don Álvaro o la fuerza del
sino* (*Don Álvaro, or The Power of Destiny*). He too
took advantage of the amnesty proclaimed on Ferdinand's death; for, as I have explained, the Queen
Regent was obliged to solicit liberal support in order
to combat Don Carlos and the Salic law. His play
may be regarded as a sort of bill-of-rights of the romantic school. The Beginner must read it. It was
acted at the Teatro del Príncipe in Madrid (March
22, 1835), barely a year later than *La Conjuración
de Venecia*. The scene opens in Seville; various persons are sitting about — a *canónigo*, an officer, a
majo, a gypsy girl, and peasants. You pick up from
their conversation that Don Álvaro, a mysterious
gallant, famous for his courage in duels and bullfights, has recently come from America, very rich,
and that he is in love with the daughter of a poor
nobleman so proud of his lineage that he has rejected
Don Álvaro's suit. The hero soon comes in, booted
and spurred, with great white sombrero and silk
cloak, looking about him *con dignidad y melancolía*.
There are five acts of prose and verse, with much
declamation. The hero — without his fault — kills
his ladylove's father and two brothers, causes her

death, and finally leaps over a precipice. But the public was not prepared for so revolutionary a performance, or perhaps the play was not very well acted, and it did not attain its acknowledged rank till much later. After Saavedra had become the Duque de Rivas he occupied a very distinguished position, both social and literary. Academician, ambassador, and minister, he acted as master of ceremonies in all academic functions, the undisputed figurehead of Spanish literature.

Our conventional notion of a romantic poet, however, is far better represented by José de Espronceda (1808–1842), who has been authoritatively stated to be the *verdadera encarnación del romanticismo*, the Byron of Spain. Espronceda was born a few weeks before *los Dos de Mayo*, and the ensuing events seemed to have rocked his cradle. When scarcely fifteen his school-days were interrupted. That was the time when the Holy Alliance sent the Duke of Angoulême and one hundred thousand French soldiers to put down the liberal discontent. Ferdinand VII became absolute once more, and young Pepe Espronceda gave himself to poetry and revolutionary plots. For a time he was shut up in a monastery away from Madrid. Released, he went back to school for a couple more years, grew restive, escaped to Lisbon, and there, aged eighteen, fell in love with a Spanish girl, Teresa Mancha, *soberanamente hermosa*. The girl's father, also an exile, wandered on to London. Espronceda followed. He studied Byron and Shakespeare and taught fencing. Teresa married a rich Spanish merchant; nevertheless, romantic love triumphed. She abandoned husband and baby and went off with Espronceda. Legend, however, has been busy with the poet's career, and the story of his youth is uncertain.

It is said that he fought at the barricades in Paris in 1830; that he attempted to return with other emigrants to Spain, but was driven back by Ferdinand's troops; that he enlisted in an expedition to liberate Poland; at any rate, on Ferdinand's death he also took advantage of the amnesty and went home to Spain, taking Teresa with him. He was enrolled in the guards, expelled, banished from Madrid, back again and so on, with his *mirada de águila, amarga sonrisa, cabeza digna del cincel de Fidias* and his *manos finas, nerviosas y bien cuidadas,* journalist, poet, orator, radical politician, and what not, with further imprisonment and exile, and *da capo.* By this time his love for Teresa had become cool: there was jealousy, neglect, discord. In 1839 she died. The next year he composed a great part of *El Diablo Mundo,* in which he dedicates to her memory what are said to be the finest pages he ever wrote. After this there were other women, more poetry, and more politics. He was elected deputy and took his duties seriously; but death cut short his career at the age of thirty-four. Espronceda wrote all sorts of things — plays, an epic, a novel, poetry of one kind and another. He was an improvising, imitative poet, and critics discover the influences of Byron, Victor Hugo, Lamartine, and others. It is obvious that he had Goethe's *Faust* and Byron's *Don Juan* in his mind when he wrote *El Diablo Mundo,* which is an extraordinary work, a medley of satire, philosophy, comedy, sentiment, and vagaries.

¡Todo es mentira y vanidad, locura! The accomplished and cultivated Juan Valera rates it very high.

I now come to the fourth representative of the school. On the afternoon of February 15, 1837, all Madrid that cared for literature attended the funeral of Mariano José de Larra, an eminent man of letters who had committed suicide. Addresses were made at the grave. Pushed forward by his friends, a pale, slender young man, with a bushy head of hair and expressive eyes, stepped out and read a poem in honor of the dead. I quote some critic: "As one luminary of literature sank to its setting, another arose." This rising luminary was José Zorrilla (1817–1893) of Valladolid. You will see his statue in the park as you drive from the station. Zorrilla's father, *furibondo absolutista*, had destined his son for the law, but the young man slipped away, caught a mule in the pasture, galloped bareback to Valladolid, sold the mule, fled to Madrid, and plunged into liberal politics. He drew to himself the attention of the authorities, but escaped from an attic window, disguised in gypsy dress, just as a policeman entered the front door. He went back to Madrid in time for Larra's funeral. He was so poor that his clothes were too shabby for the occasion. One friend lent him pantaloons, another a jacket, a third a poet's cravat, a fourth a sombrero, a fifth (he says, "I don't remember who") a pair of boots.

Zorrilla had already flung himself into the romantic movement. He had read all of its literature that he could lay hands on, in English, French, and Spanish, and now that he had the public ear he recounted in verse old legends of Spanish history, filling volumes with patriotic declamation. He himself says: "An ignorant child of Nature, I sang of my country as best I could, as birds sing in the woods, as bees hum at work over their honey." He has been compared to Lope de Vega for fertility, a *nuevo monstruo de la naturaleza épico-lírica*. He wrote many short poems too, and plays. Of the latter *Don Juan Tenorio*, our old friend in a new dress, — acted in 1844, — is the most celebrated. Altogether his poetry fills four large volumes, in double column, of five hundred pages each.

In 1855 he went to America, full of *pesares y desaventuras*, — caused, it seems, by poverty and love, — hoping that yellow fever would end them. He was away eleven years. On his return (I am quoting his words), he was welcomed like a Roman conqueror. Barcelona, Saragossa, Burgos, carpeted his path with flowers; Valladolid greeted him like the returned prodigal; Valencia, comparable to a foolish girl in love with an old man, adopted him as a son. At Granada there were revels, sweetmeats, and champagne. "In short, [I am still quoting him] my country could not have done more for a poet whom it undoubtedly rates higher than he deserves, solely because his poetry is an expression of the national character and the national tradition."

XLII

FOREIGN TRAVELERS, 1818–1845

SPANISH writers, familiar with their native land and
its ways, pass over much that strikes the foreigner's
eye, and therefore I shall make a digression to take
some account of what travelers report.

George Ticknor, whose *History of Spanish Literature* (1849) is the most distinguished book on the
subject, visited Spain in 1818, when he was twenty-
six years old. He went by diligence from Barcelona
to Madrid: Abominable roads, impossible to make
more than twenty-two miles a day; the country
desolate and deserted; no taverns, "for I do not call
the miserable hovels where we stopped by that name,
because it is not even expected of them to furnish
anything but a place to cover you from the weather."
The lower storey was always a stable, the upper
always full of fleas. But he enjoyed himself. His
companions had "that genuine, unpretending courtesy and hearty, dignified kindness, for which their
nation has always been famous." He read *Don
Quixote* aloud to them. At Madrid he lodged with
people who were honest and neat,

the two rarest virtues in Spain. . . . There is more national
character here, more originality and poetry in the popular
manners and feelings, more force without barbarism and
civilization without corruption than I have found anywhere else. . . . What seems mere fiction and romance in

other countries is matter of observation here, and in all that relates to manners Cervantes and Le Sage are historians. . . . When you have crossed the Pyrenees . . . you have gone back a couple of centuries in your chronology. . . . The pastoral life . . . is still found everywhere in the country. I never come home in the evening that I do not pass half a dozen groups of the lower class of the people dancing to their pipes and castanets some of their beautifully original national dances, for . . . the Spaniards are the most remarkable people in the world for a natural and inherent propensity to dance, and have the most graceful movements and manners.

Of the government there is very little good to say. The king personally is a vulgar blackguard. . . . What a government! Such a confusion of abuses never existed before since society was organized. [The King issues decrees, nobody obeys,] and this independence leads to such a train of abuses and corruptions as nobody can imagine. [Nevertheless] a more quiet, orderly people, a people more obedient and loyal, I have not seen in Europe. . . . In Catalonia they are industrious and active; in Aragon, idle, proud, and faithful; in Castile, cold and rude; in Andalusia, light-hearted, giddy, cruel, and revengeful. . . . These different characters are so distinctly marked in the different provinces that it seems as if you had changed country every time you pass from one to another, [but all have] a kind of instinctive uprightness. [Genuine, faithful kindness is the rule;] if you really want assistance, if you are really suffering, you are sure to meet nothing but good will. . . . The highest class . . . is deplorable. I can conceive nothing more monotonous, gross, and disgraceful than their manner of passing their day and their life."

Ticknor went south to Cordova and Granada. He says that the Alhambra is "a name which will make my blood thrill if I live to the frosts of a century." But the word "Alhambra" reminds me that I must move on to Washington Irving.

Irving went from St.-Jean-de-Luz over a mountain pass to Vitoria in February, 1820. He seems to have been particularly impressed by shabby hidalgos and shabby houses with armorial devices over the doors. Beyond Burgos —

villages dismal dirt-holes . . . country arid and dismal . . . mountains bleak and barren . . . a miserable inn . . . mountain passes overlook great tracts of arid country . . . Castilian seated on his mule, with his great wrap and mantle flowing round him . . . his montero cap . . . and his swarthy face looks with vast hauteur on all the world. . . . Hire soldiers for dangerous part of road.

He made Madrid his headquarters for over two years, I think, then went to Granada, and, as all the world knows, lodged in the Alhambra. Altogether he passed three years in Spain; of which the fruits were his *Life of Columbus*, the *Conquest of Granada*, and *The Alhambra*.

Ticknor and Irving were in Spain during the reign of the blackguard Ferdinand VII, in the period of peace between the struggle for independence against the French and the Carlist wars. George Borrow was not so fortunate. After the death of Ferdinand (1833) conditions were very different. Don Carlos claimed the throne by right of the Salic law; the Queen Regent Cristina held it for her infant daughter Isabella; and the ensuing Carlist war made life well-nigh intolerable in many parts of Spain. Aragon, Catalonia, the mountainous parts of Navarre, sided with Don Carlos; so did the

Emperors of Russia and Austria, the Kings of Prussia and Naples, and the Pope; whereas the Liberal parts of Spain, supported by England, rallied round the Queen Regent. There was desultory fighting between Carlistas and Cristinos. On the Carlist side two generals, Zumalacarregui and Cabrera, distinguished themselves for victories or brutalities, — I forget which, — and General Espartero did the same on the Queen's side. The Carlist cause collapsed in 1840.

It was during these years that Borrow wandered about, disseminating Bibles among benighted papists with a persistence and intolerance that conformed to the difficulty of his task. He gives a brilliant picture of the condition of the country, with its gypsies, Carlists, brigands, illiterate priests, bad roads, neglected fields, barren deserts, ignorance, poverty, and lawlessness.

In Madrid he had occasion to see members of the Government for permission to print and circulate Bibles, among others "a certain Duke of Rivas, Minister of the Interior." As Borrow is prejudiced, let me interpolate what Ticknor says of the Duke (1818):

Don Ángel [this was before he inherited his title] is certainly one of the most extraordinary young men I have met in Spain. He has a fine person, a beautiful face, full of genius, has written several plays that have been well received in Spanish theatres, painted a large piece that made much noise in the last exhibition in Madrid; is as brave as Cæsar, since he has eleven severe wounds in his body received from the French; and, with all this, is very modest, simple, and elegant in his manners.

George Borrow, again:

The duke was a very handsome young man, of about thirty [he was forty-five], an Andalusian by birth. . . . He had published several works — tragedies, I believe — and enjoyed a certain kind of literary reputation. He received me with the greatest affability; and having heard what I had to say, he replied with a most captivating bow and a genuine Andalusian grimace: "Go to my secretary; go to my secretary — *el hará por usted el gusto* (he will do what you want).

The secretary, however, had other views, and dexterously brought forward in opposition to Borrow's plans a hindering article of the Council of Trent. Borrow then tried to see the Duke again, but that gentleman warily slipped out of a side door (1837).

Borrow thought ill of the upper classes, but —

a Spaniard of the lower class . . . is not a common being; he is an extraordinary man . . . he possesses a spirit of proud independence which it is impossible not to admire. He is ignorant, of course; but it is singular that I have invariably found amongst the low and slightly educated classes far more liberality of sentiment than among the upper. . . . The bigotry of the Spaniards, their mean jealousy of foreigners . . . chiefly holds good with respect to the upper classes.

In spite of an imprisonment, and wearisome loitering in the antechambers of ministers, Borrow finds Madrid the most interesting capital that he has ever seen, and salutes it with this apostrophe:

Within a mud wall scarcely one league and a half in circuit are contained two hundred thousand human beings, certainly forming the most extraordinary vital mass to be

found in the entire world . . . and this mass is strictly
Spanish. . . . Hail, ye *aguadores* of Asturia. . . . Hail, ye
caleseros of Valencia. . . . Hail to you, beggars of La
Mancha. . . . Hail to you, valets from the mountains,
mayordomos and secretaries from Biscay and Guipuscoa,
toreros from Andalusia, *porteros* from Galicia, shopkeepers
from Catalonia. . . . And lastly, genuine sons of the
capital, rabble of Madrid, ye twenty thousand *manolos*,
whose terrible knives, on the second morning of May,
worked such grim havoc amongst the legions of Murat!

Among his brilliant pages he has drawn a wonderful picture of the revolution of La Granja (August,
1836), which overturned the Conservative (*moderado*)
Government. He was strolling about the Puerta del
Sol when he heard shouts of "*¡Viva la Constitución!*"
"*¡La Granja, La Granja!*" An angry, mischief-
making revolutionary mob crowded together. But
Borrow's description of the scenes in the Plaza and
in the coffee-house in the Calle d'Alcalá must be
read in his own words.

If I have not mistaken the chronology, Théophile
Gautier arrived in Spain from St.-Jean-de-Luz a
few months before Borrow sailed from Gibraltar
for Tangier. It was high time for so distinguished
a member of the Romantic group in France as
Gautier to say something about Spain. Hence the
Voyage en Espagne. Every subsequent traveler has
taken a copy of this book in his portmanteau and
everybody quotes it. Open him anywhere; for instance at the chapter on Madrid; "Allons au Prado!"
he means the park, not the museum. He describes
the fashionable crowd collected there from half-
past seven until ten, the squeezing pedestrians side

by side with the odd procession of vehicles, such
as are still seen in Latin countries, proceeding slowly
on the fashionable drive. The equipage of the
Queen Regent was *très-simple, très-bourgeois; un
Anglais un peu millionnaire le dédaignerait assurément.*
He noticed, as one does to-day, the noble riding-
horses from Andalusia. Then he discourses on the
ladies' headdresses, their mantillas, with flowers at
their temples, a *coiffure qui est la plus charmante qui
se puisse imaginer. Avec une mantille, il faut qu'une
femme soit laide comme les trois vertus théologales
pour ne pas paraître jolie.* Then every woman had
a fan; he had seen them in satin slippers without
stockings, but never without a fan. Much, too, about
the owners of the fans:

*Elles sont petites, mignonnes, bien tournées, le pied mince,
la taille cambrée.* [In Seville] *Lorsqu'une femme ou jeune
fille passe près de vous, elle abaisse lentement ses paupières,
puis elles les relève subitement, vous décoche en face un regard
d'un éclat insoutenable, fait un tour de prunelle et baisse de
nouveau les cils.* [Nevertheless, this means nothing; the
same glance falls on an ox cart.] *La petitesse des mains et
des pieds ne laissent rien à désirer.*

But I refer the reader to his Gallic pages.

Richard Ford is as typically English as Gautier
is French; and his *Murray's Hand-Book* (1845) is a
treasure-house of information concerning Spain in
the middle of the last century. He lived continu-
ously there, I think, from 1830 to 1837. The charm
of the book, aside from the immense amount of information in it, is Ford's vigorous, honest, British
personality. He tells you what he thinks. It is

instructive to compare his opinions of national events with those of Spaniards. Take, for instance, the Battle of Bailén (1808), a victory won by a Spanish general over the French. It is perhaps the most celebrated national victory since Navas de Tolosa in 1212. The Duque de Rivas, Zorrilla, and a host of other Spanish poets, speak of it as Scotchmen speak of Bannockburn. Ford says, "This hap'orth of triumph covers a multitude of intolerable defeats, such as in no history can be paralleled." The First Division of the army, "little more than nominally Spanish," was Swiss, commanded by a Swiss; the Second was commanded by a Frenchman; the Third by Jones, an Irishman; "and the best troops were Walloons. . . . The Fourth Division, which really consisted of Spaniards, never fired a shot." I merely refer to this episode to put the reader on guard against national sympathies. Spaniards are intensely patriotic; on the other hand, Richard Ford will allow no military glory except to his hero, the Duke of Wellington. The truth concerning the battle of Bailén seems to be that the French were very badly commanded, and the Spaniards very fortunate.

XLIII

IN THE REIGN OF ISABELLA II
1833–1868

The period from the accession of Isabella II (1833) to her final overthrow (1868) is by far more turbulent and confused than any since the reign of Enrique IV, four hundred years earlier. In this historical drama, the Queen and her mother are secondary personages; the Constitution is the protagonist; the plot forms a wild picaresque story that might be called "The Adventures of a Foundling." It is like Quevedo's *El Gran Tacaño: rien de plus difficile à entendre.*

In 1812 a set of patriotic doctrinaires met at Cadiz and adopted a Constitution containing all sorts of Liberal articles, but quite over the head of popular sympathy. When Ferdinand VII, reëstablished by Wellington's victories, abolished it in 1814, he acted in accordance with the wishes of an ignorant, bigoted majority. The priesthood, the religious orders, the nobility, the rural population, wished the King to enjoy his own. But the Liberals were the more intelligent, and they dominated the army. In 1820, Liberal officers, taking advantage of their soldiers' dislike — or rather, refusal — to go to America to suppress rebellions in Mexico and Colombia, took the King into custody and reëstablished the Constitution. In 1823 the French army came in, and the Constitution went out. On the death of Ferdinand, as I have said, the Queen Regent was obliged to lean on the Liberals. You would have expected them to take advantage of her needs, and reëstablish the Constitution; but the Liberals, instead of uniting solidly, divided into *moderados* (Conservatives) and *progresistas* (Progressives), and fell foul of one another. Our literary acquaintance, Martínez de la Rosa, became Prime Minister, but he was a *moderado* and timid, and did little more than enact the scaffolding of a constitution. Times were hard, poverty great; the populace were discontented, ascribed their troubles to the Conservatives and their supporters, — especially friars and monks, — and took to pillage, arson, and murder. Martínez de la Rosa fell, and the new Government had to pacify the populace. Mendizabal, a minister familiar to us in Borrow's pages, — Borrow recognized in him at once "the keen sight of the Beni Israel," — proposed various radical measures: to suppress monasteries, to sell their lands, to diminish nunneries, to banish the Jesuits again, and so on. Then his Government fell, and the *moderados* came back; but the army lost patience, and the military revolt at the royal palace of La Granja (which enacted its later scenes at Madrid before Borrow's eyes) forced the reluctant Queen Regent to re-adopt the Constitution.

It is idle to seek a path in this political labyrinth. The Carlists were beaten in the field, and finally driven from Spain (1840); but that did not do much to restore law and order, for the Liberals quarreled the more fiercely with one another. Into the seething

pot of confusion the Queen Regent tossed the
scandals of her private life. The pot boiled over,
and she left the kingdom. General Espartero, hero
of the Carlist war, became Regent in her stead. In
three years he was lucky to get away in safety to England. Isabella, but thirteen years old, was proclaimed
Queen. From then till 1868, when she too was
driven into exile, the skein of politics is virtually
inextricable. A series of soldiers rose to power:
General Narváez, General O'Donnell, General Ser-
rano, and General Prim. The last is rather better
known to the ordinary traveler than the others,
because of Henri Regnault's brilliant portrait in the
Louvre. Prim is mounted on a horse, in the thunder
of battle, very heroic and theatrical, after the fashion
of Spanish generals in sculpture and pigments.
During this period, military politicians mounted on
the crest of military revolts and receded with their
ebb. And at the same time the series of the Queen's
lovers rose and fell; for the unlucky girl, having
been obliged by politicians and her powerful neighbor
Louis Philippe to marry a nincompoop, had promptly
got rid of him and followed her mother's and grandmother's examples and her own fickle inclinations.

In 1868 the Queen went. Republicans appear on
the scene, among them, most conspicuous, the ex-
traordinarily voluble Emilio Castelar; but Spain was
not ripe for a republic, and the politicians cast about
for a sovereign. Napoleon III would not consent
to the election of Leopold of Hohenzollern, and
Prince Amadeo of Savoy, second son to Victor
Emmanuel, was chosen. This poor fellow endured his
kingship for somewhat over two years, and with-

drew. Then followed a brief Republic with a rapid succession of presidents: Pi y Margall, a man of note among Spaniards, Salmerón, and the oratorical Castelar. But the Republic failed, and in the person of Queen Isabella's son, Don Alphonso XII, the House of Bourbon was restored to the throne (January 1875).

Let us now take breath, look back over the reign, and see what — if anything — worth while was going on in art or literature during this period of civil war, riot, and rebellion. As to painting, the chronicle shall be brief. After Goya's death there is an aspect of winter and desolation. Vicente López (d. 1850) was *pintor de cámara* to Charles IV and lived on long enough to paint General Narváez. Don José Madrazo (1781–1860), another court painter, followed Charles IV, after his deposition, to Rome, and stayed even when that impoverished ex-monarch could pay him no salary. On his master's death he returned to Spain. He happened to make one of the party that went with George Ticknor from Barcelona to Madrid, and listened with the greatest joy while Ticknor read *Don Quixote* aloud. He became director of the Prado Museum. His son Federigo de Madrazo (1815–1894) painted creditable portraits, among others a picture of Queen María Cristina, as a nun, at her husband Ferdinand's bedside — which indicates imagination; and his son-in-law Mariano Fortuny made for a time a world-wide reputation.

Fortuny (1838–1874) was a Catalan. The reader probably knows his pictures. He studied in Rome, served on the staff of General Prim in the famous campaign in Morocco, and witnessed the victory of Tetuan. He went to Paris and painted genre pictures. An English critic says: "The sudden appearance of Mariano Fortuny in the art of Spain may be likened only to some bloom of startling hue in a waste of indistinguishable colors." And an American speaks of his "miracles of luminosity" and "marvels of naturalistic characterization, flooded broadly with glowing luminosity." The Spanish Marriage (1869), usually, I believe, considered his best picture, brought him great celebrity. It is a little canvas that contains portraits of Madame Fortuny, Meissonier, and Henri Regnault, very highly finished, and shows a mastery of technique. Théophile Gautier said: "It is a Goya drawing painted in by Meissonier." Alas for the inconstancy of fashion! A later critic calls it "that consummate triumph of rococo artificiality."

With an adieu to the transitory Fortuny I leave painting, in order to catch up some dropped threads in the domain of letters.

In my last chapter on literature, too intent perhaps on finding some central thread, I confined myself to the prominent members of the romantic school, to the exclusion of various notabilities who now come claiming some recognition. Manuel José Quintana (1772–1857) was an eminent poet true to the rules of the neo-classical school, and also a historical writer and literary critic, as well as a lawyer and politician. But I must pass on to mention other men, some of them much less distinguished than he. Spanish literature has always been rich in plays

beyond the dreams of the Beginner's avarice. It was
so in Lope's time, and so in Calderón's. It was
so in the middle of the nineteenth century. I find
on the yellow-paper cover of a play, dated 1842,
an announcement by the publishers that they will
furnish the public with copies of three hundred plays
by the following playwrights:

D. Manuel Breton de los Hereros	(1796–1873)
D. Antonio Gil de Zárate	(1793–1861)
D. Juan Eugenio Hartzenbusch	(1806–1880)
D. Antonio García Gutierrez	(1813–1884)
D. Mariano José de Larra	(1809–1837)
D. Ventura de la Vega	(1807–1865)
D. Angel Saavedra (Duque de Rivas)	(1791–1865)
D. José Zorrilla	(1817–1893)
D. Miguel Augustin Principe	(1811–1863)
D. Patricio de la Escosura	(1807–1878)
D. Eugenio de Ochoa	(1815–1872)
D. Francisco Martínez de la Rosa	(1787–1862)
D. Manuel Eduardo Gorostiza	(1789–1851)
D. Mariano Roca de Togores	(1812–1889)
D. José de Castro y Orozco	(1808–1869)
D. José García de Villalta	?
D. Isidoro Gil	(1814–1866)
D. José de Espronceda	(1809–1842)
D. Tomas Rodriguez Rubí	(1817–1890)
D. Eugenio de Tapia	(1777–1860)
D. Ramon Navarrete	(1822–1897)
D. Gaspar Fernando Coll	
and others.	

If the Beginner has a taste for plays, there is no
constitutional obstacle between him and satiety.
Some of the names on this list I have already

mentioned. I shall only speak of four others. Hartz-enbusch (1806–1880), son of a German joiner, was a literary scholar and wrote one of the famous plays of the century, *Los Amantes de Teruel* (1837). Antonio García Gutierrez (1813–1884) wrote *El Trovador* (1836), a romantic play that, as *Il Trovatore*, on the wings of Verdi's music has put a girdle round the world. Manuel Breton de los Herreros (1796–1873) was a popular playwright who, at the very height of the romantic movement, struck out a path of his own, composing plays on ordinary life, gay, humorous, and very Spanish. The public was delighted. He wrote a hundred original plays, beside many adaptations.

But I must keep some space for Mariano José de Larra, whose death in 1837 I have already mentioned. Larra was a playwright by the way; his chief work consisted of political journalism, literary criticism, and above all of satirical essays. It is said that after a gay, happy boyhood, for some unknown cause, perhaps a girl's disdain, he became a pessimist, sad, suspicious, immersed in self. He was fairly well read in French literature, not unfamiliar with the classics, had some knowledge of physics, but was by no means a scholar. He lived in Madrid, frequented the popular literary club *El Parnasillo*, that held its reunions in the *Café del Principe*, close to the theatre. Richard Ford speaks of this café as one of the best, where national drinks, chocolate, and "what is called tea," are served, and "where people who have little to do but to kill time play at dominoes." Larra's satirical essays appeared in various journals, usually under the pseudonym

"Figaro." They remind one a little of Swift's papers. He was deeply interested in politics. Although he professed Liberal opinions, he attacked Mendizabal of "the Beni Israel," why, I do not know. On the latter's fall, he was elected deputy for Ávila, and for a few days his future looked brilliant, but the revolution of La Granja (August 15, 1836) brought back the Constitution and changed everything. He then gave himself wholly to his pen. An incident of the time was a banquet where he and Breton de los Herreros were the lions. The two were not on speaking terms, for Larra had criticized Breton, and Breton had introduced Larra on the stage as a reprehensible character. At the banquet each had to practise great circumspection in order to look everywhere except at the other.

One of Larra's most famous essays appeared in an issue of November 2, 1836, on Madrid as a cemetery:

Each house a family's sepulchre, each street the grave of an event, each heart the funeral urn of a hope or a desire. . . . My heart is but a tomb. What is the epitaph? Let us read: HERE LIETH HOPE.

That has a romantic note. Others of his essays are more characteristic. "*Vuelva usted mañana*" (Come back to-morrow). A visitor comes to Madrid, says that he shall despatch his business within a week, see the town, and be off on the tenth day. At this Figaro reminds him that in Spain there is no *hoy* (to-day) only *mañana* (to-morrow), and invites him to dinner that day fifteen months hence. "*La Vida de Madrid*" (Life in Madrid):

As I go about, I wonder, I wonder at the great power of the Supreme Being, who has been able to make all men discontented. I wonder at His great wisdom in making life short. I wonder at the way everybody endures this wretched life. This last is enough to confound any atheist, for only an omnipotent God could make a man love life.

"Las Palabras definitivas" (Definitive Words):

There are words that seem things. For instance, the word *conspiración* makes you think you are at a tragic play; the word *libertad*, that you are at a farce. . . . See that crowd of puppets in commotion, shoving, fighting, killing one another? That is the word *honor*.

In the beginning of the year 1837 it seems that a lady — a married woman, with whom he had been passionately in love — stopped writing to him. She was afraid of malevolent gossip. Such matters are always hard to unravel. One scholar says *era casada y cumplía con su deber;* another more liberal-minded, thinks her hard-hearted. There was an interview, apparently at his house. She said good-bye. He shot himself (February 13). He was then but twenty-seven years old.

XLIV

CAMPOAMOR, BECQUER, ECHEGARAY

In this chapter I shall continue to enumerate some of the more famous figures in Spanish literature of the nineteenth century. Ramón de Campoamor (1817–1901) filled eight good-sized volumes with poetry and prose. Volume one is devoted to philosophy and metaphysics, and contains a great deal about man, society, law, politics, ontology, psychology, cosmology, and other high-sounding matters. All these writings of his are, I presume, of no value whatever. Another volume contains poetry, and he explains how he classifies it. His explanation is said to cast a shadow on darkness. The classification is roughly this: *Humoradas*, epigrams of two or four lines; *Doloras*, little genre poems of which the best known are *Grandes hombres*, and *¡Quién supiera escribir!* The first is a picture of Charles V at the monastery of Yuste, not contemplating eternity, but cross with an old woman, who mutters under her breath, "What a little, ugly old man!" The second tells how an illiterate girl asks a priest to write a letter, and he, to her astonishment, anticipates all that she desires to say, it being a love-letter. The *Pequeños poemas* are of the same character, but longer.

I shall quote one of his political judgments, partly because it is typical, and because a foreigner, looking

back more than fifty or sixty years, is likely to be
unfair to actors who gained much applause in their
day. General Narváez (whom I have mentioned), it
seems, had won a victory in civil war over a much
more numerous army. Campoamor describes his
action in the battle:

Narváez, with the mysterious power that only men of
genius possess, turned into a kind of snake, crawled
and wriggled through the masses of the enemy, and in
the very midst of them, just as they were about to blaze
away, arose erect and with an imperious cordiality said,
"Stop!"

Campoamor was an excellent man. He spoke ill
of matrimony but adored his wife; he accompanied
her to mass every day, carrying her folding-chair.
As to his poetry critics disagree. Fitzmaurice-Kelly
says, "He is not in any sense a national poet, a characteristic product of the soil"; but Don Julio Cejador
contradicts this:

He was Spanish through and through, from head to heel.
[I translate the sense rather than the words of his phrase.]
His lyrical poems are purest Spanish. . . *la lírica más
castizamente española.*

However that be, Campoamor was considered one
of the first, if not the first poet of his time, a position
somewhat analogous to that of Longfellow in this
country. Benavente, the distinguished playwright,
tells this anecdote: When, in his young days, he was
presented to the aged poet as a writer of talent,
Campoamor turned toward him, with his stern mouth
and his kindly, clear blue smiling eyes, looked for a

time and asked, "¿*Mucho, mucho talento?* Because if he does not possess much talent it is better to be a good man."

Perhaps I should give some notice to Gaspar Núñez de Arce (1832–1903), whose book of poems *Gritos del combate* is memorable, and whose historical play, *El haz de leña,* that concerns Philip II and his son Don Carlos, is the best of the century, but there seem to be so many nineteenth-century Spaniards who, as statesmen, held positions in the government and busied themselves with politics and reforms, and, as men of letters, wrote lyrics and plays, that I pass him by to take up a man whom I find much more interesting.

In the charming public garden at Seville, not far from the rose garden, the flower-girdled pools, and the tea house where white doves gather to pick up your crumbs, the carriage road passes a wide-spreading tree. Under the branches of this tree is a marble statue that reminds you of the statue to Alfred de Musset outside the Comédie Française in Paris. A young poet, sensitive, delicate, imaginative, communes with the ideal images of his fancy. One recalls one's own youth and Musset's boyish lines,

> *Et le seul bien qui me reste au monde*
> *Est d'avoir quelquefois pleuré.*

Bécquer is more commonly likened to Heinrich Heine and there can be little doubt that Heine influenced him, but his blood was Latin, and to me he is really much more like Musset.

¿ Qué es poesía? dices mientras clavas
en mi pupila tu pupila azul;
¿ Qué es poesía? ¿ Y tú me lo preguntas?
Poesía . . . eres tu.

Por una mirada, un mundo;
por una sonrisa, un cielo,
por un beso . . . ¡ yo no sé
qué te diera por un beso!

Gustavo Adolfo Bécquer (1836–1870) belongs to
the poets of the romantic school who love "twilight
and the darksome lawn." His brother Valeriano, a
painter, painted his portrait: a sad, wistful face,
with handsome eyes, rounded eyebrows, well-shaped
mouth, and hair clustering in careful carelessness
about his intellectual forehead. His life was as sad
as his poetry. He left Seville at seventeen to earn a
livelihood in Madrid. He was poor, unsuccessful,
suffered from ill health; and his marriage was not
happy. He tried his hand at various literary employ-
ments. What is left consists of two or three slim
volumes of prose and verse. There are eighteen weird
tales, after the manner of Hoffmann. Mrs. Humphry
Ward, who had her own definite notions of what
fiction should be, says "his stories of midnight cathedrals, of the ghostly presences which inhabit the
woods and streams, of the horrors of haunted castles
. . . are like hundreds of others. . . . We know it
all by heart, and its spell has departed." Professor
Mérimée is more kindly: "*On notera une certaine*
puissance d'évocation des temps disparus, une imagi-
nation poétique," and so on. But Mrs. Ward is right
in this — the spell has departed. The volume of
poetry is even slenderer; there are sixty-six short

poems. It seems to me as if Bécquer had tried to express Musset's sentiments in Heine's manner. But my opinion is worthless. Professor Cejador — who, to be sure, has but one notion of eulogy — says that Bécquer "*es el lírico . . . más español y castizo*" — (the most essentially national lyrical poet that Spain has produced). On the other hand, Professor Mérimée seems to be more of my way of thinking: "*Ce qui frappe tout d'abord, c'est l'accent personnel, intime, douloureux, et ce n'est point là précisement la manière espagnole: la note est bien nouvelle.*"

The most popular poem of all, number LIII, begins:

Volverán las oscuras golondrinas
en tu balcon sus nidos á colgar,
y, otra vez, con el ala á sus cristales
Jugando llamarán:

Pero aquellas que el vuelo refrenaban
tu hermosura y mi dicha á contemplar,
aquellas que aprendieron nuestros nombres . . .
esas . . ¡no volverán!

As romance is of the essence of Bécquer's life, I will quote the story, told by a friend, of how and where the poet saw the lady that inspired his muse. This was two years before his marriage. The two friends were strolling through the Calle de la Flor Alta, near the broad street of San Bernardo: "As we were going along we saw, in one of the second-storey balconies, two girls of extraordinary beauty, just alike except that the elder, so she seemed, who was about seventeen or eighteen, displayed in the expression of her eyes and the modeling of her features something of Heaven. Gustavo was all admiration at seeing her; and after we kept on down the *calle* he could not keep from turning time and again for the bewildering joy of looking at her. He had discerned in her the incarnation of Shakespeare's Ophelia or Juliet, Goethe's Charlotte, and, more than all, the ideal woman of the legends that seethed in his mind." This friend got Bécquer an invitation to the house of these young ladies, but he refused. The lady was his ideal inspiration, and he would not mar that ideal by any less perfect reality.

A contemporary of Bécquer's, of very different tastes, talents, and fortunes, José Echegaray (1832–1916), came into much more direct relations with his time. Bécquer was a poet and man of letters, indifferent to the doings and misdoings of the world of politics and business; but Echegaray was a civil engineer, a mathematician, professor, economist, and politician. He became a deputy, received a portfolio, and served on the committee that welcomed Prince Amadeo of Savoy to his throne of thorns in 1870–1871. He was an eager, active spirit, with wings like an ostrich — not to fly, but to cover the ground very fast. Fitzmaurice-Kelly turns up his nose at him, but that was before 1904, when Echegaray, together with Mistral, received the Nobel Prize in literature.

Echegaray's career is threefold: as a man of science, as a politician, and as a playwright. I concern myself only with the third rôle. He did not begin to write plays until he was over forty; then he made up for lost time. Some are romantic plays, some melodramas, some touch social questions. They are like

Sardou's, extravagant, exaggerated; bang the emotions, and make the top gallery hold its breath. A Spanish critic speaks of his *"gran robustez en el mover los mas fieros afectos."* The struggle between passion and duty is usually the mainspring of his action, and his success lies in our interest in the ethical questions raised by impossible adventures. *Éste es el triunfo de Echegaray, triunfo pasional, romántico, mediterráneo, muy de la raza.* I have only read, like all the world, *El Gran Galeoto*, his best, and one of the most famous of Spanish plays. The plot is simple. Don Julian, a man of forty, and his wife who is barely twenty, have taken into their house a young poet Ernesto, the son of a man to whom Don Julian owes all his prosperity. Gossip soon interests itself in the companionship of the two young people. Julian refuses to listen. Nevertheless the seed of slander begets the corruption of jealousy; and by most unlikely misadventures the young pair are often found together. Gossip becomes noisy. Ernesto insists on taking lodgings elsewhere. It is too late. A young man at a club talks vulgarly. Ernesto challenges him; but Don Julian, poisoned by the seeds of jealousy, pushes in and fights first. He is desperately wounded and carried, of all places in the world, to Ernesto's rooms. By evil chance the young wife has gone there to stop the duel. She tries to hide in the bedchamber. She is discovered. Her dying husband curses her. The upshot is that poet and young wife do fall in love and go off together. All this is due to Gossip, *El Gran Galeoto*, the "go-between," you remember, in Dante's phrase. The play has been highly eulogized and translated into various languages. To me it reads like Sardou, with touches borrowed from Ibsen and phraseology borrowed from Victor Hugo. It does not sound like the play of an eminent civil engineer, or, for the matter of that, of an eminent statesman. Echegaray was an extraordinary man.

XLV

THE NOVELS, 1840–1890

WE have now come to the principal achievements of
Spanish literature in the last half of the nineteenth
century, its novels. As the harvest of Spanish novels
is very rich, and as they are recent and have been
much discussed, I shall do little more than call the
roll.

Cecilia Böhl de Faber (1796–1877) was the
daughter of a German father and a Spanish mother.
Ticknor knew the father when he was Hanseatic
consul at Cadiz. She was born in Switzerland. She
changed her name several times by marriage, but
always, I think, made use of the pseudonym "Fernán
Caballero." She wrote her first novel in German, her
second in French; but in spite of her cosmopolitan
relations and attainments, she is thoroughly Spanish.
She says herself: "I have tried to give a truthful,
genuine, exact picture of Spain and its social life, to
describe the inner life of our people, their beliefs, their
feelings, their wit. . . . *La novela no se inventa, se
observa.* . . . And I have tried to do more: to re-
vivify what is spiritual, sacred, tender, and sublime
in our religious practices; to rehabilitate our genuine
old Spanish ways, our character, our national sentiment." Here, then, was a double purpose of realism
and reform. Spanish critics are in accord that nobody
has depicted better than she intimate family scenes

or popular manners. The Duque de Rivas said that the personages in her novel, *La Familia de Alvareda*, are like portraits by Velásquez. So she takes the proud place of pioneer in novels of contemporary life, or, as the Spanish usually say, of reviver of the old Spanish realism of Cervantes and others.

Pedro Antonio de Alarcón (1833–1891) was born in the province of Granada. He plunged with a right good will into the troubled life of the time; he was journalist, politician, deputy, ambassador, soldier, as well as man of letters. As a politician he seems sometimes to have swum with the current, sometimes against it. He wrote an account of his military service in Africa, and many novels and tales, some with proselyting purpose, others merely for the sake of an agreeable story. There are sixteen volumes and more of his writings. *El Capitán Veneno* appeared to me, I regret to say, a little slow; but *El Sombrero de Tres Picos* (*The Three-Cornered Hat*, 1874), which Emilia Pardo Bazán compares to a picture by Goya, is really a pleasure to read, and deserves its reward of being the first novel put into the hands of Beginners. Mérimée says that it is "*pittoresque, amusante et papillotante comme une aquerelle de Fortuny.*" *El Escándalo* raised a great commotion when it appeared and has been said to be his best.

Leopold Alas (Clarín), the distinguished writer, says of Alarcón:

There can be no doubt but that there is something antipathetic about Alarcón as a writer; but it is obvious that he is one of our best novelists . . . he has shown, outside his novels, that his ideas are commonplace, that his mind has

not been trained by large reflection or deep sentiments.
. . . But in compensation for these and other unattractive
qualities in Alarcón's literary personality, there is in his
books a rich, original, fresh inventiveness; there is amenity,
grace, passion, strength, vitality; and if his style lacks
polish and training, if he has little art, it has agreeable
ease, spontaneity, and variety. He is not and never can
be a novelist of the first rank.

Alarcón continues to be very much read. Cejador
says that he is like a public garden where everybody
goes for recreation.

Juan Valera (1824–1905) is a much more important
person. Born near Cordova, he was educated to be a
lawyer, but he became a diplomat and served in
various embassies, at St. Petersburg, Lisbon, Washington, Brussels, Berlin, Vienna, and Rio de Janeiro.
His position in Spain was like that of James Russell
Lowell with us: he was a poet, a finished gentleman,
an accomplished critic, a highly cultivated man, if
not technically a scholar, a *conversacionista* without
a rival in Spain. An enthusiastic English lady says
that in his sweetness and humanity he has something
of the ancient Greek, with the Hellenic love of beauty
and æsthetic sense of balance and proportion. The
beauty of his style is said to be incomparable. He is
best known in America, and all over the world, as the
author of *Pepita Jiménez* (1874), a novel given to
masculine Beginners (I refer to days of old-fashioned
conventions) immediately after *El Sombrero de Tres
Picos*. A charming young widow falls in love with a
theological student, who is absorbed in the great
Spanish mystics and intends to be a priest. He falls
in love with her; nevertheless he holds to his purpose,

until she takes matters into her own hands, and they are married. W. D. Howells says: "What took me in the book was the charm of an exquisite art . . . and a fresh and joyous sympathy with human nature. My own impression is that the book is better suited to the young, interested in romance and the mystical religion that belongs to adolescence and ideal beliefs, than to older persons cramped in their sympathies by experiences of ordinary life." Valera wrote various other novels; Fitzmaurice-Kelly thinks that *Doña Luz* and *El Comendador Mendoza* are even better than *Pepita Jiménez*. In 1885 Clarín said: "Valera has attained the foremost place among our men of letters."

José María de Pereda (1833–1905) had, I should suppose, more talent as a novelist than Valera. Cejador says: "*Pereda es después de Cervantes, el primer novelista español.*" In his life, and in his art too, Pereda was as far from Valera as his birthplace is from Cordova. He was born at Polanco, a hamlet near Santander. He loved this country. He lived there almost all his life, and his fame is rooted to the soil. The book that first drew attention to him, *Las escenas montañesas* (1864), concerns the people of the upland pastures, describes their lives, their ways, and the country roundabout, while his most famous novel, *Sotileza* (1884), does the same for the fishermen on the coast. Spaniards appropriate to the mountain range there near the coast the name *montaña*, and the adjective *montañés* to a man that comes from there; hence Pereda is always known as *el montañés*. He deserves the title. Comfortably off, he built a mansion, *llena de comodidades*, it is said, opposite the family house where he and twenty brothers and sisters had been born. He is to Santander what Thomas Hardy is to Wessex. He was a conservative of the conservatives, — "The liberty of the press, the parliamentary system, it is they that kill us," — always staunchly loyal to an absolute King and an absolute Church. For a time he sat in the Cortes as a Carlist deputy. But in spite of his opinions he was a close friend to Galdós, who was as stout a Liberal as Pereda was a Tory. He is described as tall and thin, of distinguished bearing; "*sa courtoisie est exquise . . . c'est un causeur admirable.*" *Sotileza* is undoubtedly the book to read of all his novels. The Town Council of Santander in their pride and gratitude named an avenue after it. But I warn the Beginner that it contains a great many words usually of a local character, that he will have to look up in the glossary at the back. So far as the admiration of his contemporaries can confer it, Pereda's fame is immortal.

Pérez Galdós (1845–1920) is more important, in the general estimation of the world, than any of the others. He was born in the Canary Islands, went to Madrid to finish his education, studied law, essayed journalism, and then took to writing novels and stories. He began with a long series of historical novels, *Episodios nacionales,* that present a mingling of fiction and history, as he saw it, in romantic episodes from the time of Godoy to his own days. If one has leisure and a taste for Spanish history of this period, perhaps one could not do better than read these multitudinous volumes. They will require a voyage round the Horn and back again, and diligent reading at that: first series, second series, third, and fourth. You will find volumes that bear the names of personages that I have skipped over: Zumala-carregui, the Carlist guerrilla chief; Mendizabal, the clever Jewish financier; Narváez, the Liberal general whom Campoamor admired; O'Donnell, the Irish military politician; Prim, magnificent in Henri Reg-nault's painting; Amadeo I, and others. But the author's great reputation rests upon his novels.

Galdós belongs to the literary category of the realists. His compatriots are very eager to distinguish Spanish realism from French naturalism; and many a battle royal has been fought over this field. The gist of it all is, according to patriotic Spaniards, that Zola and his French followers see Nature as something gross and bestial, whereas Galdós and Pereda paint Nature as she is, half animal, half divine. This does not mean that Galdós did not write novels in support of a definite thesis; he did. His famous novels, *Doña Perfecta* (1876) and *Gloria* (1877), are blows at intolerance. But when not swept away by a desire to proselytize, Galdós adhered to the great Spanish tradition of painting what the eye sees, and telling what the ear hears. "The novel," he said, "is a picture of life; and the art of novel-writing lies in reproducing the characters of men, their passions and weaknesses." The formula is familiar. When I read Spanish novels, long ago, I was told that everyone interested in modern Spanish literature should read, *El Sombrero de Tres Picos* and *Pepita Jiménez* and (before *Sotileza*) these four novels: *Doña Perfecta*, *Gloria*, *Marianela* (1878), and *La Familia de León Roch*. But those were days when Spanish reading was guided by Mr. Howells' advice.

Mr. Howells admired Galdós very greatly. From Ohio and the "blue Canary Isles" they met in a common ideal of the novelist's art. "No book," Howells says of *Doña Perfecta*, "if I except those of the greatest Russians, has given me a keener and deeper impression; it is infinitely pathetic and full of humor . . . and since he has worked into such realism as that of *San Roch*, his greatness leaves nothing to be desired." Menéndez y Pelayo, in his discourse of welcome when Galdós was taken into the Spanish Academy (1897), expresses the accepted Spanish opinion; he compares Galdós' work for its great scale, its wide extent, its breadth of composition, and its wealth of material, to Balzac's *Comédie Humaine*. Certainly Galdós deserves all the praises due to fecundity; but in the face of these serried ranks of books that file before you on the bookcase, a doubt suggests itself. Is not this very fecundity a hindrance to quality? Would not Lope de Vega have done better had he written, say, but forty plays or a hundred? Would not these fluent lyrical poets, Espronceda, Zorrilla, Campoamor, have produced verses of more permanence if they had submitted to self-discipline, and stopped to look before they leapt so lightly from page to page? "*In der Beschränkung zeigt sich erst der Meister.*" Menéndez y Pelayo most truly says: "In Spanish literature power always manifests itself by abundance; instead of concentrating on one masterpiece, it scatters all over. Every Spaniard in science, in art, even in politics, is essentially an improvisatore."

Emilia Pardo Bazán (1851–1921) is another conspicuous figure. She too was wonderfully prolific. At sixteen she wrote a critical study on Padre Feijóo; then she wrote on Dante, Milton, Tasso, Darwin, Saint Francis of Assisi. Next she came under Zola's influence, and took up the cudgels for his theory of novel-writing, swung her shillelagh, *La Cuestion Palpitante* (1883), round her head, and started a Donnybrook Fair among the bewildered literati of Madrid. I presume that her reputation will rest on her two best novels, *Los Pazos de Ulloa* (a family named after a château in Galicia) and its continuation, *La Madre Naturaleza* (Mother Nature). Galicia is her native province, for she came from Coruña, and her strength lies in her pictures of the place and people. Her relation to it is like Pereda's to Santander or Blasco Ibáñez's to Valencia. Cejador picks out for praise "her power of expressing the tender, obscure, mysterious, Galician soul." The kind and enthusiastic Mr. Howells says: "I have read one of the books of Emilia Pardo Bazán, called *Morriña*, which must rank her with the great realists of her country and age." I think that the Beginner had better read *La Madre Naturaleza*, and then he can judge whether he wishes to read another or not.

Armando Palacio Valdés (born 1853) is the last man on my list for this period. He is still living, at home the most popular of Spanish novelists. Mr. Howells says: "I think *Marta y María* (1883) one of the most truthful and profound fictions I have read, and *Máxima* one of the most pathetic, and *La Hermana de San Sulpicio* one of the most amusing." The Beginner is certain to read *La Hermana de San Sulpicio*, a very pleasant love-story, the scene of which is laid in Seville. I should say that it might be put into that category of which *The Vicar of Wakefield* stands at the head: lively, gay, kindly, innocent, and amusing. *La Alegría del Capitán Ribot* is another popular book, but, to my thinking, much inferior to the others. There are many of them.

XLVI

THE GENERATION OF 1898

THE BOURBONS had been put back on the throne
because there was nothing else to do, and, oddly
enough, Alfonso XII turned out to be a good king.
The Carlists gave trouble at first, the pretenders —
old Don Carlos, his son, and his grandson — calling
themselves kings; but they were beaten back, and
a régime of what one may call comparative quiet
followed. Pereda says: "We are an ungovernable
people." The dominating statesman is Cánovas del
Castillo. He could not escape the gifts that nature
conferred on all Spanish statesmen of the period;
he wrote poetry, a novel, and was a "*fácil, brillante
e imperioso orador.*" But he was also the best Spanish
statesman of the century and, between him and
Sagasta, politics at home went on fairly well. Cánovas was a Conservative, Sagasta a Liberal, and the
two agreed that the dynasty should be supported
and that the government should advance, more or
less slowly, in accordance with ideas current in the
rest of Europe. Then they took turns as prime
minister, and seem to have been as much interested
in the public good as a due consideration for their
own fortunes warranted. The great evil at home was
what we call the boss system and they call *caciquismo.*
Local politics were controlled by the cacique, and the
government in power virtually depended on the sup-

port of the caciques. There were difficulties enough. The old centrifugal tendency to assert the rights of the province against those of the national government showed itself strong, especially in Catalonia. There was the question of the religious orders: Should they or should they not be allowed free foot in Spain? Should monks or friars engaged in business be taxed? and so on. But the dominating problem was the government of the Philippines and the West Indies, especially of Cuba. Spanish colonial government was more or less corrupt,— usually more, — and worked wholly in the interests of the mother country. The Cubans had been in revolt from 1868 to 1878 or thereabouts, and the United States, highly annoyed by this nuisance at her front door, was full of sympathy for Cuba. General Grant, years before, had expressed the American views to the Spanish Government. Some sort of home rule was proposed at last by Spaniards who understood the situation; the Government rejected it (1894). Marshal Campos was sent out, but accomplished nothing. General Weyler followed, and established his famous system of concentrating the inhabitants within certain limited districts. The kind-hearted Americans — who afterward adopted a similar military policy in the Philippines — grew hotly indignant. Filibustering expeditions were supported by popular approval; no American jury would convict even the most flagrant offenders. Finally Cánovas saw the dangers ahead and attempted to set up real reforms and a fair system of home rule; but it was too late. The United States cruiser Maine was blown up, accidentally perhaps, in Havana Harbor (in

February 1898) and war became inevitable. Admiral
Dewey won the battle of Manila Bay, Admiral
Sampson that of Santiago de Cuba. Spain was
forced to give up Cuba, Porto Rico, and the Philippines. A little later she sold what scattered islands
were still left her, and the last glow of the Spanish
Empire sank below the horizon into the darkness
of things that are past.

The disaster of 1898 was a rude shock. This
proud, unwitting people, to their amazement, sud-
denly woke to the fact that they were of no account
in the modern world, no more than supernumeraries
in a theatre that display picturesque costumes in
the background and say nothing. Like a bankrupt,
this ancient nation had been turned out of its seat
at the great gaming-table of international politics.
Old Pereda, for one, is said to have taken it very hard.
However, I am not going to speak of politics but of
literature, or rather of the literary group spoken of
as the "Generation of 1898." They and their ideas
were not exactly the product of what they call "The
Disaster," but it aroused them to take thought about
the condition of their country and of what they could
do about it. The leaders in the Generation of 1898 are
Unamuno, Martínez Ruiz (Azorín), Benavente, Baroja, Valle-Inclán, Bueno, Maeztu, and Rubén Darío.

Up till now these young men had scarcely been
aware of Spain's decay. The general state of the
country — fields uncultivated, great stretches without a dwelling, cities unsanitary, population illiterate, political knavery, *caciquismo*, social injustice,
bigotry for Crown, bigotry for Church, all draped
and festooned in bird-of-paradise oratory — had

been so familiar that it had escaped their notice. And now they were brought up with a round turn, face to face with its fruits. *¡Oh tragedia de España!* At the same time these young men had been rendered sensitive by high influences, their idealism had been stimulated by various forces that strove for better things, and in particular, according to Azorín, by Campoamor, Echegaray, and Galdós. Then came the Disaster, picked them up by the scruff of the neck, and shook their drowsy numbness broad awake. They started a renascence; and because they set out to change things they are sometimes called *iconoclastas*. This literary renascence (I am following Azorín) was quickened by foreign thought. Nietzsche imparted a spirit of protest and rebellion; Gautier's *Voyage en Espagne* opened their eyes to the poetic charm of Spanish land; Verlaine's delicate music captivated the poets, especially Rubén Darío, and so on.

Miguel de Unamuno (*b.* 1864) comes from Bilbao, and for years occupied a chair of Greek literature at Salamanca, and until recently was Vice-Rector of the University. He is a man of many ideas, wandering perpetually from one to another, examining, questioning, and moving on. It is said that he is a sort of lay director of youth; that he makes older people think, and altogether exercises much influence on contemporary Spanish thought. He has written various novels; I have read *Abel Sánchez*, which seemed to me a distinct failure. His really important work consists in his essays, which are serious and stimulating. He has also written poetry. On account of a certain vague, non-orthodox religious attitude, he is sometimes called, quite improperly, a mystic.

Lately he has been written up in American news-papers that took an interest in his acrimonious quarrel with Primo de Rivera. Since his exile, his philosophy seems to have failed him. "La Roche-foucauld says: "*La philosophie triomphe aisément des maux passés et des maux à venir, mais les maux présents triomphent d'elle.*"

In Spain, like other people, Unamuno has his critics and his friends. Benavente is reported to have said:

If the history of literature were to be written to suit Don Miguel de Unamuno, it would be easier to learn: Before him, no one; after him, nothing. . . . I have the greatest enthusiasm for those people who, whatever the subject, always take the contrary opinion; so I don't have to say how much I admire Don Miguel de Unamuno.

On the other hand, an admirer sums up his qual-ities as follows:

Unamuno is paradoxically at odds with himself. He is combative as a soldier, austere and fervent as Ignatius Loyola, and as jovial as creatures without faith. Like a compass he has pointed the direction of all the winds of the spirit. He represents the course of æsthetic and philosophic ideas in Spain for twenty years.

José Martínez Ruiz (Azorín) (*b.* 1874) studied law in Valencia, went to Madrid in 1896, and be-came deputy in 1907. He has been a journalist, and is widely known as a literary critic. Blasco Ibáñez accuses him of anarchical propaganda in earlier days, and Cejador, who does not like him, says that, as chief of the Generation of 1898, he broke with the Spain of tradition and "insulted her."

Cejador also says that Azorín, after being an anarchist, joined the Conservative Party, became a follower of the Conservative Prime Minister, Maura, and obtained a seat as deputy. In answer to this it may be said that political conditions in Spain are peculiar, in that there intellectuals seldom join the Labor Party. If a radical professor, for instance, goes into politics, he would join either the Conservative or the Liberal Party, as a matter of course. Cejador goes on to say that Azorín lacks imagination, but possesses delicate sensibility and a clear intellect, and that he judges everything subjectively. An admirer agrees that Azorín is a literary rebel, but asserts that he is rebellious against rhetoric and "copious lyrical exaltation."

Pío Baroja (b. 1872) is a Basque from San Sebastian; he studied medicine, practised it for two years, and then, together with his brother, who had been an engraver, set up a bakery. Just how he became a novelist, I do not know. He possesses the national gift of profusion, and has written more than thirty novels, besides other things. Baroja is certainly one of the iconoclastic group, but he denies that there ever was a Generation of 1898, or that he ever belonged to it. Like the others, he shows the influence of Nietzsche in his reëxamination and condemnation of all the old values that had obtained in Spain. It is for this reason that some people think him unpatriotic. He says of himself:

I describe myself as Dionysiac (that is, impelled *al turbulencia, al dinamismo, al drama*), turbulent, anti-traditional, an enthusiast for action and for the future, an arch individualist, an anarchist, a romantic, and in my youth brutal and visionary. . . . Others speak of me, less amiably, as an erotic jackass, a gross Basque ox, an atheist, a toper, a plagiarist, and so on.

He is a man of talent with greater gifts but less fluency than Blasco Ibáñez. He belongs to what the Spanish call the Zola school of naturalism, and looks at the more sordid, or at least the less prosperous side of society: at the inmates of dirty dwellings, at frequenters of taverns, vagabonds, and so forth. As to his work, he says:

I make no plan. Generally a type or a place suggests a book. I see an unusual person who is new to me, a town, or a house, and I feel a desire to write about them.

There is a picaresque quality in his stories, and he hates rhetoric just as Azorín does. He too has drunk at foreign sources, and the curious say that he is an intellectual debtor to Dickens, Poe, Balzac, Gautier, Zola, and the Russian novelists; he himself admits that most of these, adding Stendhal, are his favorite authors. You will find what he has to say about himself — and he is not unduly reticent — in the prologue to *Páginas escogidas* (1918) and in *Juventud, Egolatría* (1917). I am not sure that you will like him, but you will find that he has a very distinct quality, what is usually known in our newspapers as an "aggressive personality."

Ramón del Valle-Inclán (*b.* 1869) is a very different sort of person, except on the one point that he too belabors tradition. He seems to belong to this group rather in order to round it out and give it imagination and fantastical scope than because he is really of it. Azorín calls him "*Nuestro gran prosista y exquisito poeta.*" To the ignorant beginner he appears as far away from the solid stuff of ordinary literature, novels, plays, or verse, as Maeterlinck or Lord Dunsany. He comes from Galicia, and is distinctly what we should call Celtic, but not of the sunny Irish kind; on the contrary he is cruel, both to his characters and to his readers. He says that "youth should be arrogant, violent, passionate, iconoclastic"; that when he was young he thought meanly of "those young men who, forgetting that life and art are an eternal renewing, respected too blindly the great traditions of *el Siglo de Oro*":

Nevertheless [he says] this conventional respect did good in that it kindled the iconoclastic fury that possesses all young minds to-day. In art, as in life, to destroy is to create. Anarchism is always a breath of regeneration, and for us the only regeneration possible. . . . I have preferred to toil hard for a style rather than to take a ready-made style, imitating the writers of the seventeenth century. . . . My profession of modernist faith is: Seek within thyself, and not in others. . . . If there is in literature anything that can properly be called modernism, it is the fresh breath of personality, and that is no doubt the reason why young writers try to express sensations rather than ideas. . . . The characteristic of all modern art, and particularly of literature, is a tendency to refine sensations and increase their number and intensity.

Azorín says that Valle-Inclán has been influenced by d'Annunzio and Barbey d'Aurévilly; and I should suppose, also by the French symbolists. He has been charged with borrowing from Casanova's *Memoirs*. But this is taking us into niceties that are not appropriate to the rough outlines of this book. His prose is said to be *encadenada, blanda, cadenciosa, llena de luz,* and to possess as much despotic power in modern Spanish literature as Rubén Darío's verse; but I imagine Cejador is right to find his art a little decadent, too exquisite, and overrefined. Valle-Inclán is not familiarly known in this country, probably because he is difficult for Beginners to read, and his style is lost in translation; also, the ordinary American likes decency and would find most of his books hopelessly uninteresting. "Let Gryll be Gryll."

Of them all, Rubén Darío (1867–1916) of Nicaragua is by far the most distinguished outside of Spain. At the time of his death he was easily the foremost poet in Spanish-speaking countries and, setting aside the admirers of Mr. Hardy in England and of d'Annunzio in Italy, the foremost of the world. His feelings toward the United States are instructive. But he lies outside my limits.

XLVII
OUR CONTEMPORARIES

On the death of Alfonso XII his widow acted as regent until her son, the present King, attained the age of sixteen (1902). Four years later he married the Princess Victoria of Battenberg. Among ministers of the early years of the twentieth century, Señor Maura is easily the most eminent; even after Primo de Rivera's coup d'état in 1923, Maura was deemed a force to be reckoned with. The chief political questions that confronted him, or his opponents, were these: the religious orders, the Vatican, civil marriage, compulsory education, obligatory voting, the breach between the industrial North and the agricultural South, the separatist tendency in Catalonia, the radical discontent in Barcelona, the budget, and Morocco.

In 1909, when Maura was in office, the question of Morocco became all-absorbing. The Government was building a railroad from the coast of Melilla into the back country, where Spanish concessionaires were opening mines. Unexpectedly Riff tribesmen made a fierce attack on soldiers and workmen and drove them away. The Government called out the Catalan reserves. Barcelona answered the call with a general strike. There was street fighting for three days, and military terrorism for two months. Francisco Ferrer, an anticlerical educator and, I believe, a philosophical anarchist, was accused of high treason and shot. Order was finally restored; and during the next ten years the various governments in power went slowly ahead with the invasion of Morocco, won back the lost territory up to a certain point; and then again, in July 1921, the Riff tribesmen rushed out and drove the Spanish army, said (with probable exaggeration) to number one hundred thousand men, in headlong rout, pell-mell back to Melilla. The massacre was horrible. Somebody was to blame. There had been timidity, hesitation, incompetence, dishonesty, and lack of discipline. A general outcry demanded punishment; and everybody in positions of authority accused everybody else. You get an impression of officials running away from responsibility, *sauve qui peut*. Altogether, the whole situation was bad. "When one looks at it [I quote a deputy, May 1923] one feels all the anguish of pessimism." The Government took some feeble steps to recover the lost territory and lost prestige, but the cost was great, and taxation, very high ever since the American war, could not go up indefinitely. The whole matter was a nightmare. Nobody knew what to do. Some people regarded the invasion of Morocco as a cancer that ate into the nation's life, and others as "the sacred accomplishment of a centuries-old purpose of the Spanish people."

Such, roughly indicated, was the situation on the twelfth of September, 1923. Primo de Rivera, Marquis of Estella, can hardly receive justice for years to come. Unamuno — who is in exile — says that he is a dissipated, incompetent, unsuccessful

military adventurer. Blasco Ibáñez is reported to
have shown a similar acrimony against him. On
the other hand, the dictator is still in power and has
many supporters. I read that he is *"un homme d'une
brilliante carrière militaire"* and has given proof of
his courage on the field of battle; that his intelligence is alert, his will assertive, his temperament
one of continual activity; and that in days gone by,
when other men trimmed, he had the courage to
speak out and say that the occupation of Morocco
was a mistake. I may add that during the Great
War he sympathized with the Allies.

At the date named he was Captain-General of
Catalonia. The situation demanded vigorous action.
The country was discouraged, the Red Radicals full
of hope. Some said that there would be a syndi-
calist reign of terror. It seemed as if a choice must
be made between Bolshevism and arbitrary power.
The army, with Rivera at its head, acted. All the
conservative forces in Spanish society sympathized
with their action. Rivera abolished the Cabinet,
appointed a military directory, and took upon himself the rôle of dictator, responsible to the King.
He exercised absolute power with vengeance. There
was military law — no trial by jury, no parliament,
no town councils, no freedom of the press. And it
was all done without any resistance, without any
disturbance. Rivera said: "We must carry this out,
for no other plan is thinkable — and if this fail, we
are on the brink of chaos." Men of property agreed
with him. In their eyes, this destruction of constitutional liberties was the overthrow of a sham.
The Cortes, the local councils, and — in part — the

judiciary were the creatures of political bosses; the jury system *"s'est montrée à l'expérience absolument condamnable"*; the press expressed, not public opinion, but the wishes of party chiefs; and so forth.

Primo de Rivera had hoped to be ready to re-establish a constitutional government within a few months, but that state of readiness has not yet (1925) been reached. So I go back to literature.

Blasco Ibáñez (*b.* 1867) comes from Valencia. As a youth, he thought of entering the navy, but changed his mind and began life as a journalist. In politics he was a republican. Part of the time he was deputy, part of the time in exile. He was imprisoned thirty times and fought a dozen duels. His early books found such favor that in 1909 he abandoned politics and traveled about South America, lecturing and studying the different countries. During these years he made frequent trips to Paris, where his early liking for modern French literature, for Hugo, Stendhal, and Zola, was strengthened and developed. He liked the French; they liked him; and the publication of *Terres Maudites* (a translation of *La Barraca*) in the *Revue de Paris* in 1901 launched his European reputation. Since then he has been translated into many languages and is as well known as d'Annunzio. His friend, Eduardo Zamacois, the novelist, describes his appearance at the age of forty-three (1910) as follows:

He is tall, broad, solid; his dark, bearded face might belong to an Arab. Above his high forehead, that displays restlessness and ambition, hair that should be thick and curly is struggling against baldness. Between his brows in deep vertical lines you see the wrinkles of thought. His eyes are large and frank and look straight at you. His nose is aquiline. A bushy moustache covers a smiling, epicurean mouth, and a flicker of insatiable thirst flits over his big lips. His short round herculean neck is bursting with vital energy. His handshake is like that of a boxer with his adversary before opening a bout. His voice is strong, a sailor's voice. His speech is copious, brusque, richly studded with exclamations. He looks like an artist, and at the same time like a conquistador — like one of those legendary adventurers that, holding in either hand shield and lance, guide their horses with their heels.

Such Ibáñez looks and such I think are his novels; he is an energetic, intelligent, vigorous animal. He said (I quote Zamacois again), "'I don't like men that eat little,'" and as he spoke, "his eyes shone with an expression of triumphant gluttony. . . ."
To me the epithet "conquistador" seems well chosen — not a conquistador of romance, but rather of modern industry. Ibáñez has a strong will and complete self-confidence. His eye, like a searchlight, sweeps over great regions; his intelligence is statistical. He treats his dramatis personæ like an employer who assigns his workmen to different jobs at his good pleasure, with little or no regard to their personalities. He has the talents of a great advertiser, who knows how to select incidents, situations, and phraseology to catch the multitude. He has also the fatal Spanish facility of the improvisatore, and when he starts he cannot stop. He may be a son of Valencia and Aragon, but he is a grandson of Arabia. "I am an impressionist," he says; "the terrible struggle between thought and form, over which

other authors groan, hardly exists for me. It is a matter of temperament." There speaks the Arab. But he is very intelligent; he has reflected upon his art; and his discourse upon it, which you will find reported, is admirable. The Beginner, of course, will read him. Probably the Beginner has read in translation *The Four Horsemen of the Apocalypse* or *The Cathedral*. Whatever their merits, these two books are not good novels. Critics seem to agree that the early stories about life in Valencia, *Arroz y Tartana, Cañas y Barro, La Barraca* (1894–1902), are his best. His recent philippic upon King Alfonso is singularly poor vituperation; it displays gross prejudice and contains neither evidence nor reference to evidence. Take him all in all, he is a vulgar, vigorous, masculine man, quivering with energy and the need of action; possibly these qualities would have been better employed in some other occupation.

Next to Ibáñez, of all living Spanish writers Jacinto Benavente is best known to the world at large. Benavente was born in Madrid. He studied for a time at the university there, traveled abroad, went around the country with a circus, and tried his hand — with no great success — at acting. According to a friend's description, he is "short, slight, and delicate, so that you might take him for a man of feeble physique and puny character; but the appearance of physical and moral weakness is misleading, for he is as strong as an oak, eats less than a bird, smokes like a Cuban muleteer, and sits up later than the moon, and his strength of will is as tough as his body. His little eyes lift their little lids and see very deep."

His first successful play, *Gente Conocida*, was

acted in 1896. Others followed in rapid succession. Like all other Spanish writers of his generation, he learned much from Paris, in particular from the successful Parisian dramatists, Lavedan, Donnay, Capus; but he has written plays well outside the domain of their Parisian interests — romantic plays, fairy plays, farces, comedies, and dramas of many sorts. True to his breed, he is very prolific; I think that he has written nearly a hundred plays. As I have not seen any of them acted, it would be absurd to hazard a judgment on him from the mere reading; but I find these plays far more true to life and far more interesting than such novels of Ibáñez as I have read, and I should recommend the Beginner who wishes to read for pleasure, to read almost any of them. Mr. John Garrett Underhill has translated a dozen or more.

A few years ago Benavente received the Nobel Prize. Is he a great dramatist? Is Brieux? Is Shaw? Is d'Annunzio? This is a question easier to put than to answer. To my mind, the one playwright of genius since Ibsen is Synge, and I should not think of putting Benavente in the same plane with Synge. Others think differently. I say this merely to indicate my own prejudices. The Beginner must decide for himself. In the first place there comes the question of Benavente's own point of view. Mr. Underhill quotes this passage from the playwright's statement of his own theory:

The function of the artist is to tranquillize emotion through the intelligence, and it is only in so far as he is able to do this that his work becomes good art; his aim is to bring serenity, not to create a tempest in the mind.

This, I think, is not the point of view usually accepted. But Benavente is too important a personage for my space. Let us take leave of him on his note of patriotism:

What [he asks] is most Spanish? [And he answers] The modesty of our women not contaminated by feminism; the well-bred courtesy of our men; a frank and easy intercourse with equals or inferiors — for our people are the most democratic in the world. . . . True patriotism does not lie in boasting that we are sons of Spain, but in so living that wherever we are, and wherever we go, there shall be justice, loyalty, self-denial, honorable purpose, and a noble goal.

I have no space for the two poets, Manuel (*b.* 1874) and Antonio (*b.* 1875) Machado, brothers — you will find poems by each in the *Oxford Book of Spanish Verse;* nor for the two brothers, comic playwrights, Serafín (*b.* 1871) and Joaquín (*b.* 1873) Álvarez Quintero; nor for Manuel Linares Rivas (*b.* 1867), another playwright, to whose plays I commend the Beginner. Nor shall I speak of Don Ramón Pérez de Ayala (*b.* 1882), who published his first book in 1903 and has written novels, poetry, and essays that have procured for him the reputation of being "a standard-bearer of the Spanish intellectuals," and "the most distinguished figure of the younger generation of Spanish writers"; nor of Doña Concha Espina (*b.* 1877), who has written a number of novels: *La Esfinge Maragata, La Rosa de los Vientos,* and so forth. There are, of course, various young or younger writers to be readily discovered by inordinate curiosity. I turn to two painters whose world-wide reputation rivals those of Benavente and Blasco Ibáñez.

In the sequence of Spanish painters, Joaquín Sorolla (1863–1923) stands as the first of any importance since Fortuny. His life began in humble circumstances. By day he worked for his uncle, a locksmith, and by night he drew or painted. At twenty he obtained his first success with his El Dos de Mayo, which was exhibited in Madrid (1884). Soon afterward he won a *prix de Rome* of some sort. He went to Rome, and to Assisi, rather — I surmise — to live in an economical and beautiful place than to study Giotto's frescoes; and, what proved of greater importance, to Paris, where he studied the painting of Bastien-Lepage and of the Barbizon school. On his return to Spain he was by no means disregardful of what his fellow artists there were doing, but, as he says:

Firm on my own feet, I began to create for myself my own way of doing (I don't know whether well or ill), but truthful, sincere, realistic, the reflection of what my eye saw and my heart felt.

He originated the modern fashion of painting in Spain, which is really a return to the great Spanish tradition of painting what you see. He discarded the old historical canvases, once so much in fashion, the artificial genre pictures in which Fortuny had excelled, and conventional modes in general. He painted fishing boats with gaudy sails, careened on the Valencian sands; boys and girls running on the beach or swimming in the glorious, spray-flecked, blue and green waters of the Mediterranean; whatever best embodied, at the moment, light, color, and beauty. His motto is *El arte por la vida y la vida por la belleza.* His execution has the brilliant rapidity and fluency

that mark the lyrical poets, "the most prodigious
[it has been said] in the history of pictorial art."
One admirer says that his painting is "a vibrant
hymn to light." And indeed one seems to listen to
a canticle:

Blessed be the Lord our God for his servant the Sun,
For it is glorious, and clothes the earth in the beauty of color.

Beside his outdoor scenes, Sorolla painted many
portraits — the King, the Queen, Echegaray, Pérez
Galdós, Menéndez y Pelayo, Blasco Ibáñez, María
Guerrero, the eminent actress familiar on the list of
actresses in Benavente's plays. His pictures have
been exhibited in Paris, London, New York, and
Chicago (1905–1911), and are to be found, scattered
here and there, in many museums.

Ignacio Zuloaga (b. 1870) is a Basque, and comes
from a family of artists. His grandfather chiseled
damascene patterns on sword blades; his uncle was
a famous potter. At Segovia, in an old abandoned
church, this uncle established his factory for tiles,
pottery, mosaics, and enamel, and there his daughter
and his niece maintain the furnace, together with
warehouse and salesrooms. These artists are well
known in Europe and America for their wares, and
especially in Boston, because the painter's picture,
Uncle Daniel and His Daughters, hangs in the
Boston Museum of Fine Arts. In this picture you
see the painter's skill in all its amazing dexterity.
An English critic, in a comparison between Sorolla
and Zuloaga and their predecessors, says:

What do we find in Fortuny, Zamacois, and their like?
Unerring draughtsmanship, a capacity for pictorial design,

an appreciation of the harmonies of color, and a daring handling of its brilliancies; whereas in Goya and his revivers, Zuloaga, Sorolla, and others, we observe a breadth of expression, sufficient exactitude in drawing, an impulsive realism, and a certain disregard for pictorial balance. The two sets of men are irreconcilable.

I may interpolate here that another critic says Zuloaga is "always sensitive to the efficacy of a well-balanced design." Alas for us poor Beginners, the doctors too often disagree. However this may be, to the Beginner Zuloaga is a very brilliant painter, telling him more about Spain, I think, than either Blasco Ibáñez or Benavente. He loves whatever is truly Spanish. He selects for his canvas *toreros* or a gypsy where he can; but a sombrero, a mantilla, a fan, a stark hill, a tawny wall, or better still, an Andalusian eyebrow or a well-modeled Castilian cheek is enough. Whatever it may be, there you see a bit of pure Spain. His painting is like a patois, so inseparable it seems from its Spanish soil.

Zuloaga is now famous the world over; but in his early days there were struggles and discouragements enough. Days of scantiness at Montmartre, days of unbought pictures at Seville, a brief season as bookkeeper, an apprenticeship as a *torero*, until a toss by his eighteenth bull terminated that career. In 1898 his picture, Víspera de Toros, at an exhibition in Barcelona won the gold medal. Then he leaped into renown.

I should say that while Sorolla and Zuloaga are both independent, truth-telling, honest painters, preferring what Nature presents to any imagined *mise-en-scène*, nevertheless Sorolla loves the sun, the circumambient air, joy, beauty, and finds delight in life everywhere; but that Zuloaga is a little wayward in his vision, and emphasizes, by some dextrous manipulation of the brush, whatever seems to be most typically Spanish.

I have no room here for the sculptor, José Clara (*b*. 1878), who has lived most of his life in Paris—you will find two statues by him in the Musée du Luxembourg; nor for the wayward painter, Pablo Picasso (*b*. 1881), who, I understand,—if I may use that word for my relation to him or his work,—founded cubism; nor for Picabia. All such artists lie beyond the horizon of this elementary book. But as to them I have read this:

Pablo Picasso . . . whose basic idea may be found in Pythagoras, and the principles of whose methods were long since formulated by Plato. Sublime elementalism here gives place to divine geometrizing, with the result that we are at last freed from all taint of nature-imitation and watch unfold before us a world of visual imagery existing of and for itself alone. The austere Iberian temperament of Picasso, which makes appeal almost exclusively through an inherent plasticity of design, is supplemented in the work of Picabia by a warmer, more sensuous tonality, and a kindred desire to create, not to copy.

Picabia, I ought to add, says of his own painting: "The objectivity of the subjectivity is in every case superinduced by the original sensation."

There are other painters, as well as authors, to whom I hope the Beginner will proceed after laying down this book. And now I have come to the end of my irregular and halting chronicle, and I must end. In Spanish fashion, *He dicho*.

EPILOGUE

AND what shall I say for a summing-up? What is the spirit within, that gives to Spain so definite and vigorous a personality? How different she is from her Latin sisters, France and Italy; and yet the Roman foundation is much the same. Were the Iberians a peculiar people? Did the Visigoths accomplish more than I think? Or was it the interpenetration of Arabian and African ways of life, habits of thought, and modes of expression, that wrought the divergence?

As one cannot draw up an indictment against a people, so one cannot say that a nation is this or this. Spain's element of superiority over other nations does not lie in achievements, great as hers have been. Her empire was no vaster than England's, and hers is gone, while England's encircles the earth. Her literature is rich and splendid, but is it really comparable in quality to the Greek? The cathedrals of Toledo, Burgos, Leon, and Seville are noble, but think of Amiens, Rheims, Beauvais, Paris, and Chartres. Velásquez, Ribera, Murillo, and Goya are mighty masters, but will you compare them with the heavenly host of Italian painters? Is Andalusia comparable in smiling beauty to Ireland? Are the Pyrenees as majestic as the Alps?

No; the superiority of Spain does not lie in Spanish land or in Spanish achievement. There is some quality there, of which I do not know the like, that I can but indicate. You are aware of it in a thousand ways: in pigment, in masonry, in ruins, in a muleteer, in a fishwife, in a barren prospect, in a poem. I think of some gentleman of the old school walking down my village street, let us say a little like Colonel Newcome. He is very much of a gentleman, but his clothes are shabby. There is something very masculine and soldierly in his appearance, some hauteur. You take your hat off to him instinctively. When a child passes, his face becomes as radiant as an April morning. The rich pass near him, and their gold loses its lustre. A poor old lady passes, and rejoices to perceive what gallant gentlemen are still abroad. A girl goes by, with half a blush to find a man so charming. A laborer comes, stops, chats, touches his hat with a "God bless you, Sir."

What is it — this charm, this gallantry, this sense of breeding and chivalry, and this obvious failure in a material world?

Well, the Beginner must continue the search for explanations under wiser guidance. Let him tarry several days in the cathedral of Burgos; read *Don Quixote* twice from cover to cover; read *La Vida es Sueño, Las Coplas* de Jorge Manrique; sit for hours in Velasquez's salon in the Prado; go visit the Immaculate Madonna by Ribera in Salamanca, the Burial of Count Orgaz in Toledo, the Casa de Cervantes in Valladolid; wander for a week in and about Segovia; and then he will do well to forget my tastes and prejudices, and enjoy, unvexed by officious guidance, his own delightful memories.

APPENDICES

ABBREVIATIONS

Alt. = Altamira, *Historia de España y de la civilización española*, 4 volumes (1913)

Cej. = Cejador y Frauca, *Historia de la lengua y literatura castellana*, 14 volumes (1915-1922)

F.K. = Fitzmaurice-Kelly, *Spanish Literature* (1901)

E.M. = Ernest Merimée, *Précis d'histoire de la littérature espagnole* (1908)

R.H. = *Revue Hispanique*

APPENDIX A

AUTHORITY FOR STATEMENTS IN TEXT

CHAPTER I

CHAPTER II

CHAPTER III

PAGE   LINE

CHAPTER XXX

CHAPTER XXXI

CHAPTER XXXII

CHAPTER XXXIII

CHAPTER XXXIV

CHAPTER XXXV

CHAPTER XXXVI

CHAPTER XXXVII

CHAPTER XL

CHAPTER XLI

CHAPTER XLII

CHAPTER XL

CHAPTER XLI

CHAPTER XLII

CHAPTER XLIII

CHAPTER XLIV

CHAPTER XLV

The novels referred to speak for themselves, but comment and criticism upon them are very voluminous. Valera, Emilia Pardo Bazán, Leopold Alas, as well as more recent Spanish writers, have expressed their opinions freely. Wm. Dean Howells gives some place to them in *My Literary Passions*. Cejador, as usual, gives statistical details and opinions, both his own and others'.

CHAPTER XLVI

I have followed, in the main, Martinez Ruiz (Azorín) in his analysis of the "Generation of 1898;" others, Pio Baroja, for instance, dissent from his views, and I have not neglected more recent criticism.

CHAPTER XLVII

For Primo de Rivera's *coup d'état*, see the French and Spanish reviews of the time. Mr. Underhill's translations have made Benavente

a familiar figure, and Blasco Ibañez announces himself.   For Sorolla and Zuloaga there are brief notices prefixed to catalogues of an exhibition of their works held in the Hispanic Museum in New York some years ago, and various references in magazines on art.   Clará, Picasso, and Picabia are noticed in the *Burlington Magazine*, and such.

APPENDIX B

CHRONOLOGY

Kings of Castile

Ferdinand I, 1037–1065

Sancho II, 1065–1072   Battle of Hastings, 1066

Alfonso VI, 1072–1109   Capture of Toledo, 1085
                                        Death of Cid, 1099

Urraca, 1109–1126
    (married Don Raimondo and
    later married Alfonso I of Ara-
    gon)

Alfonso VII, 1126–1157

Sancho IV, 1157–1158

Alfonso VIII, 1158–1214   Las Navas de Tolosa, 1212

Enrique I, 1214–1217   Alfonso IX of Leon, 1188–1230
                                            (married daughter of Alfonso
                                            VIII and is then numbered
                                            among the Castilian Alfonsos)

Ferdinand III (St.), 1217–1252   Jaime I of Aragon, 1213–1276
                                        Capture of Cordova, 1236
                                        Capture of Seville, 1248

Alfonso X, El Sabio, 1252–1284   Aragon acquires Sicily, 1282

Sancho IV, 1284–1295

Ferdinand IV, 1295–1312

Alfonso XI, 1312–1350   Death of Dante, 1321

Don Pedro, 1350–1369	Battle of Nájera, 1367
Enrique II, 1369–1379	Death of Petrarch, 1374
	Death of Boccaccio, 1375
Juan I, 1379–1390	
Enrique III, 1390–1406	Death of Chaucer, 1400
Juan II, 1406–1454	Aragon acquires Naples, 1443
	Execution of Don Álvaro de Luna, 1453
Enrique IV, 1454–1474	
Isabella, 1474–1504	Ferdinand of Aragon, 1479–1516
	Morte d' Arthur, Malory, 1485
	Capture of Granada ⎫
	Discovery of America ⎬ 1492
	Expulsion of Jews ⎭
	Conquest of Naples, 1503–1504
Philip I (regent), 1504–1506	
Ferdinand of Aragon (regent), 1506–1516	Annexation of Spanish Navarre, 1512
Charles V, 1516–1556	Luther nails up theses, 1517
(Charles I of Spain)	Conquest of Mexico, 1519–1521
	Death of Raphael, 1520
	Conquest of Peru, 1532–1537
	Death of Ariosto, 1533
	Death of Henry VIII, 1547
	Death of Francis I, 1547
	Death of Ignatius Loyola, 1556
	Death of Michelangelo, 1564
Philip II, 1556–1598	Battle of Lepanto, 1571
	Invincible Armada, 1588
	Portugal united to Spain, 1580–1640
	Death of Titian, 1576
	Death of Paolo Veronese, 1588
	Death of Tintoretto, 1594

Philip III, 1598–1621	Expulsion of Moriscos, 1609
	Death of Shakespeare, 1616
Philip IV, 1621–1665	Death of Lope de Vega, 1635
	Death of Rubens, 1640
	Death of Van Dyck, 1641
	Death of Quevedo, 1645
	Recognition of independence of Holland, 1648
	English capture Jamaica, 1655
	Death of Velasquez, 1660
Charles II, 1665–1700	Death of Molière, 1673
	Death of Calderón, 1681
	Death of Corneille, 1684
	Death of Racine, 1699
Philip V (Bourbon), 1700–1746	English capture Gibraltar, 1704
	Death of Louis XIV, 1715
Ferdinand VI, 1746–1759	
Charles III, 1759–1788	Expulsion of Jesuits, 1767
	Death of Voltaire, 1778
Charles IV, 1788–1808	French Revolution, 1789
	Battle of Trafalgar, 1805
Joseph Bonaparte, 1808–1814	Dos de Mayo, 1808
	Peninsular War, 1808–1814
	Colombia independent, 1811
	Constitution of Cadiz, 1812
Ferdinand VII, 1814–1833	Fall of Napoleon, 1814
	Waterloo, 1815
	Argentina independent, 1816
	Chile independent, 1818
	Florida sold to U. S. A., 1819–1821
	Mexico independent, 1821
	Peru independent, 1821
Isabella II, 1833–1868	First Carlist War, 1833–1839

(Interregnum) 1868–1871

Amadeo, 1871–1873   Second Carlist War, 1872–1875

Republic, 1873–1874

Alfonso XII, 1874–1886

Alfonso XIII, 1886–   War with U. S. A., 1898
                                     Great War, 1914–1918
                                     Coup d'état, Primo de Rivera,
                                        September, 1923

INDEX

INDEX